Learning
for Organizational
Development

Learning for Organizational Development

How to design, deliver and evaluate effective L&D

Eileen Arney

KoganPage

First published in Great Britain and the United States in 2017 by Kogan Page Limited

2nd Floor, 45 Gee Street	c/o Martin P Hill Consulting	4737/23 Ansari Road
London	122 W 27th Street	Daryaganj
EC1V 3RS	New York, NY 10001	New Delhi 110002
United Kingdom	USA	India

© Eileen Arney 2017

The right of Eileen Arney to be identified as the author of this work has been asserted by her in accordance with the Copyright, Designs and Patents Act 1988.

With thanks to Rebecca Page-Tickell for contributing Chapters 3 and 6.

ISBN   978 0 7494 7744 8
E-ISBN   978 0 7494 7745 5

British Library Cataloguing-in-Publication Data

A CIP record for this book is available from the British Library.

Library of Congress Control Number
2017001498

Typeset by Integra Software Services, Pondicherry
Print production managed by Jellyfish
Printed and bound in Great Britain by CPI Group (UK) Ltd, Croydon CR0 4YY

CONTENTS

For my sons,
Eddie and Tom

Introduction

This book is written for learning and development professionals and for those following programmes of study in this field. The changing nature of learning and development work and roles will be an important theme; another will be the development of thinking about learning itself, with all this implies about approaches to helping others to learn, whether in groups, teams or across the whole organization. Underpinning both these themes is a recognition of the constantly changing contexts within which organizations operate.

The acronym VUCA is widely used to describe a global environment which is volatile, uncertain, complex and ambiguous. Developments in information technology, social media and mobile communications are changing the way individuals, groups and teams work, with virtual working between geographically dispersed groups of individuals increasingly common. This means that rapid learning is needed about how groups and teams can communicate, work together and learn together in a virtual world. At the same time the pressures of globalization are pushing organizations to jostle for position in a crowded marketplace and to find new ways of achieving competitive advantage.

For many this can only be achieved through making the best possible use of the skills and talents of those who work for them. This means both recruiting talented individuals and also nurturing and developing their talents so that there is a steady supply of those with the right skills to take on key roles. It also means that employers need to create a relationship with those who work for them so that they are fully engaged in pursuing the organization's objectives and are willing to commit extra effort to achieve high performance. In a labour market where highly skilled workers are in short supply, employers are drawing on marketing techniques to create their own employer brand to attract and retain employees.

New approaches to learning

Pressure to learn quickly and to keep on doing so has led to changes in thinking about learning itself. There is an increased emphasis on individuals' responsibility for managing their own learning and recognition of the personalized nature of the knowledge and understanding needed in different contexts. Helping others to learn now often means supporting them in developing the skills they need to manage their own continuous learning. There is still a place for a structured approach to training, based on analysis of training needs, design and delivery of training interventions and evaluation of outcomes but this is very much the smallest part now of the work of learning and development professionals in most organizations.

There is a strong emphasis too on workplace learning so that what is learned can be applied immediately to improve performance. This can take a number of forms, many of which will be discussed in this book; these include coaching and mentoring, team development and leadership and management development. Workplace learning can also be provided in conjunction with external providers. These may be universities, which can provide accredited learning tailored to meet the organization's needs. In this case, programmes of study can be designed to draw on workplace experience and to develop the skills, through practice-based learning, of applying what is learned in the workplace. They may also be consultants, including coaches, who may provide services to complement those provided internally and who may also help those in the organization to develop skills such as coaching and mentoring, for example.

Peer learning is also increasingly popular. This can take the form of peer mentoring, where colleagues support each other by sharing their greater experience in particular areas, or where peers with similar levels of experience simply help each other by providing opportunities for discussion, each offering a willingness to listen and help the other to think through issues of concern. It can also take the form of working together to develop new understandings, for example through action learning or action research projects.

The relative importance of each of these approaches to learning is a matter of judgement. However, one top-tier consultancy firm plans for 70 per cent of employees' learning to take place on the job, 20 per cent to come from peer learning and 10 per cent to come from formal training courses, and this is not untypical of leading-edge companies.

Perhaps most fundamentally of all, new approaches to learning are being developed to take advantage of the opportunities offered by developments in digital technology. With broadband now very widely available to both individuals and organizations there is great potential to offer learning in virtual environments and with the growth of home working and of organizations whose work spans large geographical areas there are great incentives to explore the potential offered by online learning. The advent of Massive Open Online Courses (MOOCs) has demonstrated the potential of online learning. At the time of writing the MOOC learning platform, FutureLearn, which offers free online courses created by a number of universities, claims on its website (https://www.futurelearn.com/) to have 4,275,423 students enrolled. These courses are entirely free to students (although fees are payable for certification of completion or achievement) and they are accessible by organizations who want to use them as part of their employee development. This has thrown down a gauntlet to learning and development professionals who in many organizations have not yet embraced online learning.

A new role for learning and development professionals

For learning and development professionals, new thinking about learning and its role in organizations has produced both challenges and opportunities. As well as skills in identifying training needs and designing and delivering training, most also now need well-developed skills as facilitators, coaches and mentors. In these roles they will work with individuals, groups and teams, helping them to reflect on experience and practice in order to improve future performance. They may also be asked to facilitate meetings or problem-solving groups in the workplace. Increasingly they will need to be able to offer these skills in virtual environments and to be able to design and deliver online learning.

All this, however, constitutes only a small part of what learning and development professionals can and do offer in the workplace. They will often be responsible for sourcing providers of learning services, whether hiring consultants to take on training, facilitation or coaching services or purchasing online learning. They will also be responsible for managing budgets in relation to these and evaluating and reporting on the outcomes of the investment made.

It is also an important part of their role to contribute to the design of systems and processes which support learning in the wider organization. They need both a good understanding of the business and the ability to develop a learning and development strategy which aligns with the organization's strategy. More than this, they should be able to contribute to the development of that strategy, showing how their work can contribute to achieving business objectives. The term human resource development has been introduced to describe this new strategic role for learning and development professionals, although it is not universally accepted and is perhaps more widely used in academic writing than among practitioners.

How to use this book

This book will outline some of the ways in which learning and development professionals can contribute to the success of the business. It provides a mixture of theory and very practical ideas about skill development. The purpose of this book, however, is not to provide prescriptions for practice but to introduce a range of theories and ideas from which readers can choose those which are most relevant and helpful to their personal context. Exercises throughout the text invite the reader to think about how the ideas and theories introduced can best be applied to their own practice, encouraging reflective and practice-based learning.

Readers who are not currently working in organizations might choose to draw on their experience as volunteers or as members of social groups as they think about how to apply their reading to the workplace. Those who are self-employed might find it helpful to look at practice in organizations for which they provide services.

There are also case studies in practitioner journals such as *People Management* or *Training Journal* and these can give very helpful insights into organizational life.

There is encouragement for the reader throughout this book to consider and practise continuing professional development. There are suggestions for how to go about developing some of the skills introduced in this book, for example, and a suggested format for a skills development plan is provided in Chapter 4.

Understanding organizational development 01

Introduction

Organizational development (OD) describes a set of ideas, theories and skills which are increasingly important for learning and development professionals. There are specialist OD practitioners (and academics) but there is also an increasingly widespread recognition that OD skills and understanding are needed by a much wider group, and there has been a considerable flow of ideas from the work of writers and thinkers about OD into the worlds of learning and development, human resource management and even line management. For this reason, even if you have never studied or thought about OD before, you are very likely to recognize some of the ideas and theories you read about in this chapter.

Learning and development professionals increasingly adopt a strategic role in organizations, contributing to thinking about change and OD and designing learning and development interventions to support these. Learning may take place at the level of the individual, groups or teams, or organization-wide, and will often be self-managed and directed; many of the ideas about the nature of learning and how it can best be supported are drawn from OD.

This chapter will consider what we mean by OD and will examine some of the ideas and theories of its writers and thinkers. These address motivating individuals to give of their best, improving the performance of groups and teams and managing change and cultural change. It will explore the changing role of learning and development professionals and the implications of this for OD as a separate discipline and will introduce debate between OD practitioners about the nature of their work. The chapter will introduce reflective and practice-based learning and, finally, will suggest ways in which learning and development professionals can develop their own OD skills as part of their continuing professional development.

What do we mean by organizational development?

Organizational development is the name given to a body of processes and techniques drawn from the behavioural sciences and applied to organizations to improve their effectiveness. There is a strong emphasis on improving the skills and abilities of members of the organization so that they can contribute to this improved effectiveness, and there is a strong association with change management. For these reasons, there are close links and overlaps with learning and development and human resource development, and organizational development is an important skill area for all HR practitioners (it is one of the professional areas in the Chartered Institute of Personnel and Development's Profession Map).

OD practitioners have a remit which spans the whole organization and their interventions are intended to address this whole remit. Fundamental to this approach is systems theory, which emphasizes the interrelatedness of all parts of an organization and its place, in turn, in the wider environment (or system), to which it belongs. Any intervention in one part of the system impacts inevitably on others, and systems thinking means thinking through and taking into account the wider effects of these interventions. Senge identified systems thinking as a fundamental attribute of organizations that are designed to support continuous learning. He called these 'learning organizations' and you will read more about them in Chapter 2. He explained systems thinking like this:

> Business and other human endeavours are…systems. They…are bound by invisible fabrics of interrelated actions, which often take years to fully play out their effects on each other. Since we are part of that

lacework ourselves, it's doubly hard to see the whole pattern of change. Instead, we tend to focus on snapshots of isolated parts of the system, and wonder why our deepest problems never get solved. Systems thinking is a conceptual framework…to make the full patterns clearer, and to help us to see how to change them effectively (Senge, 2006:6).

Schein echoed the importance of systems thinking in OD, defining OD simply as 'about building and maintaining the health of the organization as a total system' (Schein, in Cheung-Judge and Holbeche, 2015:10).

Equally fundamental to OD are the ideas about learning that underpin it. OD interventions are based on the assumption that change and development are fundamentally about encouraging individuals and organizations to learn. Much of the early work of writers about OD, therefore, was focused on how to learn, in particular how to learn from experience and how to support learning in organizations. These ideas about learning are explored later in this chapter.

OD has also long been associated with a commitment to values which support human development more generally. Cheung-Judge and Holbeche (2015:19) note that these include 'democracy and participation', 'openness to lifelong learning and experimentation' and 'enduring respect for the human side of enterprise'. There are currently debates, however, about whether these values can endure as defining characteristics of OD, as it becomes seen as the responsibility of a range of people management professionals and not simply the domain of OD specialists.

The origins of OD

The development of the body of theory and practice which has come to be known as OD grew out of requests for help from businesses in understanding how organizations work and how to make them work better. From the 1950s and initially predominantly in the United States, practice-focused academics such as Lewin, Likert and Argyris began to research and develop theories about the human aspects of organizations and about how to use this new understanding to improve and develop those organizations. From this research emerged ideas about individual motivation, about management and leadership styles, about the dynamics of groups and teams, and about ways of supporting the organization-wide change and learning needed to implement improvements to practice in these areas.

The pressure on organizations to compete more effectively, which gathered pace in the United States and Europe from the 1950s and 1960s, also produced new ideas in the field of human resource management (HRM). The term HRM itself emerged in recognition of the importance of taking a strategic approach to managing people, in which people would be regarded as being as important a resource as any other – recognizing that it is people who can give the organization a competitive advantage. From this it follows that organizations need to organize themselves in ways which engage and motivate their employees, and there is a premium on good leadership and management skills, particularly among line managers who significantly influence the way workers experience their working lives. The same influences produced changes in the work of learning and development specialists, and the term Human Resource Development was coined to express their new strategic role.

Applying these ideas to your practice

Spend some time now thinking about an organization you know well. Who takes responsibility for developing leadership and management skills, for supporting team development and for managing change and culture change?

Feedback

You are quite likely to have identified that a number of different players contribute to these areas. Only very large organizations are likely to employ OD specialists in-house, but external consultants who are OD specialists may be brought in contribute to particular areas of work. You may also have found HR specialists, learning and development specialists and perhaps also leaders and managers who demonstrate the skills to lead in some or all of these areas. See for example the case study later in this chapter where Peter Horrocks, newly appointed vice-chancellor of the Open University, speaks about his role in leading change in the University.

For all these reasons, the ideas of OD thinkers came to be seen as important and attractive to HR and learning and development specialists who have drawn on them in a number of ways. For example, ideas from OD have been used in developing leadership and management skills, in advising on organization-wide approaches to creating cultures in which individual potential is nurtured and supported, and in supporting effective team and group working. Ideas about managing change have been adopted too, and as the pace of change has quickened in organizations, so it has become increasingly important to be able to manage change in a way that supports individual motivation and growth.

Motivating individuals to give of their best

Where people are recognized as an organization's most important asset it follows that it is important to motivate them to want to give of their best. Writing in the 1950s and 1960s, industrial psychologists explored what really does motivate individuals in this way, and produced insights and models of motivation which marked a distinct departure from ideas previously widely accepted. Taylor had argued in 1947 that:

> what the workforce want from their employers beyond anything else is high wages and what employers want most from their workers is low labour costs of manufacture... (Taylor, 1947 in Thomson and Arney, 2015:53).

By contrast, new research began to show that what individuals really seek in their work is meaning and fulfilment and that to achieve improved performance organizations and managers need to take this into account.

Herzberg (1968) distinguished between the factors which improve motivation (he termed these 'satisfiers') and those whose presence could not motivate, but whose absence (or presence in an unsatisfactory form) could dissatisfy. These he termed 'dissatisfiers' or 'hygiene factors'. 'Satisfiers' included high levels of achievement, recognition, opportunities for advancement and responsibility. 'Dissatisfiers' or 'hygiene factors' included supervision, salary, interpersonal relations and working conditions. Where 'dissatisfiers' could be improved and 'satisfiers' increased, performance should improve.

Likert, an American social psychologist, conducted research into the effects of different management styles. He pointed out, in a marked departure from Taylor's position, that managers who focused on task rather than people tended to be least effective. By contrast, the best results were achieved when managers adopted a more people-centred approach. This could mean, for example, involving workers in setting goals and agreeing work methods, and was associated with a close relationship between employees and their managers (Pugh and Hickson, 2007).

McGregor, writing in 1960, identified the role of the manager in motivating individuals to perform well. He distinguished between Theory X managers who believe that employees should be controlled and directed in the workplace, with sanctions in place to deter poor performance, and Theory Y managers who believe that people can usually be, and should be, trusted to accept responsibility for their work and encouraged to seek to reach their full potential. This was an important departure from ideas then widely accepted about management which tended to emphasize managers' responsibility to plan, organize, command, co-ordinate and control. This approach was associated with the work of Fayol (Pugh, 2007) and is still found in some workplaces.

Likert pioneered the use of employee surveys to measure how employees feel about their work and their organization, measuring for example their feelings of loyalty and commitment to it. These surveys produced information which allowed managers and the wider organization to understand the effects of their behaviours and, where necessary, to consider how to alter these. While some organizations continue to use annual surveys, others have now moved to much more frequent sampling of worker responses.

Research into the impact of people management practices on organizational performance has since confirmed the importance of McGregor's and Likert's early work. Guest and Conway (1999) pointed to the importance of employees having a sense of the fairness of their employer and observed that a climate of employee involvement and consultation seems to have a positive influence on performance. Purcell *et al.* (2003) researched the relationship between people management practices and performance and identified that a number of policies and practices could be shown to be linked to improved performance. These included: having some influence on how the job is done; having a say in decisions that affect the job; working in teams; being able to raise matters of concern; having a manager who shows concern (Purcell *et al.*, 2003:71).

Workers who are willing to contribute over and above what is required of them to achieve a good result in the workplace are sometimes referred to as 'engaged' and employee engagement is seen today as critical to high performance in the workplace. Factors which can contribute to this include good communication and leadership and supportive and motivating management styles (MacLeod and Clarke, 2009). You will read more about employee engagement in Chapter 2.

Applying these ideas to your practice

Spend some time now thinking about your own experience of working for an organization, and in particular times when you have felt motivated to make an extra contribution. Can you identify behaviours in individual managers and in the organization as a whole which made you feel motivated to do this?

Improving the performance of groups and teams

Human behaviour in organizations and our experiences of the workplace are shaped by the groups and teams in which we work, and membership of these groups and teams in turn influences our behaviours. They can satisfy social needs as well as contributing to a sense of identity, and when social aspects of groups are working well their ability to manage the task can be improved. For these reasons, groups and teams and the dynamics within them are of importance to leaders and managers, and have been the focus of important research by organization development professionals.

Lewin wrote about the way groups influence their members and about group dynamics, the 'forces operating in groups' (Cheung-Judge and Holbeche, 2015:33). He argued that an understanding of the behaviours of individuals in groups depends on an understanding of these dynamics. These ideas are at the root of his field theory (Cheung-Judge and Holbeche, 2015:34) and they also underpin his three-step model of change, discussed later in this chapter.

Tuckman undertook a review of literature about the developmental stages in small groups, and discerned from this a common sequence. He admitted that the fit was not perfect (Tuckman, 1965:397) with some studies identifying more than four stages of development and some fewer. His model of group development has been widely used and remains a popular way of thinking about group development.

The first stage, which he termed 'forming', was characterized by uncertainty and behaviours designed to test boundaries. This was followed by a period of conflict and challenge, both to group influences and the task itself. This he called 'storming'. In the third stage, 'norming', the group establishes how it expects group members to behave and how the task will be addressed, and in the fourth and final stage, 'performing', when the issues of the previous

Tuckman's stages of group development (Tuckman, 1965)

Forming

In this first stage the members of the group are testing out the limits of acceptable behaviour and making judgements about these on the basis of feedback from the other group members and the group leader or leaders (whether formal or informal) about what is acceptable. At the same time they may be looking for guidance, perhaps from a group leader, about what is permissible, so that this stage of group formation is typically characterized by a degree of dependence on this source of guidance.

Storming

In this phase there may be resistance to the formation of the group itself and to the demands of the tasks facing the group. This may be expressed in tension or hostility between members of the group and the leader or leaders, between members of the group or between sub-groups within the group. This tension may be accompanied by high levels of emotion.

Norming

In this stage the group members move on from resisting and the group begins to cohere. Group standards are agreed and individuals take on new roles in the group.

Performing

In this final stage, group members have learned to work together in ways which enable the group to work towards achieving its objectives.

stages have been resolved, the group is able to perform and to be productive.

Edgar Schein drew attention to the importance of allowing time for groups to form and for individuals to find their place within the group or team. He identified these challenges for all individuals joining a group (Schein, 1988:41):

- What role will I take in the group?
- Will I be able to control and influence others?
- Will the group's goals include mine?
- Will I be liked and accepted by the group?

Schein identified that, once established, the group has a series of responsibilities. These include managing the task, helping the group itself to work well and managing its boundaries. This last responsibility includes managing its relationship with the environment.

Applying these ideas to your practice

Choose a group or team you are currently working in or which you have worked in recently. This could be drawn from your experience of studying or working or it could even be drawn from your social life. Make notes on the following questions:

Can you recognize any of the stages Tuckman identified in group development?

Did you experience any of the challenges Schein identified for individuals entering a group?

Feedback

Tuckman's model may (or may not) fit your experience perfectly. However, if you find yourself in a group where there is a lot of conflict in the early stages, for example, it can be very helpful to recognize that this is often a very normal part of group formation. Similarly, if you feel uncomfortable joining or working with a new group it can help to recognize that there are always challenges to be met.

Helping groups and teams to work more effectively

Teams can be helped to work more effectively by skilled practitioners who understand team dynamics and are able to recognize and give feedback to them on both interpersonal and task-related issues and behaviours. The consultant may be an external or internal consultant, with experience of working with teams and a good understanding of team dynamics. This could be an OD practitioner, but could equally be a specialist in learning and development with OD experience and skills (or an HR manager with well-developed OD skills and understanding).

One popular way for consultants to work with groups and teams is through workshops designed to develop an awareness of how they are performing and of the issues that may be going on in the team. The consultant is likely to notice and give feedback on group dynamics as outlined above. He or she may also address relationship issues within the team. Where the group or team is having difficulty working together, for example, psychometric instruments such as the Myers-Briggs Type Indicator and Firo B can be used to raise awareness of different personality traits within the team. Belbin's self-perception inventory is also often used to help team members to understand the particular role they can adopt in a team. This inventory is based on a model of team development which proposes that a team works best when its members bring a range of skills and mental abilities and each member is operating in a role which is a match for his or her natural skills. You will read more about Belbin's team roles and about team development in Chapter 4, and team coaching is covered in Chapter 5.

Managing change

Managing change is an important focus of OD work – perhaps its most important focus. This section will outline ideas and theories about change drawn from OD and will consider how these ideas have changed over time.

Lewin, writing in the 1940s, developed ideas and models of change which are still widely used today. These were drawn from his analysis of group dynamics and his belief that groups (rather than individuals) are the most important unit to consider in organization development and change. His force-field analysis and three-stage model of change are set out below. Both are still important and influential models, but later in this section you will read about more recent thinking about change which tends to emphasize the individual rather than the group.

Force-field analysis and the three-step model of change

Force-field analysis is a technique for analysing a change situation and planning a response to it. It begins from an assumption that the current situation is always produced by a balance of opposing forces and that an alteration or change requires a shift in the balance of those forces. It can form the basis of an exercise in which a group participates in the change process by identifying

Figure 1.1   Force field analysis

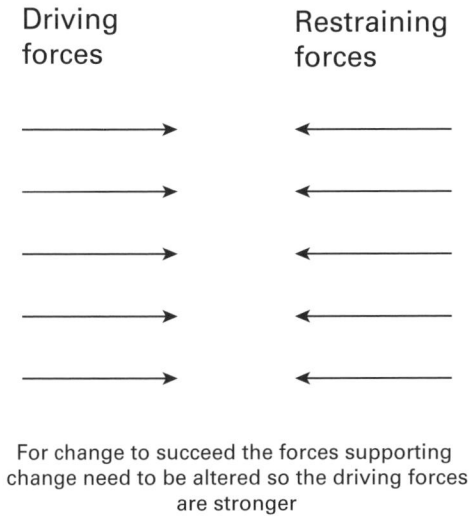

Driving forces → ← Restraining forces

For change to succeed the forces supporting
change need to be altered so the driving forces
are stronger

those factors which are supporting a proposed change (the 'driving' forces) and those which are preventing it (the 'restraining' forces). In this model (see Figure 1.1) the 'driving' and 'restraining' forces could be any internal or external factors, including individuals or groups. For change to happen, the driving forces (that is the forces supporting change) need to be stronger than the restraining forces (that is, the forces which are preventing or blocking change). This can only be achieved by strengthening the former and/or weakening the latter.

Lewin (1951) identified the three stages of any change process as 'unfreezing', 'moving', and 'refreezing'. In the 'unfreezing' stage the status quo is challenged so that the ground is prepared for change; in the 'moving' stage the change is put in place; and in the 'refreezing' stage the change is reinforced and consolidated so that no regression to the previous stage is possible. In the last stage, new practices need to be supported by new group norms and behaviours and, at an organizational level, might require changes in the organization's culture, policies and practices (Burnes, in Gallos, 2006:143).

Kotter (2012) suggested that there are eight stages in any major change process. These are as follows, using Kotter's own words to describe each step (Kotter 2012:23) because these are so widely known and referenced:

Step 1: 'establishing a sense of urgency'.

Making sure that everyone understands the need for change and that it needs to happen soon.

Step 2: 'creating the guiding coalition'.

Identifying and bringing together these who will lead the change and who have the influence or power to make it happen.

Step 3: 'developing a vision and strategy'.

Showing what the change will achieve and setting out the steps that will be taken to make this happen.

Step 4: 'communicating the change vision'.

Making sure the vision and strategy are understood throughout the organization. Kotter notes the importance of ensuring that those leading the change model the new behaviours now expected in the organization.

Step 5: 'empowering broad-based action'.

At this stage potential obstacles to change, such as structures, processes and practices are replaced by those which support new ways of working.

Step 6: 'generating short-term wins'.

Early and noticeable benefits from the change process provide encouragement and it is worth looking for opportunities to identify and celebrate these.

Step 7: 'consolidating change and producing more change'.

Ensuring that the right people and processes are in place to reinforce and build on what has been achieved.

Step 8: 'anchoring new approaches in the culture'.

Change will be sustained by behaviours and leadership and management practices which support it.

These eight stages of Kotter's model are compatible with Lewin's three-step model. The first four steps can be seen as challenging or 'unfreezing' the status quo and preparing for change while 'empowering broad-based action' and 'generating short-term wins' put the change in place. 'Refreezing' is represented by 'consolidating gains' and 'anchoring new approaches in the culture' (Stewart and Rogers, 2012). Hendry comments:

> Scratch any account of creating and managing change and the idea that change is a three-stage process which necessarily begins with a process of unfreezing will not be far below the surface. Indeed, it has been said that the whole theory of change is reducible to this one idea of Kurt Lewin's (Hendry, 1996 in Open University, 2015:74).

Why organizational culture matters

If a major organizational change is to be effective, and lasting, it needs to be supported by complementary changes throughout the organization in behaviours, processes, structures and styles of leadership. Both Lewin's and Kotter's models of the stages of change make this clear. In practice, however, most major organization change programmes fail – Cheung-Judge and Holbeche (2015) suggest a failure rate of about 70 per cent. One important factor which can contribute to this high failure rate is culture – or at least the failure to make sure that the newly implemented change is anchored in and supported by the organization's culture (Kotter, 2012).

Schein pointed to the central role in organizational culture of 'the taken-for-granted, underlying and usually unconscious assumptions that determine perceptions, through processes, feelings and behaviour' (Schein, 1990:112). These 'deeply held assumptions' are at the root of behaviours, processes, attitudes and much else in an organization, and changes which are in conflict with this culture are destined to fail, as noted above. Given, though, that many of the assumptions which lie at the heart of a culture are unconscious, it can be very hard indeed even to understand and characterize the existing culture, let along to shift it so that it can be supportive of a desired change, rather than opposed and hostile to it.

Schein (1990) identified three distinct elements in a culture: artefacts, norms and values. The artefacts are the physical and outward manifestation of the culture. They include the way people dress, the way they behave towards each other and address each other and even the physical environment created by the organization. These artefacts, however, are the tangible expressions of more deeply rooted aspects of culture which cannot be seen and are less easy to identify. There are two levels of these more deeply rooted levels of culture: the first and more easily accessed level is the organization's values, but these in turn express the deeply held and deeply rooted assumptions in the organization which are often held unconsciously and are very difficult to surface and to change.

Schein's three levels of culture

Artefacts

Those aspects of the culture that can be seen. Is the dress code formal or informal (or mixed, in the case of dress-down Fridays)? Are offices designed to encourage working together (as in open plan offices) or are many staff working separately in their own offices?

Values

The organization's values are not immediately visible but can be detected with some investigation. They are expressed in agreed norms of behaviour, for example about punctuality, honesty, commitment to working hard for the organization. Values will also often be expressed in the organization's mission statement.

Assumptions

These lie at the heart of the culture and are expressed in both the values and the artefacts. These are taken for granted and often held quite unconsciously. They can include assumptions about whether people can generally be trusted or whether their performance needs to be monitored, and whether authority should be shared through participative decision making or reserved for senior employees.

One way to understand this way of thinking about organizational culture is to try to envisage it as an iceberg, of which only the uppermost portion can be seen. The larger part of an iceberg is, of course, always submerged and this is also true of cultures. The assumptions and values which underpin and frame the culture are unseen and often unrecognized even by those who are part of that culture and this helps to explain why cultural change is so difficult and so prone to failure.

The cultural web

Johnson and Scholes (2002) suggest that there are external manifestations of the organization's culture which can help to illuminate the hidden assumptions that underpin it. These are:

- the rituals and routines of organizational life;
- the stories that members of the organization tell;
- the symbols of what is valued – such as innovation or respect for authority, for example;
- where power lies and who has power;
- control systems which identify what is considered worth monitoring;
- the organizational structure itself.

Taken together, these represent 'a cultural web... a representation of the taken-for-granted assumptions, or paradigm, of an organization and the physical manifestations of organizational culture' (Johnson and Scholes, 2002:230).

There is an obvious appeal in using these visible aspects of organizational life to understand a culture and identifying and analysing them can provide opportunities for individuals and groups to develop an understanding of shared assumptions. This can be a helpful early contribution to a cultural change programme. However, there are challenges in this too; it can take considerable insight and skill to interpret and make sense of a cultural analysis, whether based on the cultural web or using other techniques. Cultural change cannot, needless to say, be achieved simply by changing the external manifestations of the culture.

Applying these ideas to your practice

Choose an organization you know well and spend some time thinking and making notes about its culture, drawing on your reading about Schein's levels of culture and the cultural web. Make some notes about any insights you get into the organization in this exercise.

Feedback

Trying to understand organizational cultures is complex and easy to get wrong, as noted above. It is further complicated by the fact that there can be quite different cultures in different parts of the same organization. However, Schein's levels of culture and the cultural web can be very helpful in raising awareness of the nature of an organization's culture. They can also help you to be aware of the messages others may pick up from the symbols, artefacts and behaviours on display in your own organization.

Building engagement with the change process

Current thinking about change management emphasizes the active involvement of those affected by it so that they can be motivated and encouraged to support it. This means much more than simply communicating to individuals about change; it means encouraging them to contribute to the change process and building a shared understanding of what it is about.

Techniques for involving individuals in the change process include narratives and storytelling, which help to build common understandings. Leadership within the organization can also play a key role in supporting cultural shifts, and leadership development activities are used by many organizations to support and promote culture change (CIPD, 2015). Those within the organization can also be involved in attempts to understand and intervene in the culture through action research, which is often led by learning and development practitioners. You will read more about action research later in this chapter.

It is very often line managers who can have the greatest impact in encouraging engagement with organizational change and this argues for the inclusion of managing change and cultural change in leadership development programmes. In the following case study, you will read about the way the newly appointed vice-chancellor of the Open University (Peter Horrocks) sees his role in leading change in the organization. This is an edited extract from a discussion between him and Professor Jean Hartley of the Open University's Faculty of Business and Law. In it, you will see how he emphasizes the importance of involving members of the organization in discussions about the changes taking place. He also acknowledges the dilemmas for leaders about when to be participatory and when to move to a more directive form of management.

CASE STUDY

Peter Horrocks: My approach to change is to try to help the group of people I am working with or who are working with me to think ahead, to be able to deal with tough external challenges like reduced resources and to be able to think through together the way things can be changed and improved at the same time as well as potentially having to save money.

Jean Hartley: And as a leader, how might you help people to deal with this change intellectually but also emotionally and psychologically?

Peter Horrocks: Well just by talking about it in this way, acknowledging that it is difficult. I have plenty of uncertainties as it were, in terms of my understanding of the external environment. Maybe it is an odd thing to admit as a leader, but it is true, so all of us are experiencing these similar circumstances and so discussing it together has got to be a good thing. This is fundamentally about sharing the problem.

Jean Hartley: When you arrived here, and consistently since, you have been very open and have invited people to give you comments and ideas. You have opened up things on Yammer and so on. What is the balance between participation and decision making from the centre?

Peter Horrocks: I wanted to be participative. I see sharing information and sharing the problem as being a better way of trying to achieve, if not consensus, at least for people to feel as though their views have been included and respected. The dilemma in relation to being participative or being determinative about one's leadership approach, is fundamental. I have to rely on the evidence that is being put together by a group of people who have got the interest of the University at heart and who have examined the problem and in my view (I know not everyone will agree with this) they have looked at range of options and said this is a way that things can be better in the future and I agree with the logic of that and so in this particular context I am putting, and the Executive are putting a greater weight on that than on the strongly argued views of the people who are expressing their views on Social Media. Sometimes you have to make a choice between those things.

Jean Hartley: So how do you work with, or harness, opposition?

Peter Horrocks: By sharing the problem more. Helping people to see the context of the senior people in the organization and asking people whether, when faced with that information, they can come up with something better.

This case is reproduced with permission from both speakers.

Learning and development, change and OD

All change and OD interventions involve new learning for individuals, groups and teams, and throughout the whole organization. For this reason, learning and development professionals are closely involved in their design and delivery – or at least they should be. This means that they need a good understanding of OD and change. They also need the skills to identify learning and development needs and to design (and sometimes deliver) activities to enable these to be met. In addition to all this, learning and development professionals need to be able to work as internal consultants and to work at strategic level with CEOs and senior executives.

Some of the skills needed to support successful OD and change will be covered in later chapters of this book. They include talent management and development, facilitation, coaching and mentoring, and leadership and management development. This section, however, will cover the provision of consultancy services, developing thinking about OD and the changing role of learning and development professionals.

Providing consultancy services

Consultancy is central to the purposes of OD. Whether internal or external to the organization, OD practitioners will work in a consultancy role, for example in supporting change or development. In OD literature, these interventions are usually held to follow a particular pattern with a set of specific phases, which are examined in this section. These phases are not peculiar to OD interventions and in fact you will find that they are echoed in the establishment of coaching interventions, as outlined in Chapter 5. Cheung-Judge and Holbeche (2015) also point out that OD consultancy is characterized by a commitment on the part of the consultant to working collaboratively with the people in the organization in ways which support the development of their understanding, insights and capability. In this way, not only are they engaged with the development process but they are able to support and sustain its continuation and progress.

Although the definitions of the phases of an OD intervention vary slightly they are generally agreed to include entry and initial contracting, a process of diagnosis based on data collection and analysis, then feedback to the client followed by planning for action and taking action. The last stage is evaluation of the intervention to establish what has been achieved. Cheung-Judge and Holbeche point out, however, that as thinking about OD evolves, some argue that this process is being superseded by new and less structured approaches.

Entry and contracting

In the initial stages the consultant and client will need to explore together the nature of the task or issue to be addressed. Both will probably want to explore the fit between the consultant's skills and the task, and there may also be some testing of 'chemistry' – that is whether both can really work together well and whether there is likely to be a good fit between the consultant and the organization. In the case of internal consultants, however, there may be less freedom of choice about whether they will take on the contract. Where both client and consultant agree to work together there will need to be some sort of contract, whether verbal or written, expressing the objectives of the OD intervention and how the consultant will work with client and the other individuals in the organization who will be involved as it progresses.

Agreeing this contract is an important exercise and is likely to involve the consultant helping the client to think through what the real issues may be. You will see echoes of this in Chapter 5 when you read about creating contracts with coaching and mentoring clients. In OD consulting, as in coaching and mentoring, it may be necessary to revisit the contract more than once as circumstances change or as new understandings or insights emerge.

Data collection analysis and feedback

Gathering information is an important step to understanding the situation faced by the organization. However, the process by which data is collected will itself have an impact on the organization and on the issues being addressed. It is normally a collaborative process which involves those who will be affected by any subsequent actions. Involving interested members of the organization in this way encourages their engagement with the activities undertaken as a result of the data collected.

The data collected may be a combination of quantitative date such as financial information about the organization and HR metrics such as staff turnover and statistical data from staff surveys. There may also be qualitative data from discussions or interviews with stakeholders, including staff and also customers. To be useful this data will need to be analysed and this may mean using statistical analysis (for quantitative data); for qualitative data the task is more difficult and the consultant may simply summarize the main points made.

A full analysis will need to be fed back to the client in a way that is useful; this means that the analysis has to be transparent. However, the feedback session may call on a range of skills on the part of the consultant, to enable him or her to provide support to the client in dealing with any challenges presented by the feedback.

Planning an intervention and putting it into effect

The success of the planning and implementation of an intervention depends to a large extent on the success of the preceding phases; it depends on having successfully engaged the client in recognizing the issues and making sense of the data which has been collected and analysed. The techniques used to intervene depend on the issues to be addressed and a number of the techniques which could be used are described in this chapter.

Stewart and Rogers (2012:47) point out that if OD interventions are to be successful they must be 'designed to meet the needs of the organization, be based on valid knowledge, skills and experience, and through active participation in the design and implementation of the interventions develop and enhance the organization's capacity to manage change.'

Evaluating the outcomes

Measuring the benefit to be achieved through an OD intervention is often challenging given the complexity of the environment in which OD interventions are carried out. It can certainly help if the benefits sought and the indicators of success and failure are agreed at the outset. Evaluation is covered in Chapter 6 of this book.

The fact that change interventions have a poor success rate, as already noted, demonstrates the challenge of managing an OD intervention. At each stage the consultant will need to draw on well developed facilitation skills in order to build successful and collaborative relationships. These skills are explored in Chapter 4 of this book.

Process consulting

Schein identified that in OD consultancy roles it is nearly always best to adopt a mode of consulting which he called 'process consulting' in which the consultant helps the client both to identify the problem which needs to be solved and to work out the best solution to that problem. He contrasts this with the 'content expert' and 'doctor' modes of consulting (Schein, 1988). In the content expert mode, the client is buying expertise which may not be available in the organization, but it may well be that the client has misdiagnosed the problem and/or selected the wrong sort of expertise to address it. In the 'doctor mode' the consultant both diagnoses the problem and prescribes the solution. Here there is a danger that the consultant may misunderstand and misdiagnose the problem and hence prescribe a solution which does not really help.

In the process consulting model the consultant enters into a relationship which supports the client in solving his or her problem and, importantly, by supporting the learning this involves, leaves the client better able to diagnose and address problems in the future.

Dialogic and diagnostic OD

This section will explore the difference between two quite distinct approaches to OD. While OD practitioners disagree about how clearly these approaches are distinct from each other, the debate is important in understanding and evaluating approaches to OD. Fundamental to 'dialogic' OD is the belief that, both in consulting and in managing change, attention must be paid to the meanings individuals themselves ascribe to their experiences, and they must be involved in shaping the outcomes. The purpose of this engagement is to generate and explore different understandings and options, even at the risk of initially seeming to create more complexity and confusion, and with the intention of creating new and changed (and shared) understanding between participants.

Bushe and Marshak contrast this approach with what they term 'diagnostic' OD, in which the focus is on groups rather than individuals and in which there is an emphasis on rational analysis and an assumption that there is a correct answer to be found. In this approach, there is an emphasis on best practice and benchmarking (Bushe and Marshak, 2015:13). By contrast, in the dialogic approach there is a belief that the practice which will work best can be identified by the individuals involved. This means that in this approach there is an emphasis on supporting individuals in finding these solutions and in both supporting the creation of shared understandings and also sharing of these new understandings through discussion and collaborative learning.

Underpinning these two very different approaches are distinct philosophical beliefs about the nature of reality (ontology) and what this means for ideas about how to provide OD consultancy services. These differences, which are set out in Table 1.1, are worth examining closely, because they also inform decisions about how to help people to learn more generally, and you will come across them again as you work through this book.

Table 1.1 Differences between dialogic and diagnostic OD

	Ontology (what do we understand by reality?)	Helping people to learn	Supporting organizational change	Providing consultancy support
Dialogic OD	The most useful way to understand reality is to see it as socially constructed. It is the meaning we give to our experiences which creates the world we need to deal with.	It is important to help individuals to create their own meanings and to develop their own understandings.	It is important to help individuals to create and share their own understandings of the change process and the new changed reality.	Consultants should help their clients to engage in developing solutions to the problems that confront them.
Diagnostic OD	Reality exists independently of our experience of it, and it follows that there are facts which need to be identified and understood.	Learning can mean passing on the knowledge of experts, since that knowledge has an independent existence and value.	Change can be planned by experts and rolled out according to that plan.	Consultants bring expert skills which can be used to diagnose problems and identify solutions.

Edgar Schein (in Bushe and Marshak, 2015) argues that the distinction between these two approaches to OD is not absolute and points out that 'dialogic' OD is in any case not new. For example, the importance of handing to individuals responsibility for managing their learning was recognized in the early days of OD and was characteristic of the T-groups, or training groups, in which many OD practitioners learned their skills (you will read more about these later in this chapter); it was often the members of the T-groups themselves who decided what they would learn. Schein also identified process consulting, which you read about earlier in this chapter, as an early example of dialogic OD, while both 'content expert' and 'doctor' modes of consulting are examples of dialogic OD. Schein argues that most OD consulting should be process consulting, but that in his own OD consulting he moved flexibly between all three modes (Schein, in Bushe and Marshak, 2015).

The changing role of learning and development professionals

It should already be clear why OD is so important for learning and development professionals. Many of the ideas about learning regularly used by learning and development professionals are drawn from the work of writers on OD. However, in OD there is a strong emphasis on taking the impact on the whole organization into account, while in the past specialists in learning and development would often focus on discrete activities, such as individual training programmes. Today, though, learning and development is recognized as a strategic issue in organizations, so learning and development specialists are expected to contribute to strategy development and implementation in the organization. It is for this reason that the organization-wide remit of OD is now seen as so important for learning and development specialists and in fact there is now rather an overlap between OD and learning and development, which will be explored further later in this chapter.

There has also been a significant shift from the idea that learning is best achieved through instruction by an expert. This traditional model of learning still has its place but it is now widely agreed that learning has to be, most of the time, the responsibility of the learner, with the learning and development practitioner providing support, for example through coaching, mentoring or facilitation of learning activities, and also by helping individuals to learn how to learn and how to manage their own learning.

This emphasis on learning rather than training is a response to the need for individuals and organizations to learn constantly in order to keep abreast of a constantly changing environment, to cope with constant internal as well as external change and (often) to achieve competitive advantage in the workplace. With this new emphasis on learning rather than training has come a change in thinking about the nature of what is to be learned. Training has traditionally been based on an assumption that what is to be learned is already known and can be specified (and that the trainer, being more expert, can transmit this knowledge to the learner). A very different and increasingly widely used approach to learning assumes that what is to be learned cannot be specified in advance, or even known; the understanding and knowledge to be achieved will be created by the learner or learners themselves. This approach to learning is known as constructivism, and it is an approach which produces important benefits when new ideas and understandings are needed (Tallantyre, in HEA, 2008).

The open-endedness of constructivist approaches to learning offers profound challenges to those who help others to learn. What is the role of the learning and development professional in supporting this learning, and how can the benefits of this learning be defined and measured? The first of these questions will be addressed in Chapters 2–5 of this book which cover leadership and management development, coaching and mentoring, and facilitation. The second question will be addressed in Chapter 6, 'Evaluating learning and development in a knowledge economy'.

It should be added that this approach to learning can offer profound challenges to learners too, who still often hope for someone to tell them what they should know and learn. Unfortunately, this isn't always even possible given that individual contexts vary so widely and given the rate of change in the environments in which we mostly operate.

Social constructionism assumes that learning and knowledge will be created through social interactions and that learning is therefore a social activity in which participants (for example in a learning event) co-create learning, knowledge and understanding. This idea is fundamental to dialogic OD, which you read about earlier in this chapter.

A new strategic role for learning and development practitioners

The need for learning and development specialists to adopt a strategic role has already been discussed in this chapter and the term Human Resource Development (HRD) has been introduced. Widely used since the 1980s, definitions of HRD vary but it is generally used to emphasize the strategic role of learning and development and its contribution to improving organizational effectiveness and performance. Hamlin and Stewart (2011:41) reviewed 20 definitions of HRD and identified from these four purposes of HRD:

- improving individual or group effectiveness and performance;
- improving organizational effectiveness and performance;
- developing knowledge skills and competencies;
- enhancing human potential and personal growth.

The overlap with OD is obvious and indeed Hamlin and Stewart (2011:47) have argued that OD and HRD (and also coaching) might move to being 'a new, all-embracing field of study and practice', although this is a controversial and contested view. The term HRD is in any case more widely used among academics than practitioners, but there is no disagreement about the principle that learning and development practitioners must be able to think strategically and to contribute at all levels of the organization and that they need an understanding of OD skills. Cheung-Judge and Holbeche (2015) note that an increasing number of learning and development specialists already operate as OD experts.

Supporting learning in the workplace

Just as OD concerns itself with organization-wide interventions, so the learning which supports these interventions must be organization-wide. This section will explore the idea of learning organizations and will go on to explore cultures and practices which support learning in the organization and workplace. These include action research and action learning and reflective and practice-based learning.

Learning organizations

A learning organization is one which grows, develops and learns in response to changes in the external environment. The term 'learning organization' was coined by Senge (2006), although many of the ideas about learning fundamental to this concept can be traced back to earlier OD theorists. He argued that organizations should be seen as systems in which all parts work together in synergy to create a whole greater than the sum of its parts (this is systems thinking, which was introduced earlier in this chapter). In a learning organization, individuals would learn how to learn, they would work with others to create learning and the organization's structures and processes would support this continuous learning (Thomson and Arney, 2015).

Senge drew on the work of Argyris, an important contributor to OD thinking and research, particularly about learning and development in organizations. Working with Schön, he distinguished between single-loop learning and double-loop learning. In the former, learning takes place within the constraints of current thinking and assumptions, while in double-loop learning these assumptions are challenged so that real understanding and learning can be achieved. Double-loop learning is necessary if real change is to be achieved but can only be achieved by managers who have developed the skills of testing assumptions and avoiding defensive responses (Argyris and Schön, 1974).

Arie de Geus, former corporate planning director at Shell, also argued for the importance of constant learning in organizations, identifying it as one of the factors enabling companies to adapt to a changing external environment and to survive – he called this a 'living company' (de Geus, 1997). He emphasized the importance of social learning in organizations, drawing an analogy from the natural world: 'Birds that flock learn faster. So do organizations that encourage flocking behaviour' (de Geus, 1997:57).

For social learning to happen there must be processes in place to facilitate this. This can in part be about the type of learning events which take place in the organization and the next section of this chapter will discuss these. It can also take place informally, however, when employees are encouraged to meet regularly and discuss their work collaboratively. This can happen, for example, when offices are organized in an open-plan way or when employees are encouraged to meet regularly for coffee and lunch. All this can become much harder as organizations move to virtual working, and as this happens new ways must be found to work and learn together. This can be achieved through the use of collaborative online tools and it is increasingly important for employees to develop the skills to use these. This is discussed further in Chapter 2.

Social learning in organizations

Social learning is both created by and personal to the learner, and moulded by social relationships and cultural influences. This is also sometimes also referred to as 'situated learning' (Harrison, 2009), and it is characteristic of social learning that it is applied to real situations and (in workplace learning) to workplace practice. Ideas about social learning are closely linked to ideas about adult learning. Knowles, a leading writer on adult learning, argued that in teaching adults (andragogy) it is important to devise learning experiences which draw on and make use of their experience and their potential to contribute to the learning of others (Harrison, 2009). Both practice-based learning and reflective learning are important elements of social or situated learning and both are dealt with later in this chapter, as are the skills needed by learning and development practitioners who support this learning.

The products of social learning in organizations include human and social capital and the knowledge which is the outcome of learning. 'Human capital' refers to those who create and share knowledge, and many organizations do now measure and report on human capital issues. However, there is no agreement yet on a common approach to measurement (CIPD and ACCA, 2009).

Social capital, which is a closely related idea, describes the value to an organization of internal networks (for example between individuals and departments) and trusting relationships. Both of these help to create an environment in which social learning can take place, and both can be the products of social learning (Harrison, 2009).

The knowledge that is the product of learning is equally of value to the organization. Nonaka distinguished between explicit knowledge, which can be relatively easily identified and recorded, and tacit knowledge, which may be more ambiguous and thus harder to capture; it describes those things which are known, but may never have been recorded anywhere (Thomson and Arney, 2015). It is this tacit knowledge which is most troublesome to manage and, potentially, most valuable to organizations. Learning and development specialists have an important role in surfacing this knowledge and finding ways to capture and share it. These can include informal conferences, workshops and, importantly, communities of practice (Armstrong, 2012:84), and can be the outcomes of action research and action learning, covered later in this chapter.

Communities of practice are an important feature of social learning and can make an important contribution to the development of an organization's human and social capital. They may be communities which come together spontaneously or which are encouraged and supported by the organization, but they are characterized by a common interest among participants in a concern, issue or topic. Members of the group work together over a period of time to develop their knowledge and expertise in relation to this (Wenger, McDermott and Snyder, 2002:4).

While communities of practice may be informal and spontaneous, there are a range of more formal ways of engaging groups to explore issues of common concern, based again on peer learning and reflection, and these are important OD tools for any learning and development practitioners. Two of these, action research and action learning, are discussed next.

Action research and action learning

Action research was developed by Lewin, but he had left only a limited account of what he meant by it at the time of his death in 1947. It has since been refined and developed in a variety of ways, so that there is no one definitive action research process (Dickins and Watkins, in Gallos, 2006).

It is generally accepted, however, that action research is a collaborative and democratic process which combines research into practice (focusing on a chosen issue of concern) with reflection on both the practice being researched and the research process. Those taking part in the inquiry work together to understand their chosen issue or problem and to change it (Dickins and Watkins, in Gallos, 2006). In doing so they develop an understanding of the issue or problem and of how to achieve change, and through reflection on the research process and their role in it they can increase their own capacity for continuous learning and for contributing to future change processes.

Action learning

Action learning is a widely used development method which relies on social and peer learning and draws to some extent on the ideas of action research (Raelin, in Gallos, 2006). Mainly associated with the work of Reg Revans, action learning is widely used in management development and professional development, for example in teaching, nursing and HRM (Stewart and Rigg, 2011). Participants identify a complex project which is of value to their organization, to which they may apply new learning, either drawn from earlier professional studies or (if they wish to) from specialist advisers. Participants work in a group, or set, normally not smaller than 4/5 people or greater than 7/8 people, which meets regularly to provide support, encouragement and sometimes challenge for each member. Each is allocated time to explain progress on his or her project and is in turn questioned by other members of the group. There may be a set facilitator to support this process and to encourage reflection, which is an important element of this learning method. The outcomes should go far wider than simply learning about the problem the individual is working on. There are opportunities too, through reflection on the process, to address the chosen problem and to develop a better understanding of how to address workplace problems more generally. There is also potential for each individual to develop an improved ability to manage his or her own learning and, through observing behaviours in the learning set, to develop an understanding of group dynamics.

Reflection and practice-based learning

The ability to reflect on and learn from experience is fundamental to individual and organizational learning. In professional development, it is reflection on practice which bridges the gap between generic and decontextualized theory and the complex and often ambiguous realities we all face in the workplace. In a complex and fast-changing workplace it is also a tool for creating new and original thinking, understanding and knowledge.

Schön (1983) argued that professional development founded on academic and theoretical study alone could not adequately prepare individuals for practice. Using a series of case studies drawn from architecture, psychiatry, engineering and town planning, he demonstrated how professionals could use reflective practice to learn how to apply theory to the complex and ambiguous situations they encountered in the workplace. In doing so, they developed a store of tacit knowledge which helped them to be effective.

Perhaps the most widely used model of effective practice is Kolb's learning cycle (Kolb, 1976 and 1984). This identifies four stages of reflective learning. The first two stages are, as might be expected, having an experience and reflecting on that experience. Kolb identified two further stages, however: drawing out the learning from the experience, so that it can be applied more widely, and finding new ways of trying out the learning and applying it to practice. These stages are usually referred to as 'theorizing' or 'generalization' and 'action' respectively.

Part of the value of this model is that it draws attention to the importance of completing all four stages of the reflective process. In practice, learners may find that they are stronger or more comfortable in certain stages than in others. In the following case study, you can see that John demonstrates a strong preference for putting his energy into experience and, when change is needed, deciding quickly what needs changing and putting it into practice (action). Notice how his colleague Georg encourages him to spend time reflecting on that experience and using that reflection to draw out the learning from it (theorizing) before moving on to draw conclusions about how to change his practice.

CASE STUDY

John had just finished leading a presentation skills course and was disappointed by the feedback sheets from participants. The ratings were average at best and the comments were lukewarm, but he struggled to understand why. He had had poor feedback on a previous presentation, but he had responded by really throwing himself into this one; his visual aids were meticulously prepared and during the course he had put a great deal of energy into being friendly and convivial with his students. What more did he need to do?

John spoke to his friend and colleague Georg, hoping for more suggestions about what he might do. To his surprise, Georg suggested doing rather less for a while. Just have a good think, he said, about whether there is anything you have missed. What did you notice about participant reactions in each of these courses? Perhaps you could also read the feedback sheets again for both and consider what they are telling you.

John wasn't terribly enthusiastic but he did as Georg suggested and spent some time running through the experience of both courses. He did remember that participants had seemed rather disengaged when he gave his presentation on how to present, and his film clips of how not to present had not gone down as well as he had hoped. He also noticed when he reviewed the feedback sheets again that several had given better feedback for the sessions where they themselves had been practising their skills. He began to wonder whether he might need to rethink the whole course, although remembering Georg's advice he resolved to reflect a bit longer before he did so.

In the next case study you will see how Mina, unlike John, shows a strong preference for reflection and theorizing. Like John, she needs help (which again comes from a colleague) to use the other stages of the learning cycle and to draw the maximum benefit from her reflective learning.

CASE STUDY

Mina had been working as a coach for a number of senior managers. One manager in particular had been quite challenging and Mina struggled to make their time together productive. She spent some time reflecting on what had happened. She also did some reading about different personality types and the different ways in which individuals communicate. She spent some time writing on her personal blog about her experiences and heard from a number of others about similar experiences. She concluded that her personality type was probably very different to her coachee's and concluded that this was why they were having difficulty communicating with each other. She felt quite pleased that she had reached this conclusion and was quite satisfied with this outcome. She reported her reflection and the theory she had developed to her a group of peer coaches and was quite surprised to find herself challenged by one of her colleagues who asked what she proposed to do next and how she would respond when she came across another coachee with whom she found it difficult to communicate.

Applying these ideas to your practice

Choose an example of an experience you have learned from recently. Make notes about each of the stages of the learning cycle, noting whether you carried out that phase and if so what you did. Could you have improved your reflection by paying more attention to any of the stages?

A well-known learning styles inventory, developed by Honey and Mumford (1992), is designed to help learners to develop their awareness of their own reflective practice by identifying how they perform in each of the four stages. This awareness can help to find ways of completing the whole cycle in a satisfactory way. Learning styles inventories generally are sometimes criticized, for example on the grounds that learning styles are difficult to measure because they seem to vary in different situations (Harrison, 2009). However, they can be very helpful in raising awareness.

A rather different way of looking at reflective practice is offered by Pedler, Burgoyne and Boydell (2001). They emphasize the importance of developing awareness of how emotions can influence the way we reflect on experience and the sense we make of this reflection. They use the term 'action tendencies' to describe the ways we habitually respond. It can be helpful to develop an awareness of our own action tendencies and to understand those of others.

Schön (1983) distinguished between reflection-on-action and reflection-in-action. Reflection-on-action takes place after an experience has happened and provides an opportunity to think back on how you dealt with a situation, to identify what learning you can draw from it and how you can apply this learning in the future. Reflection-in-action is reflection which takes place as the experience is unfolding and Schön identifies this as an important skill in complex and ambiguous situations, helping to develop insights and understanding which inform developing practice. Reflection-in-action is not always possible – sometimes action is required quickly and there is no time to pause and reflect.

Skilled reflection means more than simply reflection on personal experience. Gray (2007) distinguishes between this and reflection on the wider social and political context within which personal experience and management practice are situated. He argues that those who are managers or leaders in the workplace should practise reflection in this wider sense, thinking critically about the aspects of society, culture and politics that influence actions and the assumptions that underpin and inform them. Reflection defined in this broader way is often referred to as critical reflection.

Reflection in all the forms described above will be an important support to your learning and your continuing professional development in the workplace. It will help you to make sense of the ideas and theories you read about in this book and elsewhere and to work out how they can best be applied to your practice. Many programmes of study in the fields of Human Resource Management and Human Resource Development and in business studies more generally very explicitly require students to demonstrate that they are able to apply the theories they have studied to their workplace practice and also that they are able to draw learning from their experience of trying out ideas and theories in the workplace. This approach to learning, often referred to as 'practice-based learning', starts from an assumption that decontextualized study of theories and ideas about workplace practice makes no sense unless it is allied to the study of the application of these ideas to practice and their use in varied contexts.

Developing your skills as an OD practitioner

Learning about OD, as you are doing by reading this chapter, is a first step in developing your skills as an OD practitioner. The reflective activities in this chapter have also been designed to help you to start applying these ideas to your practice. In the remaining chapters of this book you will read about organization-wide interventions to support talent management, to develop leadership and management capability, to implement coaching and mentoring and to develop your facilitation skills.

Developing the skills to work as an OD practitioner, however, means finding opportunities to work on change and development projects and developing the personal skills and self-awareness to do so effectively.

T-groups

This chapter ends with an account of the T-groups (training groups) which many OD practitioners have attended as a part of their training.

T-groups are training groups led by one or more facilitators. Their purpose is to enable participants to learn from their interactions with each other, and their experience of forming a group together, about human relationships and group dynamics. Participants give each other feedback about their experience of others' behaviour so that they develop an awareness of their impact on others.

T-groups have been widely used in the development of OD practitioners, and the principles of enabling individuals to learn from working in groups and receiving feedback from peers have been more widely applied, particularly in leadership and management development. The intensity of feeling which can be generated in T-groups, and in personal development groups based more loosely on peer feedback, can be intense. Participants always need to be supported by experienced facilitators so that a safe learning environment is created.

Schein observed that an important characteristic of T-groups was that they were open-ended: it was not clear what participants would learn. They learned from their experiences and were responsible for managing their own learning – this was practice in 'learning how to learn' (Schein, in Bushe and Marshak, 2015).

Applying these ideas to your practice

Spend some time before you leave this chapter making a note of the areas where you might want or need to develop your skills and understanding of OD further. How might you go about doing this?

Conclusion

In this chapter you have read about the origins of OD and some of the ideas and techniques which are fundamental to its practice. These have included techniques for managing change and an outline of the phases of an OD consultancy. However, OD practitioners are strongly focused on engaging individuals in contributing to change and development initiatives and on helping them to develop their capacity to do so. For this reason, OD practice emphasizes both collaborative working and supporting learning and development, both for individuals and organizations. You have read about a variety of approaches to supporting learning, including action research, action learning, reflective learning and practice-based learning.

Many of the techniques used by OD practitioners have been drawn from the works of writers and thinkers such as Lewin, Argyris and Likert, who introduced new ideas about involving individuals in the development of the organizations they work for. Current debates among HR practitioners, however, address questions about whether traditional approaches, many of them introduced in the post-war years, are really still relevant and whether OD should focus more on dialogic approaches which start from a constructivist perspective, believing that real understanding and knowledge can only be developed by those who are participants in the organization's development and change.

More fundamentally still, questions have been raised about the future of OD itself. As learning and development practitioners take on a more strategic role in the organization, some who write about HRD have questioned the existence of OD as a separate body of knowledge and practice, seeing it as a part of HRD practice.

Reflective questions

Can you summarize what is meant by the term organizational development?

What are the most useful learning points from this chapter about helping groups and teams to work effectively and also about how you yourself can work effectively in groups and teams?

How might you go about trying to understand the characteristics of your organization's culture?

How can learning and development professionals support successful organization development and change?

Do you agree with the suggestion that OD is best seen as one part of learning and development practice and is therefore a key skill area for learning and development practitioners?

How can reflective and practice-based learning help you to develop your skills as an HRD professional?

References

Argyris, C and Schön, D A (1974) *Theory in Practice: Increasing professional effectiveness*, Jossey Bass, San Francisco

Armstrong M (2012) *Armstrong's Handbook of Human Resource Practice*, Kogan Page, London

Belbin, R M (1981) *Management Teams: Why they succeed or fail*, Butterworth-Heinemann, London

Bushe, G R and Marshak, R J (2015) *Dialogic Organization Development*, Berrett-Koehler, San Francisco,

Cheung-Judge, M Y and Holbeche, L (2015) *Organization Development and Change: A practitioner's guide for OD and HR*, 2nd edn, Kogan Page, London

CIPD (2005) Training to learning [online] http://www2.cipd.co.uk/NR/rdonlyres/52AF1484-AA29-4325-8964-0A7A1AEE0B8B/0/train2lrn0405.pdf [accessed 11 November 2016]

CIPD (2015) Organization development factsheet [online] https://www.cipd.co.uk/knowledge/strategy/organisational-development/factsheet [accessed 11 November 2016]

CIPD and ACCA (2009) Human capital management: An analysis of disclosure in UK reports [online] http://www2.cipd.co.uk/NR/rdonlyres/7C200E31-F4D8-49A7-8B89-2BE98B003869/0/human_capital_management_joint_acca_cipd.pdf [accessed 11 November 2016].

De Geus, A (1997) The living company, *Harvard Business Review,* 75 (2) [online] https://hbr.org/1997/03/the-living-company. [accessed 20 July 2016]

Gallos, J V, ed (2006) *Organization Development*, Jossey Bass, San Francisco

Gray, D E (2007) Facilitating management learning: developing critical reflection through reflective tools, *Management Learning*, 38 (5), pp. 495–517

Guest, D and Conway, N (1999) Peering into the black hole: the downside of the new employee relations in the UK, *British Journal of Industrial Relations*, 37 (3), pp. 367–89

Hamlin, B and Stewart, J (2011) What is HRD? A definitional review and synthesis of the HRD domain, *Journal of European Industrial Training*, **35** (3), pp. 199–220

Harrison, R (2009) *Learning and Development*, 5th edn, CIPD, London

HEA (2008) *Work-based Learning: Connection, Frameworks and Processes*, HEA, York

Herzberg, F (1968/1987) One more time: how do you motivate employees? *Harvard Business Review*, **65** (5), pp 109–17

Honey, P and Mumford, A (1992) *The Manual of Learning Styles*, 3rd edn, Peter Honey Publications, Maidenhead

Johnson, G and Scholes, K (2002) *Exploring Corporate Strategy*, 6th edn, FT Prentice Hall, England

Kolb, D (1976) Management and the Learning Process, *California Management Review*, **18** (3), pp. 21–23

Kolb, D (1984) *Experiential Learning*, Prentice Hall, Englewood Cliffs, N J

Kotter, J P (2012) *Leading Change*, Harvard Business Review Press, Boston, Mass

Lewin, K (1951) *Field Theory in Social Science*, Harper & Row, London

MacLeod, D and Clarke, N (2009) *Engaging for Success: Enhancing performance through employee engagement*, BIS, London

McGregor, D (1960) The Human Side of Enterprise, McGraw-Hill, London

Open University (2015) *B716 Management: Perspectives and practice book 1, exploring management*, The Open University, Milton Keynes

Pedler, M, Burgoyne, J and Boydell, T (2001) *A Manager's Guide to Self-development*, 4th edn, McGraw Hill, Maidenhead

Pugh, D S, ed (2007) *Organization Theory: Selected classical readings*, Penguin, England

Pugh, D S and Hickson, D J (2007) *Writers on Organizations*, Penguin Business Books, Harmondsworth

Purcell, J, Kinnie, N, Hutchinson, S, Rayton, B and Swart, J (2003) *Understanding the People and Performance Link: Unlocking the black box*, CIPD, London

Schein, E H (1988) *Process Consultation Volume 1: Its role in organization development*, 2nd edn, Addison Wesley, Mass.

Schein, E H (1990) Organizational culture, *American Psychologist*, **45** (2) pp. 109–19

Schön, D A (1983) *The Reflective Practitioner: How professionals think in action*, Baric Books, New York

Senge, P (2006) *The Fifth Discipline: The art and practice of the learning organization*, Doubleday, New York

Stewart, J and Rigg, C (2011) *Learning and Talent Development,* CIPD, London

Stewart, J and Rogers, P (2012) *Developing People and Organizations,* CIPD, London

Thomson, R and Arney, E (2015) *Managing People: A practical guide for front-line managers*, 4th edn, Routledge, Oxford

Tuckman, B W (1965) Developmental Sequence in Small Groups, *Psychological Bulletin*, **63** (6), pp. 384–99

Wenger, E, McDermott, R, and Snyder, W M (2002) *Cultivating Communities of Practice*, Harvard Business School Press, Boston, MA

The role of learning and development in talent management

Talent management and talent development are both seen as important activities in organizations whose people are valued as assets who can be a source of competitive advantage. Definitions of talent management vary but tend to emphasize aspects of resourcing such as attracting potential employees, recruitment, development, retention and deployment. Talent development focuses on part of this range and includes the identification of employee development needs, the design (and sometimes delivery) of learning interventions to address these and the evaluation of outcomes. More broadly, it covers policies and practices which support continuous learning and which promote employee commitment and engagement.

Both talent management and talent development imply a strategic approach in which policies and practices are aligned with and contribute to the organization's strategic objectives and are congruent with each other. Learning and development professionals therefore need a good understanding of both areas so that they can contribute to the development of broader policies and also ensure that there is synergy between their work and wider talent management strategies.

They also need to demonstrate the skills of strategic thinking and business focus. This means much more than simply ensuring that the learning and development strategy is aligned with the business strategy. It means demonstrating the credibility in strategic and business thinking which enables learning and development professionals to contribute to the development of the business strategy itself.

The responsibility for talent management and development is widely spread in the organization and senior managers and line managers have a central role to play. Here learning and development professionals contribute by supporting them in developing the skills they need to do this well. Finally, learning and development professionals contribute by identifying development needs for individuals, groups and the organization as a whole. Once these needs have been identified it is learning and development professionals who are best placed to advise on how they can be met and this means designing (and sometimes delivering) talent development interventions.

In this chapter, you will read about the different meanings ascribed to 'talent' and 'talent management' and strategic approaches to talent management and succession planning. You will also read about broader approaches to building and retaining talent in the organization through people management practices which are associated with improved performance, employee engagement and continuous learning, and how learning and development professionals can contribute to talent development through identifying talent development needs and designing interventions which enable these to be met. Evaluation of the success of these interventions will not be covered here but is the subject of Chapter 6.

What is talent?

The use of the term 'talent' dates from the reference in 1997, by the consulting firm McKinsey, to the 'war for talent' as firms compete to recruit those they believe will improve their performance (Stewart and Rigg, 2011). The term 'talent development' is now sometimes used interchangeably with 'learning and development'. Although the common-sense meaning of the word 'talent' is widely understood, its use in the contexts of 'talent management' and 'talent development' varies considerably. For example, there is disagreement about how widely the talent to be managed and developed is distributed. In other words, some employers focus on the talents of a small number of individuals identified as having high potential or as being in key roles, while others seek to develop the talents of all employees. There are differences too in the talents organizations regard as valuable and in the ways they seek to define this talent. This section will look more closely at these differences and their implications for talent management and development, and at the difficulties of identifying talent and of describing it, for example through competency frameworks.

Whose talent matters? Exclusive and inclusive approaches

There are two quite distinct ways of looking at where talent is to be found in organizations. In the first case, talent is seen in those identified as potential high performers (those selected for fast-track promotion schemes, for example) and those who are in senior management positions. Sometimes particularly important professional or technical groups will also be included (Taylor, 2014). This is sometimes referred to as an 'exclusive' approach to defining talent and by definition focuses on only a small part of the workforce. It follows that in this approach talent development activities are also focused on this same group.

By contrast, an 'inclusive' approach recognizes that all employees (other than poor performers) have the potential to contribute to the organization's success. This means that talent management and development policies are needed which can support all employees in developing their skills and in making the best contribution they can to the organization's performance. In this approach, there is investment in talent development for the whole workforce, in the expectation that there will be corresponding benefits for performance across the whole organization.

In an interview with Robert Jeffrey of *People Management* magazine, Professor Hill of Harvard University observed that very innovative organizations regard all employees as talented, adding:

> At places like Pixar, for example, where they say everyone has a 'slice of genius', there isn't that sense of a really good group of people who

are separate to everyone else... That isn't necessarily incompatible with saying that some people have greater potential to run the company in the future (Hill, in Jeffrey, 2016:41).

In practice, many organizations adopt a combination of these two approaches, that is a blended approach in which talent development opportunities are offered to all employees, with a particular emphasis on a smaller group or groups (CIPD, 2015d). This will generally mean that in practice there is a stronger emphasis on those identified as strong performers.

The talent management and development practices and interventions organizations choose will vary, depending on which definition of talent is adopted. Where the definition is exclusive there may be a stronger emphasis on leadership development for those identified as potential senior employees. There will also be an investment in succession planning to make sure those identified as having high potential are given experience in posts which prepare them for senior roles. You will read more about succession planning later in this chapter. Stewart and Rigg (2011) also point out that the employer may emphasize employee branding to attract high-potential employees and that there may be a strong emphasis on work-life balance to support retention.

Applying these ideas to your practice

Spend some time thinking about the talent management and development practices in an organization you know well. Do you think this organization adopts an inclusive or an exclusive approach to talent development, or does it adopt a blended approach of the two?

Feedback

There is no right or wrong way of defining talent. However, if you conclude that the organization you have chosen adopts an exclusive approach, it might be interesting to explore the impact on those not identified as 'talented'. Is there any sense in which they might be demotivated by the emphasis on others? Conversely, where no particular group of individuals is groomed for fast promotion, how are individuals prepared to take on the most senior posts?

Where a more inclusive approach is adopted, there is likely to be a stronger emphasis on providing a full range of development opportunities at all levels which are open to all. There may also be a strong emphasis on creating a culture in which a commitment to learning, particularly self-managed learning, is encouraged. These approaches may be combined with those associated with an exclusive definition of talent, as noted above, to form a blended approach.

What does talent look like?

It is not easy to specify the sort of talent an organization needs to identify and develop. Individuals may be talented in all sorts of ways, and not all of these may be particularly valuable to an organization. For example, an employee who has a talent for football is undeniably talented, but not in a way that is necessarily helpful to most organizations (Clutterbuck, 2012). Even between organizations working in the same sector there may be significant differences in the talent each chooses to look for in its recruitment policies and to nurture through its development policies.

Applying these ideas to your practice

Think about an organization you know well. What talent or talents do the individuals who work there need to be successful?

Feedback

Your answer to this question will depend on the organization you have chosen. For example, in a large organization the skills of managing relations between individuals and departments may be more highly valued than in small organizations. In some organizations creativity and innovation may be highly valued, while in others there may be greater emphasis on demonstrating loyalty and commitment.

You might have specified a range of talents and you might have noticed that some seem more important than others. This can sometimes be related to role. For example, in specialist roles it may be the specialist skills the individual contributes which matter most, while in more generalist roles management and people management roles may take priority.

These differences may depend partly on the purpose and activities of the organization and also on its size. The talents being sought may also vary between different roles in the same organization. In other words, definitions of talent may be context-dependent and organizations will need to decide how these should be specified.

Many organizations put considerable effort into defining what they mean by talent, so that it can be identified and nurtured. This can be done, for example, through the development of competency frameworks which are discussed later in this chapter. This does, however, presume that talent really can be defined in a meaningful way and readily identified. Gladwell (2008) highlighted the extent to which success depends on commitment and practice and in doing so, he raised questions about how much performance is really about inherent qualities or talents at all. He illustrated this with the story of the Beatles' road to fame. He pointed out that the foundations for their great success after 1964 were laid in a series of trips to Hamburg between 1962 and 1964. Here they played 1,200 live performances. Gladwell observed that this was far more than most bands ever manage and that the skills they developed through this practice were at the root of their later success.

Examples of failure to spot talent are legion. One famous example is John Maynard Keynes' relatively poor performance in the economics paper of his civil service entrance exam. Keynes went on to become one of the most famous economists of the 20th century, giving his name to the Keynesian school of economics. He later concluded simply that he evidently knew more about economics than his examiners. Here are two more examples:

- The Beatles, in 1962, failed an audition with Decca Records. The company's talent spotter, Dick Rowe, allegedly commented to their manager, Brian Epstein, that guitar groups were on their way out (Viner, 2012).

- J K Rowling's first book, *Harry Potter and the Philosopher's Stone*, was rejected by a number of publishers before going on to sell millions of copies worldwide. When she submitted later novels under the assumed name Galbraith, she received more rejections, one publisher even suggesting she should take a writing course (Kennedy, 2016).

The challenge of defining and recognizing talent is made more complex by the interference of stereotyping and prejudice. Where the qualities which are valued are particularly associated with one gender, for example, there will inevitably be barriers for those not of that gender. In the case of leadership, it is commonplace to argue that male characteristics are often given preference; however, where communication and collaboration are emphasized in the assessment process the reverse can often be true. You will read more about fairness and diversity later in this chapter.

Competency frameworks

Competency frameworks seek to identify and capture the behaviours or attributes which enable individuals to perform well. They are typically identified through analysis of those who are identified as effective performers, using techniques such as personality questionnaires, interviews or repertory grid analysis. The competencies identified will usually include communication skills, customer service, problem solving and results orientation (CIPD, 2015a).

Once a competency framework has been developed it can be used to inform a wide range of learning and development and people management activities such as recruitment and selection, induction, performance appraisal and promotion. You will read about how competencies are used in assessment and development centres later in this chapter.

There are some obvious benefits in using competency frameworks. They can make clear to members of an organization which qualities are valued, and it makes sense for these to guide decisions about selection, development and reward. It goes without saying that if the organization publishes competencies which it claims to value but which are at variance with those valued and rewarded in practice, the effects are likely to be destructive of trust and commitment within the organization.

There are two important concerns about the use of competency-based approaches. The first is that competency frameworks which capture the skills of high performers today tell us nothing about competencies which may be needed in the future – perhaps the very near future, given the rate of change facing most organizations.

The second is that by encouraging the same competencies in all employees you may lose the potential benefits of a diverse workforce, including the challenges of different perspectives (Taylor, 2014).

Competencies and competences

The terms competency and competence (and competencies and competences) are often used interchangeably. A theoretical distinction has been drawn between them in the recent past, however, with 'competency' used to describe the qualities which underpin performance and 'competence' used to describe what you need to be able to do in a particular role. The CIPD defines competences as 'broader concepts that encompass demonstrable performance outputs as well as behaviour inputs, and may relate to a system or set of minimum standards required for effective performance at work' (CIPD, 2015a:1). They note, however, that the distinction between competence and competency has reduced as awareness has grown that performance at work, in reality, depends on a combination of 'behaviour, attitude and action' (CIPD, 2015a:1).

Talent management

The term talent management is used in a variety of ways, although it is typically used to describe a range of resourcing and development activities. Learning and development professionals are most concerned with development activities (often referred to as talent development). However, they need a good understanding of the whole range of talent management activities, so that their talent development work contributes to these and is congruent with them. This section will cover definitions of talent management, strategic approaches to talent management and succession planning.

Definitions of talent management

The scope of talent management can be defined broadly or narrowly. In the first case, it is held to cover a wide range of HR activities. Taylor (2014) notes that these include HR planning, recruitment and selection, employee engagement, performance management, coaching and mentoring, employee involvement and employee retention. By contrast, narrower definitions of talent management limit its scope to a much smaller area, such as workforce planning and succession planning.

The CIPD offers the following definition of talent management:

> Talent management is the systematic attraction, identification, development, engagement, retention and deployment of those individuals who are of particular value to an organization, either in view of their 'high potential' for the future or because they are fulfilling business/operation-critical roles (CIPD, 2015d:1).

Strategic approaches to talent management

While there is a disagreement about the definitions of 'talent' and 'talent management' there is no disagreement about the importance of a strategic approach to talent management and development. It is in any case a well-established principle that all human resource management (HRM) and human resource development (HRD) should be informed by strategic thinking, as already noted in Chapter 1. It is not the purpose of this section to look in detail at strategic approaches to HRM and HRD – that is outside the scope of this book. However, this section will give an overview of some of the ideas about strategic thinking in both these areas which inform thinking about talent management.

Human resource management and human resource development

The emphasis on the importance of strategic approaches to HRM and HRD dates back to the late 20th century, when fierce criticisms of the role of personnel professionals raised questions about their ability to add value to their organizations. The term HRM, first used in writings in the United States in the 1980s, was introduced to express the importance of strategic approaches to people management. This meant that HR practices would be aligned with and mutually supportive of each other. They would also be aligned both with the organization's business objectives and the requirements of the external environment within which the business operates (Beer *et al.*, in Open University, 2015).

Fundamental to this new strategic approach to HR was the belief that the people in an organization are an important source of competitive advantage – this was then a radical idea but is now widely accepted and is a fundamental theme of this book. For this reason, considerable attention needs to be paid to selecting and developing employees and to encouraging a culture of employee commitment. There is also a strong emphasis in the HRM approach on the importance of line managers in managing people and many people management responsibilities have now been devolved to them.

The characteristics of the HRM approach have been set out by Storey (2007). Because this is an idealized model, not all the elements set out here will be present in all organizations committed to a strategic approach to HRM. All, however, are widely accepted and all are relevant to learning and development professionals who are committed to adopting a strategic approach to HRD.

Storey's model of the HRM approach

Beliefs and assumptions:

- that it is human resources which give competitive edge;
- that the aim should be not mere compliance with rules, but employee commitment;
- those employees should be very carefully selected and developed.

Strategic qualities:

- because of the above factors, HR decisions are of strategic importance;
- top management involvement is necessary;
- HR policies should be integrated into business strategy – stemming from it and if possible contributing to it.

Critical role of managers:

- because HR practice is critical to the core activities of the business, it is too important to be left to HR specialists alone;

- line managers need to be closely involved as both deliverers and drivers of HR policies;
- much greater attention is paid to the management of managers themselves.

Key levers:

- managing culture is more important than managing systems and procedures;
- integrated action on selection, communication, training, records and development;
- restructuring and job design to allow devolved responsibility and empowerment.

(From Storey, 2007)

Strategic thinking about talent management and development

Learning and development professionals are expected to have a good understanding of the organization's strategy and to be able to demonstrate that their own objectives are both compatible with and contribute to the organization's objectives. In the same way, talent management and development objectives will be aligned with wider organizational objectives and all activities undertaken in these areas will contribute to them. The alignment of objectives and activities at all levels of the organization is sometimes referred to as vertical fit. Talent management and development activities also need to be aligned with activities across the organization, so that they are congruent with each other and reinforce each other. This is known as horizontal fit.

Achieving vertical and horizontal fit is only possible if those planning objectives and activities have a well-developed understanding of what is happening in the wider organization and of what its leaders are seeking to achieve. This is much easier if the organization's strategic objectives are clearly articulated and are communicated throughout the organization. This might include setting out the strategy and its objectives in a written document, which can be referred to by heads of departments or units as they formulate their own local strategies. It can be much harder, conversely, when the organization's strategy is not clearly formulated and communicated. In this case, there may well be a strategy, but it has to be inferred from the actions and decisions of the senior team. This is sometimes referred to as an emergent strategy (Mintzberg, 1978). Ensuring alignment with this sort of strategy requires a well-developed ability to tune into what is happening at senior levels of the organization. In reality, though, even where a strategic plan exists, strategic priorities can change quickly, so it could be argued that it is always important to be tuned into senior management activity in this way.

Succession planning

Succession planning is an important part of talent management and development. This is the process of identifying the key posts in an organization and ensuring that they can be filled promptly and smoothly when necessary. The posts which are the focus of succession planning are likely to be in leadership or senior management but may also include important technical posts such as research roles, for example (CIPD, 2015c). When carried out well, succession planning will ensure that at any time the organization has sufficient numbers of people with the ability, knowledge, personal attributes and experience to step into senior roles when they become vacant (Taylor, 2014:250).

Succession planning involves short-term activities (identifying the individuals who are likely to move into particular roles) and longer-term activities (ensuring that those with potential to move into key roles are identified and offered development opportunities to prepare them for those roles.

Traditional approaches to succession planning, however, have been challenged by a number of factors, including the changing nature of the employer–employee relationship. It is uncommon now for employees to spend their whole working life in one organization (or even one career) so investment in early career entrants may not be best seen as preparation for a senior management role in the same company. There have been also been challenges to approaches to succession planning that have been largely centralized and lacking in transparency. Critics have argued that women and ethnic minorities have been disadvantaged so that some of the potentially most able have been excluded from promotion. Moreover, the elitism and lack of transparency of traditional approaches to succession planning are at odds with current approaches to managing people. These emphasize the importance of a positive psychological contract and engagement of employees in support of improved organizational performance. Open communication and trust are important contributors to both of these.

Succession planning is still widely practised and Taylor (2014) argues that interest in it is in fact increasing. However, it is now more likely to be characterized by much greater openness than in the past about the processes for identifying those seen as having high potential, whether this is achieved through performance review or formal assessment (for example through assessment centres). There is also a greater openness to diversity and there may be mentoring initiatives to support under-represented groups in preparing for assessments. There may also be much closer links between succession planning and wider talent management strategies, so that all employees are supported, and recognize that they are supported, in their personal and career development.

Clutterbuck (2012:11) has argued against traditional approaches to succession planning and advocates a more flexible and dynamic approach in which HR supports and enables the process of developing talent so that 'employee aspirations and talents' are aligned with 'the constantly evolving needs of the organization'. The role of HR in this vision is to provide employees 'with the resources and support they need to grow into new roles'.

Building capability

Talent management and development activities are designed to build the value of the workforce and this section will focus on organization-wide strategies which support this objective. These include people management practices, learning organizations and employee engagement strategies.

People management practices

Much research has been devoted to exploring whether there is a positive relationship between particular people management practices and improved performance, and a number of studies have found that there is. Huselid (1995) reviewed a number of 'high-performance work practices' including appraisal, job design, information sharing, recruitment, training and promotion, and concluded that these were associated with better productivity and performance than were found in firms not using them. Attention has also been paid to the 'psychological contract', a term used to describe the understanding between employer and employee, about the nature of their relationship and mutual obligations. This is an unwritten understanding which may never be openly articulated and is quite distinct from the written contract of employment. The expectations it describes may be 'informal and imprecise: they may be inferred from actions or from what has happened in the past, as well as from statements made by the employer, for example during the recruitment process or in performance appraisals' (CIPD, 2016c). A positive psychological contract can make an important contribution to improving performance (Patterson *et al.*, 1997). One factor which can contribute to this is a sense that the employer is fair and can be trusted (Guest and Conway, 2002).

Further research into the people management practices associated with improved performance has identified the importance of line managers' leadership and management skills. The policies and practices linked to positive results and improved performance include:

- opportunities for career advancement;
- doing a challenging job;
- having some influence on how the job is done;
- opportunities for training;
- having a say in decisions that affect the job;
- working in teams;
- working for a firm that assists people to balance home and work;
- being able to raise matters of concern;
- having a boss who shows respect.

(Purcell *et al.*, 2003:71.)

Learning organizations

Much of the emphasis in this book is on encouraging and enabling individuals to take responsibility for managing their own learning, particularly through reflection on workplace practice. Senge (2006), whose work was introduced in Chapter 1, went further than this, however, and argued that not only should individuals be willing and able to learn continuously, but organizations themselves should be designed to support that learning. He pointed to the importance of 'systems thinking' in which an organization is seen as a system, all parts of which are interrelated and need to work together to support learning, and saw the learning organization as a single system in which practices throughout the organization work in synergy to generate this continuous learning. These practices include a commitment to reflective learning (introduced in Chapter 1) and double-loop learning in which the assumptions underpinning practice are challenged through reflection (you will read more about this in Chapter 4). Other practices include: scanning and anticipating change; willingness to question, challenge and change current practices; allowing the organization's strategy to emerge from practice rather than being handed down from the top of the organization (Open University, 2016).

Employee engagement

Employee engagement policies and practices seek to encourage employee commitment to performing well in their work (this idea was introduced in Chapter 1). This is demonstrated through the extra efforts employees make (this is often referred to as 'discretionary effort'). However, importantly, this effort is directed to meeting the organization's objectives, so that employee engagement can be defined as a 'set of positive behaviours and attitudes enabling high performance of a kind which is in tune with the organization's mission' (Open University, 2014:1). McLeod and Clarke (2009:1) described its effects as 'unlocking people's potential at work'. It is clear that the effects being described here are of great importance in improving organizational effectiveness and that policies and practices which support employee engagement will play an important role in talent management and development.

Storey *et al.* (2009) point out that engaging employees is quite different to simply creating conditions in which they like or enjoy their jobs, since it is quite possible to feel this way without working hard. Some suggestions for how to promote engagement were provided by the McLeod Commission, set up by the then Labour Government to review employee engagement and to report on how it could benefit companies by improving innovation. Reporting in 2009, the McLeod Report concluded that while many organizations had high levels of employee engagement there were still many others where levels were low. Four factors the report suggested to support employee engagement were:

- leadership which helps employees to understand the organization's purpose and how their work contributes to it;
- managers who support and enable their staff, rather than controlling or restricting them;
- communication policies and practices which enable employees to express their views and to be listened to and involved in decision making;
- behaviours within the organization which engender feelings of trust because they are consistent with the values to which the organization claims to be committed.

This last point raises a particular challenge because there is considerable evidence that levels of trust within organizations are low and this is discussed in the next section.

Trust

The importance of trust in employee engagement and in achieving a positive psychological contract have already been noted. However, recent CIPD research showed that only 29 per cent of employees reported that there was strong trust in senior managers in their workplace (CIPD, 2013). The same report notes that levels of trust in line managers and colleagues are higher than those for senior managers and that levels of trust in senior leaders fell between 2009 and 2011, although there has been some improvement since.

While low levels of trust in organizations are not a new phenomenon they have probably been made worse by the challenges of the economic downturn after 2008 and the pressures of constant change. Reduced levels of trust in organizations more generally may have been influenced by public dissatisfaction with the behaviour of some, for example in relation to corporate taxation, and CIPD notes that 'public trust in big business has been falling for some time and this has implications for the trust employees place in their leaders' (CIPD, 2013:2).

One widely used definition of trust in organizations describes it as 'a psychological state comprising the intention to accept vulnerability based upon positive expectations of the intentions or behaviours of another' (Rousseau *et al.*, in Farndale, Kelliher and Hope Hailey, 2009:20). Hope Hailey, Dean of the Bath School of Management, puts it like this:

> the willingness for someone to take a risk, to allow themselves to feel vulnerable, believing the other person has an attitude of goodwill towards them (Hope Hailey, in Jacobs, 2014).

Both definitions emphasize that employees need to feel trusted by their employers as well as able to trust them in return and if this is not achieved, not only will employee commitment and engagement be compromised, but the company's ability to attract and retain new talent will be too, with obvious consequences for productivity and performance.

The challenge for many organizations now is to rebuild trust, particularly in senior managers. This is particularly the case for larger and public sector organizations where levels are lowest (CIPD, 2013). Improved communications can help, particularly by providing opportunities for employees to express their views and to feel that they have been consulted. The quality of leadership matters too. The behaviours of senior managers also make an important contribution to levels of trust. As well as being competent in their roles they need to demonstrate a benevolent concern for others, integrity and predictability. They can also contribute to effective communications through being visible, talking to staff and listening to them, and expressing their recognition of the work that has been done and efforts that have been made (CIPD, 2012).

CIPD (2012) offers a number of case studies which demonstrate how organizations have worked to improve trust levels. One of these, Her Majesty's Revenue and Customs (HMRC), is a large public sector organization which has worked at improving levels of trust in senior managers and has improved its trust scores. This work has included making a considerable investment in the organization's communications strategy 'with far more emphasis on dialogue rather than announcements' (CIPD, 2012:83). It has also invested in encouraging leadership behaviours such as being visible, talking and listening to staff, admitting mistakes and thanking people.

These findings have important implications for both talent management and talent development. They make clear the importance of attracting and recruiting candidates for senior roles who can demonstrate the qualities which engender trust and of selecting and developing those with potential for senior roles with reference to the same qualities.

Attracting talent and managing performance

Once organizations have specified the talents they need there remains the challenge of attracting individuals with those talents to work for them. Once employed they must be persuaded to stay with the organization and to put their talents fully at its service in a way that enables it to meet its objectives. Both are difficult tasks, since there is intense competition between employers to recruit and retain skilled workers. Considerable effort goes into attracting potential applicants for employment and once recruited employers face the challenge of maintaining their continuing commitment and engagement. This can be made harder by changing attitudes among younger workers who may not expect or even want a job for life.

Attraction strategies include a variety of recruitment practices such as advertising and personal searches as well as offering improved salaries and benefits or improved working conditions. Many employers also draw on marketing techniques to create an employer brand which supports the attraction and retention of talented individuals.

There is often also considerable investment, as already discussed, in people management practices which support high-performance working and high levels of engagement.

This section will look more closely at employer branding and at using performance management practices to support, direct and monitor performance and, where this is part of the organization's strategy, to identify future potential.

Employer brand

An employer brand articulates, for both prospective and existing employees, the positive aspects of the relationship they can expect to have with their employer. Its purpose is to communicate:

- the nature of the organization;
- its values;
- what it asks of employees;
- what it offers in return;
- what it is, or would be, like to work for the organization.

The proposition expressed by the employee brand should be applied consistently throughout the organization and should be experienced by the employee in every part of their working life with their employer from appointment up to and including their exit from the organization.

The Chartered Institute of Personnel and Development (CIPD) defines the employer brand as:

> ...a set of attributes and qualities, often intangible, that makes an organization distinctive, promises a particular kind of employment experience, and appeals to those people who will thrive and perform best in its culture (CIPD, 2016a:1).

In setting out these 'attributes and qualities' the employer may choose to place particular emphasis on the financial rewards they offer, or the workplace benefits, such as flexible working arrangements. Additionally, or alternatively, it may focus on the organization's values, for example by emphasizing a commitment to corporate social responsibility (CSR). In practice, many organizations will offer a mix of all these, creating a unique and distinctive brand and employee proposition. They may go further and, instead of offering a simple brand, emphasize different elements of their offering for different groups of employees (CIPD, 2016a).

Advocates of employer branding claim that it can produce impressive benefits in relation to recruitment and retention and can also support employee engagement and even performance. However, to produce meaningful results, the brand must be reflected in all aspects of employee relations so that all people management processes (including talent management and development) are congruent with it. Where this is not the case the efforts put into branding can be counter-productive, producing more negative than positive responses.

At the heart of the employer brand is the 'employee proposition' (IDS, 2013:12). In the case of the financial mutual LV (previously Liverpool Victoria) this is: 'People are at the heart of what we do. You'll need to be sharp with a heart and we'll give you a job you'll love' (IDS, 2013:2).

Applying these ideas to your practice

Spend some time searching on the internet for information on what you might expect if you were employed by an employer of your choice. You should be able to find, for any major organization, messaging provided both by the employer and by present or former employees. You could also carry out the same exercise for your own employer and compare the messages with your own experience of the employment relationship.

Feedback

If you had any difficulty in finding examples of employers communicating their proposition to employees, try looking at Google.com. At the time of writing, interviews were available, for example with employees in Google London, explaining what they thought working at Google London could offer. Their comments included references to the provision of free meals and massages, but also to: opportunities for intellectual and career development; having an opportunity to be innovative; collaborating with and learning from others; and having an opportunity to make a difference to people around the world (Google, 2016).

Income Data Services (IDS) reported that LV's employer brand was widely promoted through external media and that the company reported improved engagement. They believed that the branding exercise had contributed to low rates of turnover and improved employee engagement scores.

It is very easy, through a simple internet search, to find out what working for a particular employer is likely to involve. Employers send out their own messages, but so too do those working for organizations and those who have left. This is an obvious check on employers giving misleading advice on their offer to potential employees.

Managing performance

Performance management systems and processes are widely used to align individual and team contributions with the organization's strategic objectives. In doing so they make an important contribution to talent management and development. Performance appraisals are central to performance management and provide opportunities to support all employees in delivering effective performance and to plan learning and career development. They also provide opportunities to identify good (and poor) performance and high potential.

Performance management systems

Performance management systems seek to ensure that performance at all levels of the organization aligns with and supports its strategic objectives. This depends on effective communication so that these objectives can inform those identified for each department or unit and subsequently for teams and individuals. In this way talents throughout the organization can (in theory at least) be directed towards its most important goals. This alignment of objectives at all levels of the organization is an example of vertical fit (introduced earlier in this chapter). It tends, by its nature, to be top-down, although there can be feedback loops at all levels so that objectives can be revised in response to upward feedback.

The process of cascading objectives in this way can be challenging, not least because many organizations operate in complex and unstable environments. This means that goals and objectives at all levels may have to change very quickly and the process of objective setting needs to be agile enough to respond quickly to altered circumstances.

A further challenge in managing performance is that these processes of objective setting and review must also align with all other people management processes in the organization and with the employee proposition expressed in the employer brand (where this exists). This is an example of horizontal fit and means that performance management processes should complement communication, learning and development and reward strategies for example. One of the challenges of achieving this may be the tension between individual and team objectives which allow for personal and career development and the need to meet urgent and unanticipated organizational objectives. It can be an important part of the line manager's role to find ways to balance these competing objectives.

Performance review

Performance reviews (sometimes known as performance appraisals) are widely used and are typically carried out annually or biennially. These are normally carried out by line managers, and the reports of the review process are often signed off by a more senior manager. They provide an opportunity to discuss, monitor and measure performance and to give feedback both on what has been achieved and how it has been achieved. Just as importantly they provide opportunities to discuss development needs and for an open discussion between employees and their managers about how they see their career progressing. Performance reviews also offer opportunities to rate employee performance and to identify potential, and there may be links between the measurement of performance in the appraisal process and employee reward.

There are many criticisms of performance reviews. They create a heavy workload for managers and can be a painful process for employees. This can be moderated by helping the managers who carry out reviews to develop good skills in performance assessment and feedback. It is also helpful to have good listening and questioning skills and the ability to support employees in managing their own learning and development. These are core coaching and mentoring skills and are covered in Chapter 5. There can also be serious problems when the developmental aspects of review are mixed with measurement rating and reward, and some performance management systems separate these processes.

Many large companies are rethinking the process of annual appraisals, replacing them with more informal and more regular feedback on performance (Kirton, 2015). However, a report by an insight and technology firm, CEB, has raised questions about the effects of removing performance reviews, suggesting that this can lead to a marked decline in productivity (Arnstein, 2016). CIPD (2015b) suggests that when annual performance reviews are replaced by more regular feedback methods it is important to create the conditions in which this can work. This includes ensuring that there are high levels of trust between employers and their line managers and making sure that both parties to the appraisal have the skills they need for the process to work well. It also means 'remembering that the purpose of appraisals is to align individual performance with business objectives and improve organizational capability as a whole, rather than to find fault in the way a specific individual works' (CIPD, 2015b:4).

Measuring performance and identifying potential

Performance reviews usually include an element of performance measurement. One way to do this is to assess performance against the objectives agreed between employee and line manager at the start of the appraisal period. Some objectivity can be claimed for this approach (ACAS, 2006) because it focuses on what has actually been achieved. The involvement of the appraisee both in formulating the objectives and providing evidence of completion can also contribute to a sense of involvement, ownership and commitment to achieving results. However, since circumstances can change in unpredictable ways over the review period the difficulty (or even possibility) of achieving objectives may alter considerably. For this reason, a mid-year review is likely to be needed, so that objectives can be altered if necessary. It can also be very difficult to identify what an individual has achieved through their own efforts and what others have contributed. Clutterbuck (2012:83) points out that 'most problems (and processes) are now complex and beyond individual grasp or solution'.

Assessment of how well objectives have been achieved may be combined with assessment against competencies valued by the organization. This can be achieved through self-assessment, so that employees are invited to provide evidence of competence. This has the merit of raising awareness and understanding of valued ways of working. Ranked assessments against competencies, or against other criteria such as work quality or achievement for example, are problematic, since any rating needs to be supported by good evidence. The danger here is that line managers may have an incomplete understanding of performance, and this may in part be because significant events have been forgotten. Again, appraisees may be asked to provide their own evidence, but some will be more skilled at this than others.

Measuring potential is arguably even harder than measuring performance, because the evidence drawn from what appraisees have done so far can be a poor predictor of how they will perform in different contexts or roles. Reports from managers and self-reports from individuals themselves can be helpful, but more systematic analysis may be drawn from assessment centres which systematically assess performance on work-based tasks against agreed competencies. One-to-one interviews and 360-degree feedback can also be used to provide relevant evidence. This is a way of providing anonymized feedback from senior and junior colleagues as well as peers and is discussed later in this chapter. The techniques used in assessment centres are very similar to those used in development centres, which are described in detail later in this chapter.

In identifying individuals as candidates for succession to more senior roles, evidence will need to be provided of both performance and potential. In the traditional language of succession planning the 'stars' (Odiorne, 1984, in Taylor, 2014) are those demonstrating both to a high level.

Inclusion, diversity and fairness

The purpose of talent management and talent development strategies is to ensure that the most talented potential employees are attracted to the organization and are encouraged to work with commitment as they develop their careers with the organization so that they can reach their full potential. For this to happen, decisions about recruitment, performance review and promotion must be free of unfair bias, whether conscious or unconscious, and the workplace culture must embrace diversity and a commitment to valuing all employees.

There is a strong social justice argument that everyone should have the right to be treated fairly in their employment and in the workplace. This is reflected in a legal requirement in the UK's Equality Act 2010 to avoid discrimination on unfair grounds, including race, religion, disability, sex (including sexual orientation and gender reassignment) and age. There is a strong business case too for treating people fairly. Talent is wasted when individuals are barred from making a full contribution for irrelevant reasons, while a workplace culture which affirms the value of all members of the organization can support creativity and innovation (CIPD, 2016b). Employing a workforce which reflects the demographic structure of the local community can also make an important contribution to the organization's reputation, so that a commitment to diversity can contribute to a positive corporate reputation (CIPD, 2016b).

The 2011 Workplace Employment Relations Study (van Wanrooy *et al.*, 2013) showed the following about the UK workforce:

- 51 per cent are female;
- 24 per cent are over 50;
- 2 per cent have a long-standing health problem or disability;
- 9 per cent belong to a non-white ethnic group;
- 10 per cent are non-UK nationals.

These figures make clear how diverse the pool of potential talent in the workforce is. They illustrate the importance for employers of avoiding discrimination on unfair grounds if they are to recruit and retain the most capable employees and make the best use of their potential. However, there is still considerable evidence to suggest that discrimination on unfair grounds persists in the workplace. For example, there is a pay gap of 24 per cent between the average salaries of men and women in full-time employment (Allen, 2016b) and in 2015 less than 9 per cent of full-time executive roles were held by women (Guardian Writers, 2015).

Meanwhile, the TUC has reported that the unemployment rate for Black, Asian and Minority Ethnic (BAME) workers stands at 5.9 per cent compared with a figure of 2.3 per cent for white workers. Frances O'Grady, the general secretary of the Trade Union Congress (TUC) has commented:

> whether they have PhDs or GCSEs, BAME workers have a much tougher time in the job market. Not only is this wrong but it is a huge waste of talent. Companies that only recruit from a narrow base are missing out on a huge range of experiences on offer from Britain's many communities (O'Grady, in Allen, 2016a).

Learning and development professionals can make an important contribution to supporting a diverse workforce. At the most basic level this can include modelling good practice in their management of learning and development and assessment activities. This means, for example, thinking carefully about making development activities accessible and avoiding difficulties for those with disabilities or caring responsibilities. It can also mean leading the development and delivery of learning events which raise awareness and understanding of diversity issues. Development activities can be designed to support members of groups who are under-represented in particular roles or at senior levels in the organization. These can include providing peer support groups or coaching or mentoring support to help participants develop the skills to be able to apply for senior roles. These interventions are often provided for women or BAME workers, both underrepresented at senior levels in many organizations. These are positive action initiatives rather than positive discrimination; their purpose is to help under-represented groups to prepare for selection or promotion. This is not the same as positive discrimination in selection processes and it remains unlawful to discriminate on any of the grounds protected by equality legislation in decisions about appointment or promotion. For a more detailed account of employment law relating to fairness and diversity in talent management see Taylor (2014).

Age and generational differences in the workplace

The proportion of older workers in the workforce has significantly increased for a variety of reasons. These include disappointing returns from some pension schemes, the delay in retirement age for women born after April 1953 and the abolition of the compulsory retirement age in the UK in 2011, as well as (more positively) increasing longevity. Some observers have identified that the wide range of different age groups in the workplace have different expectations of work and that in order to engage and motivate them, employers need to respond to each rather differently. In particular, there has been a great deal of discussion about workplace 'generations' which are sometimes claimed to have distinctive attitudes to work. While there have been different definitions of the age boundaries, and even the names given to these, they are generally referred to as Baby Boomers (the post-war generation), Generation X (born in the 1960s and 70s), Generation Y (after the early 1980s) and now Generation Z (born in or after the 1990s). The *Harvard Business Review* reported in 2009 that the 'landscape of talent management' had been transformed by the changing composition of a workforce dominated by Baby Boomers and Generation Y (both larger groups than Generation X), and argued that these two groups share many distinctive attitudes and behaviours to which employers need to pay attention (Hewlett, Sherbin and Sumberg, 2009:1). The *Economist* reported in 2013 on a survey conducted by Ernst & Young in the United States which found that baby boomers were seen as hard working and productive, Generation X were seen as the best team players and Generation Y were seen as 'good at tech stuff but truculent and a bit work-shy' (*Economist*, 2013:1).

Academic research has raised serious questions about whether there really is evidence that distinct generations can be identified in the workplace and whether popular stereotypes about the character-istics of each can be substantiated (Parry and Urwin, 2011). In any case, it is important to remember that workers are protected against age discrimination and there is a very short step from stereotyping to discrimination on unfair grounds.

It may be that those in different age groups in the workplace some-times have different expectations about what they want or need from their work and that some skills (such as digital skills) may be more commonly found in those who are young enough have grown up using technology. However, there is considerable variation within age groups and this underlines the importance of responding flexibly to individual needs in the provision of talent development opportunities.

Identifying and meeting talent development needs

In identifying and meeting talent development needs, learning and development professionals will sometimes call on structured approaches to needs analysis and learning design, delivery and evaluation. In many cases, however, structured approaches have given way to arguably more agile approaches in which individuals and line managers take greater responsibility for managing their learning and development. This is particularly the case at the individual level where development needs may be identified in personal development planning or (in conjunction with line managers) as part of the performance review process.

Identifying talent development needs

A structured approach to training identifies training needs analysis (sometimes known as learning needs analysis) as the first step in identifying and addressing these needs. Needs analysis, in this approach, is followed by and informs training design which in turn informs the delivery of training and finally evaluation. Where the needs analysis has been carried out rigorously it will lead to an identification of the objectives of the proposed development. These objectives will be articulated in a way that makes it possible both to design activities to ensure that they are achieved and to assess, through evaluation, whether they have been achieved.

A needs analysis can be carried out at the level of the organization, the job or occupation or at organizational level (Steward and Rigg, 2011). The needs identified are usually expressed as Knowledge, Skills and Attitudes (KSAs).

- **At the organizational level** there will be a need to identify the skills needed now and those likely to be needed in the future, so that these can be planned for. This means identifying the job-related skills needed in the organization and aggregating these to identify how many individuals need to be recruited or trained and with which skills. Without this basic planning, production and performance can be badly damaged by skills shortage.

This needs analysis will be carried out with reference to the organization's strategy, so that the implications of changes planned or anticipated can be taken into account. Change might be produced by altered legislative requirements for example, by plans to restructure or by plans to move into new markets.

- **At the level of the job or role** a needs analysis will again usually identify the knowledge, skills and attitudes needed by the role. This analysis can inform the development of a person specification for recruitment purposes and can feed into reward planning. Where gaps are identified in the KSAs of those already in post this can form the basis of development planning.

- **At the individual level** the analysis will focus on whether there is a gap between the knowledge, skills and attitudes individuals can offer and those required for good performance in their role. A particular challenge here is to distinguish between a performance gap caused by a development need and one caused by other factors. These could include a range of possible obstacles to performance such as poor equipment, relationship problems in the workplace or simply lack of engagement or motivation. In these cases, line manager intervention is more relevant than personal development.

Development centres

Development centres can be a valuable way to identify individual development needs and to help individuals to plan their future development. They share the same methodology as assessment centres but have, theoretically at least, quite distinct functions. Assessment centres are used for selection purposes (either for new recruits to the organization or for promotion) while development centres are limited to identifying individual development needs and providing feedback to support personal development. However, in practice, assessment centres should always offer developmental benefits to participants, whether successful in the selection process or not, through assessor feedback based on the evidence collected through candidate assessment. Conversely, Stewart and Rigg (2011:184) question 'the true purpose of development centres in practice rather than intent', and there is certainly a risk that information from development centres can leak into selection and promotion practices.

Typically, both assessment and development centres require participants to take part in work-related exercises. These will normally include a group exercise which provides an opportunity for assessors to evaluate how each participant works with others as well as how they deal with the task. Each participant may be interviewed by one or more assessors. Assessors use the evidence from exercises and interviews to evaluate participants' performance against agreed competencies and this provides the basis for feedback at the end of the centre. There may also be additional information from psychometric assessments and 360-degree feedback.

Development centres (like assessment centres) are extremely expensive. They must be designed with great care so that the exercises used are genuinely relevant to workplace practice and provide reliable evidence in relation to the competencies being assessed. Also, there is a high ratio of assessors to participants and all assessors will need to be carefully selected and trained if their assessments are to be reliable.

Additional support should be provided after the assessment centre so that participants can draw maximum benefit from it. This can include coaching or mentoring support for participants to help them develop an action plan to address their development needs, and they are likely also to need further support in carrying out their plan.

360-degree feedback

360-degree feedback is widely used in personal development and leadership development programmes and can be a very helpful way to enable individuals to better understand their strengths and areas for development. This is achieved by arranging for them to receive feedback from those around them in the organization, including those who are senior to them, their peers, and those who work for them or are junior to them. Typically, those receiving feedback are asked to choose those who will provide it, but the collection and collation of feedback is undertaken by a third party so that the author of each piece of feedback is concealed. Usually the feedback will not be passed on unless enough individuals provide feedback for this anonymity to be preserved.

The assembled feedback should always be delivered through a facilitator or coach who will discuss it with the individual receiving feedback. This can provide an opportunity to provide help in interpreting feedback and support if the messages in the feedback are challenging.

Feedback is usually sought in relation to competencies agreed to be valuable within the organization (these are usually the same competencies as are used in selection, promotion and performance appraisal) with strengths and areas for development assessed in each case. This can be complemented by freestyle comments about personal areas of strength or weakness. In addition to this evidence there can be striking insights from the pattern of responses, which can sometimes reveal marked differences in the way individuals are assessed by those senior to them, junior to them or at the same level. Where an individual is rated more highly by peers than by more senior colleagues, promotion is likely to be hindered, since it is usually senior colleagues who make decisions about promotion and about access to career development opportunities. Where senior colleagues give more favourable ratings than junior staff there can also be obstacles to career development lying in wait, since most management roles require an ability to motivate and develop good relations with those being managed. Learning from individual patterns of feedback can lead to important changes in behaviour.

There are challenges in using 360-degree feedback. Even where anonymity is carefully preserved, those asked to give feedback may feel wary of doing so honestly for fear of retribution if they are identified and this can lead to anodyne feedback which does not help much. Also, since it is usual for the receiver of feedback to choose who gives it, they may take care to choose those known to be well disposed to them – again with obvious consequences for the value of the exercise. Both these challenges will be less of a problem when 360-degree feedback is understood by all to be fully confidential and used only for development purposes.

Meeting talent development needs

Once talent development needs have been identified the next step is to decide how these should be met. Harrison (2009) emphasizes the importance at this stage of developing a learning strategy. She points out that this means thinking through the learning principles which will inform the choices made, and considering how best to ensure that both individuals and the business draw maximum benefit from the proposed investment in learning. It will also be important to have a good understanding of the likely costs and of the interests of all relevant stakeholders.

There are a wide variety of options to choose from in meeting learning needs. Often some form of workplace learning will be chosen, to make transfer of learning easier, but this is not always the case and employers regularly sponsor learning in external organizations.

In any of these cases another important decision to be made is what use to make of online or virtual learning environments. These may already exist in-house or may belong to an external provider. There may also be scope for making use of Massive Open Online Courses (MOOCs) now widely available, free of charge, from a number of providers.

This section will cover workplace learning and in particular practice- and work-based learning. Collaborative and peer learning through action learning and communities of practice were covered in Chapter 1 and both coaching and mentoring are covered in Chapter 5. Online learning will also be explored, including the use of MOOCs to support both personal and corporate learning and development.

Workplace learning

There is a strong case for workplace learning since, as noted above, it can make the transfer of learning into practice much easier. It can take a variety of forms, including coaching and mentoring (both covered in Chapter 5) which remain among the most popular forms of learning and development. Development can also be provided through secondments, special assignments or projects and work or job rotation. In each of these cases, support needs to be provided to enable the learner to develop the necessary skills, and this will typically be provided by a more experienced worker. On-the-job training will often also be provided for new employees, again usually by a more experienced member of staff.

Where training is to be provided for larger groups, development programmes may be designed. These may take the form of action learning (covered in Chapter 1) or alternatively other forms of peer learning may be introduced such as communities of practice. Learning in teams may be supported through team development workshops, which are covered in Chapter 5.

It may be that some form of accredited learning is needed, perhaps in the form of a qualification such as a professional certificate or diploma, a specialist Master's Programme or an MBA. Accredited learning may also take the form of an apprenticeship programme. These might be delivered by, or in partnership with, an external body with degree-awarding powers. Any of these qualifications can be (and often are) customized to meet individual employer needs. They will incorporate practice- or work-based learning so that the learners are supported in managing the transfer of learning about theory or knowledge to the workplace.

Practice-based learning

There is an assumption at the heart of practice-based learning that knowledge and understanding are context-dependent and are constructed by the learner through reflection on practice. This sort of learning is relevant when new insights and capabilities need to be developed and it can be supported through facilitation (covered in Chapter 4) and coaching or mentoring (covered in Chapter 5). Practice-based learning can be an important way of bridging the theory-practice gap and is widely used in academic study designed to support learners in their workplace practice. This is achieved through activities (and often assessments) which encourage reflection on practice and critical thinking about theory. Critical thinking in this case means asking questions about the value and relevance of theory in the learner's context and challenging assumptions about what constitutes good practice there. This enables the learner to assess how useful theory can be if applied to practice and can make it possible to draw on theory, where appropriate, to inform practice. At the same time, learners are able to explore ideas, theories and concepts through the lens of practice and to assess how, and whether, they help them to make sense of their experience.

For the learning and development professional it is important to ask what is the nature of the learning to be achieved. Where it is open-ended and context-dependent, practice-based approaches may be the most helpful. In other cases, where the emphasis is on the transmission of existing knowledge and insights, there may be a case for training, whether face to face or online.

Online learning

Rapid developments in digital technology have created considerable potential to use e-learning to support both learning and talent development solutions and the creation and sharing of knowledge. Where learners are spread over a wide geographical area, online learning (often referred to as e-learning) has an obvious appeal. It can also offer considerable flexibility to learners, making it easier to fit learning around working (and family) life and avoiding the disruption of regular attendance at a physical venue. Further flexibility can be offered when materials are provided on a variety of platforms, including smartphones and tablets as well as computers.

There are a wide variety of ways in which online learning can be designed and delivered, the most sophisticated of which require considerable investment and expertise. Where design and delivery are poor, learners can be expected to be dissatisfied – this is likely to be the case, for example, where learners are simply provided with text to read online. This is not likely to produce a good learning experience and the variation in quality of provision may explain, at least in part, the doubts sometimes expressed about e-learning (CIPD, 2014). By contrast, well-designed e-learning provision will incorporate interactive activities as well as discussion forums. Skills training can also be provided in simulated learning environments, although a high level of investment and sophisticated learning design are required to achieve this.

Online learning can provide opportunities for learners to study materials in their own time and to come together to discuss their ideas, relevant experiences and reflections. They can also interact with a tutor or facilitator and with other students in the online environment. These discussions and interactions can be synchronous (that is, all participants come together at the same time) or asynchronous (participants contribute at different times of their own choosing, usually within an agreed timeframe).

Synchronous learning may be based in a virtual classroom and this may (or may not) include video of participants. Audio or video interactions may be complemented by a chatbox enabling learners to raise questions or comment without actually speaking. The same technology can also be used in the delivery of webinars and online meetings. Asynchronous learning may take place in a discussion forum and this may be led by a facilitator who may initiate and support discussion.

There are challenges in supporting learning in an online environment. It can be harder to build relationships, for example, than in a face-to-face environment. It can also be challenging to build a sense of community among participants who are physically separated. This can partly be overcome by using synchronous and asynchronous learning tools well: where facilitators and participants invest time and effort in working together a sense of community can be built. Synchronous discussion, especially with video links, can be very helpful, although even here the visual clues provided by facial expressions and body language may be harder to read than in a face-to-face environment, so extra efforts are needed to create mutual understanding and rapport.

It can also be very helpful if learners are able to come together at the start of the learning experience or if face-to-face and online learning are combined (this is usually referred to as blended learning). Since face-to-face learning can make relationship building much easier, it can be very helpful if this is included at the start of a programme which incorporates digital learning.

There is also considerable potential for using collaborative tools and social media to create a sense of a learner community. Wikis, for example, can be used to share knowledge, ideas and experience. They enable contributors to build a single document together, each adding to and amending the work of previous contributors. Wikipedia is a widely known and used example, available for general public access. Blogs can also be used to share ideas and are often used, for example by CEOs, to share their thoughts and perspectives with those working for their organization. Twitter can be used to share ideas and to continue discussions which complement the objectives of the learning experience. In developing the skills of building a sense of community in a virtual world, learners and facilitators are developing digital literacy skills which have direct relevance to their work in the wider organization. All the tools mentioned here are widely used in communication and knowledge building in organizations, and the ability to communicate and build relationships in virtual environments is relevant to those who work with virtual teams or in geographically dispersed organizations.

Another important challenge in e-learning can be the technology itself, since online learning (particularly synchronous learning) depends on the availability of broadband, which cannot be assumed at all times and in all locations. In asynchronous learning, this can partly be overcome by ensuring that materials can be downloaded and studied offline – and printed, if learners prefer this. Some learners

Applying these ideas to your practice

Spend some time now exploring the use of online tools in your own workplace or in another organization you know well. Make some notes about how helpful you think they are in supporting communication and about any problems you see in their use.

Feedback

As well as wikis and blogs, you may have noticed that there are tools which make synchronous (that is, real time) discussion possible. These may include video facilities and, in the case of webinars, may provide additional facilities such as online chat boxes to complement discussion. There may also be asynchronous discussion groups (such as Yammer, for example) to which individuals contribute at different times. All these tools can help to support quick and easily accessible communication. You may have identified that there can also be problems. For example, it can be very easy to overload others with information – something already widely recognized by e-mail users. Material posted online can also be circulated very widely indeed, very quickly – again, this is something e-mail users have learned to their cost. For this reason, communication in an online environment needs to be considered quite carefully. It can also be harder to communicate well when the non-verbal elements of communication, such as body language, are either absent or, in the case of video, usually harder to read.

in any case prefer not to read large amounts of text online and for this reason it makes sense to make provision for learners to be able to print off at least the most complex materials.

The skills needed to be effective in using online tools are not primarily technical, although it is obviously important to understand how they work. The skills of communicating and building relationships in a virtual world are far more important if they are to be used effectively. These have been introduced in this chapter and will be discussed further in Chapter 4.

Massive Open Online Courses (MOOCs)

E-learning is available in the form of MOOCs to anyone who has internet access. These are short courses delivered online and are free of charge to learners. They are designed to be easily accessible and attractive to time-poor learners, so there is a strong emphasis on designing learning so it is easy to follow and learners are engaged quickly. This can be achieved, for example, by ensuring that progression of learning is carefully planned and students can participate in discussion of materials as they are studying them. There may be social media features such as 'liking' materials or 'following' areas of personal interest, and there may be 'to do' lists and progress bars to encourage completion.

There are a number of providers of MOOCs. FutureLearn, for example, is a company owned by the Open University and launched in 2012. It provides MOOCs in partnership with a number of UK and international universities. MOOCs have the potential to make a considerable difference to both higher education and online learning. This is partly because they provide a model of easily accessible online learning but also they offer access to free learning which any organization can draw on. MOOCs do offer certificates of completion (although these are not free) and can provide routes into accredited higher education programmes.

Applying these ideas to your practice

Spend some time exploring what MOOCs are available and make notes on any you find which you could use to support your personal development or which might be useful in corporate learning.

Conclusion

Competition for talent is so intense that talent management and development are at the heart of people management practice in many organizations. Employers draw on marketing techniques to create a brand which is attractive both to potential and existing employees to support the recruitment and retention of the most talented individuals. This is made harder by the unwillingness of many, particularly younger, employees to commit themselves to working for a single employer, or even to a single career for their whole working life.

Strategic approaches to talent management and development tend to draw on a resource-based view of the firm which emphasizes the importance of its people as an asset to be invested in rather than a cost. Strategic planning of talent management has to achieve vertical fit, so that the objectives and activities of all parts of the organization and all individuals within it support the overall strategic objectives. It must also achieve horizontal fit so that all people management practices are congruent and supportive of each other. Learning and talent development professionals need a well-developed understanding of strategic thinking and planning if their activities are to contribute to this process. This is especially difficult when the organization's policy is emergent and must be divined from the actions and decisions of the senior management team, rather than by simply consulting a policy document.

Line managers and senior managers play an important role in talent management and development and it is important that they are supported in developing the skills to do this effectively. They need to be able to support performance reviews and for this they need the ability to create trusting relationships with employees so that open and meaningful conversations can take place, and to make judgements which are free of unfair discrimination and bias. Other important skills include the ability to listen well and ask helpful questions, to support individuals in taking responsibility for their own development, and to give feedback to support improved performance. All these are the skills good coaches can deploy and they are discussed further in Chapter 5.

Learning and development professionals play an important role in each of the areas identified above. They also make an important contribution by identifying development needs at organization, job and individual level and (where needed) by designing and delivering development interventions to meet these. Techniques for identifying development needs should include high-level research projects (at organization-wide level) as well as more individual-focused techniques such as 360-degree feedback and development centres, which can complement feedback from performance reviews.

Reflective questions

Are there circumstances in which an exclusive approach to talent management might be preferable to an inclusive approach, and if so, what are these?

What are the advantages and disadvantages of using competencies to define the talents an organization values?

In what circumstances might an organization have an emergent strategy rather than one which is set out in a written document?

What sorts of activities might an employer carry out to identify its brand and what tools might be used to advertise it?

How can line managers and senior managers be helped to develop the skills they need to support employees in improving their performance?

What arguments might be used to persuade a senior management team of the value of investing in a diversity awareness programme?

References

ACAS (2006) *Employee Appraisal*, advisory booklet [online] www.acas.org.uk/media/pdf/s/b/B071.pdf [accessed 1 August 2016]

Allen, K (2016a) BAME graduates '2.5 times more likely to be jobless than white peers', *Guardian* [online] www.theguardian.com/society/2016/apr/15/bame-graduates-25-times-more-likely-to-be-jobless-than-white-peers [accessed 26 August 2016]

Allen, K (2016b) Women earn £30,000 less than men over working life, *Guardian* [online] www.theguardian.com/money/2016/mor/07/gender-pay-gap-uk-women-earn-30000-less-men-lifetime [accessed 26 August 2016]

Arnstein, V (2016) Scrapping performance reviews causes 'significant' drops in productivity, *People Management*, 9 June [online] www.cipd.co.uk/pm/peoplemanagement/b/weblog/archive/2016/06/09 [accessed 1 August 2016]

CIPD (2012) *Where Has All the Trust Gone?* Research report, CIPD, London

CIPD (2013) *Are Organizations Losing the Trust of Their Workers?* Megatrend Report, CIPD, London

CIPD (2014) *Learning and Development: Annual survey report 2014,* CIPD, London

CIPD (2015a) Competence and competency frameworks factsheet [online] https://www.cipd.co.uk/knowledge/fundamentals/people/performance/competency-factsheet [accessed 8 June 2016]

CIPD (2015b) Performance appraisal factsheet [online] https://www.cipd.co.uk/knowledge/fundamentals/people/performance/appraisals-factsheet [accessed 8 June16]

CIPD (2015c) Succession planning factsheet [online] https://www.cipd.co.uk/knowledge/strategy/resourcing/succession-planning-factsheet [accessed 19 July 2016]

CIPD (2015d) Talent management: an overview factsheet [online] https://www.cipd.co.uk/knowledge/strategy/resourcing/talent-factsheet [accessed 26 May 2016]

CIPD (2016a) Employer brand factsheet [online] https://www.cipd.co.uk/knowledge/fundamentals/people/recruitment/brand-factsheet [accessed 8 June 2016]

CIPD (2016b) Diversity in the workplace: an overview factsheet [online] https://www.cipd.co.uk/knowledge/fundamentals/relations/diversity/factsheet [accessed 27 July 2016]

CIPD (2016c) The psychological contract factsheet [online] https://www.cipd.co.uk/knowledge/fundamentals/relations/employees/psychological-factsheet [accessed 1 September 2016]

Clutterbuck, D (2012) *The Talent Wave: Why succession planning fails and what to do about it*, Kogan Page, London

Economist (2013) Winning the generation game: Generations in the workplace, *Economist,* 28 September

Farndale, E, Kelliher, C and Hope Hailey, V (2011) High commitment performance management: the role of organisational justice and trust, *Personnel Review*, **40** (1) pp. 5–23, DOI: 10.1108/00483481111095492

Gladwell, M (2008) *Outliers*, Allen Lane, London

Google (2016) Working at Google London [online] www.google.com/ AboutGoogle/Careers/LifeatGoogle/WorkingatGoogleLondon [accessed 30 July 2016]

Guardian writers (2015) Where are the cracks in the glass ceiling? *Guardian* [online] www.theguardian.com/world/2015/dec/30/women-feminism-2015-glass-ceiling [accessed 26 August 2016]

Guest, D and Conway, N (2002) *Pressure at Work and the Psychological Contract,* CIPD, London

Harrison, R (2009) *Learning and Development,* 5th edn, CIPD, London

Hewlett, S A, Sherbin, L and Sumberg, K (2009) How Gen Y and Boomers will reshape your Agenda, *Harvard Business Review* [online] https://hbr.org/2009/07/how-gen-y-boomers-will-reshape-your-agenda [accessed 1 September 2016)

Huselid, M (1995) The impact of human resource management practices on turnover, productivity and corporate financial performance, *Academy of Management Journal* 38 (3), pp. 635–72

IDS (2013) LV= uses latest technology to communicate employer brand and attract new recruits, HR in Practice Case Study, Thomson Reuters, London

Jacobs, K (2014) How to build trust in organizations, *HR Magazine* [online] www.hrmagazine.co.uk/article-details/how-to-build-trust-in-organiszations [accessed 24 August 2016]

Jeffry, R (2016) You won't keep people if you don't develop them, *People Management,* July, pp. 40–41

Kennedy, M (2016) J K Rowling posts letters of rejection on Twitter to help budding authors, *Guardian* [online] www.theguardian.com/books/2016/mar/25/jk-rowling-harry-potter-posts-letters-of-rejection-on-twitter [accessed 27 August 2016]

Kirton, H (2015) Appraisals are finished. What's next? *People Management,* 20 August

McLeod, D and Clark, N (2009) *Engaging for success: Enhancing performance through employee engagement,* Department for Business Innovation and Skills, London

Mintzberg, H (1978) Patterns in strategy formation, *Management Science,* 24 (9), pp. 934–48

Open University (2014) BB845 Strategic Human Resource Management Unit 3 'Employee Engagement', The Open University, Milton Keynes

Open University (2015) B864 Human Resource Management in Context Unit 2 'HR Strategy in Context', The Open University, Milton Keynes

Open University (2016) B867 Workplace learning with coaching and mentoring Unit 4 'Learning and talent development in the workplace', The Open University, Milton Keynes

Parry, E and Urwin, P J (2011) Generational differences in work values: a review of theory and evidence, *International Journal of Management Reviews*, **13** (1) pp. 79–96

Patterson, M G, West, A W, Lawthorn, R and Nickell, S (1997) *Impact of People Management Practices on Business Performance*, Institute of Personnel and Development, London

Purcell, J, Kinnie, N, Hutchinson, S, Rayton, B and Swart, J (2003) *Understanding the People and Performance Link: Unlocking the black box*, CIPD, London

Senge, P M (2006) *The Fifth Discipline: The art and practice of the learning organization* (revised edition) Random House, London

Stewart, J and Rigg, C (2011) *Learning and Talent Development*, CIPD, London

Storey, J, ed (2007) *Human Resource Management: A critical text*, 2nd edn, Thomson, London

Storey, J, Ulrich, D, Welbourne, T M and Wright, P M (2009) Employee engagement, in *The Concise Companion to Human Resource Management*, ed J Storey, P M Wright and D Ulrich, Routledge, Abingdon

Taylor, S (2014) *Resourcing and Talent Management*, 6th edn, CIPD, London

Viner, B (2012) The man who rejected the Beatles, *Independent*, 12 February [online] www.independent.co.uk/arts-entertainment/music/news/the-man-who-rejected-the-beatles-6782008.htm [accessed 12 November 2016]

Van Wanrooy, B, Bewley, H, Bryson, A, Forth, J, Freeth, S, Stones, L and Wood, S (2013) The 2011 workplace employment relations study: first findings, *Gov.uk* [online] https://www.gov.uk/government/uploads/system/uploads/attachment_data/file/336651/bis-14-1008-WERS-first-findings-report-fourth-edition-july-2014.pdf [accessed 26 August 2016]

Developing leadership and management capability

03

REBECCA PAGE-TICKELL

Introduction

This chapter will address the theories of leadership and management and the options for development which emerge. Leadership and management have been studied extensively from a number of different perspectives; for example, Spillane and Martin (2005), in reviewing managerial psychology, consider perspectives as wide as psychoanalysis, anthropology, psychology and philosophy to provide an insight into the nature of leadership as well as management. Much of the research is contested, and in terms of both understanding what good managerial and leadership behaviour is and predicting what will be relevant and useful in the future, there are still more areas that we are unclear about than areas in which we have confidence.

This provides both an opportunity and a challenge for the L&D professional. Leadership and management are contextually based – that is, they depend entirely on where and how they are applied. The culture of the organization, nation, industry and perhaps even function has a fundamental impact on the effectiveness of leadership or managerial behaviour. The reason for this is that leadership is very much in the eye of the beholder – that is, it is dependent on those who are following and those who receive the results of that leadership and management, for example, various stakeholders. The opportunity for the HR professional is to identify and agree across the organization what leadership and management really mean. The challenge is to link that to measures of success and development interventions that can be demonstrated to be effective. The design and development of the organization itself will also relate a great deal to what this organization considers management and leadership to be.

Organizations of all types crave good leaders, and for their sustainable success it is indeed essential that they have them. We will consider the nature of leadership and identify the differences between leadership and management. The value of each and their appropriate place within the organization will also be discussed. The previous chapter discussed the importance of managing talent across the organization. In this chapter, we will go on to consider the importance of developing that segment of talent that will shape and direct the organization, ie management and leadership.

I will go on to discuss the various different approaches to developing leaders and managers and the role of the learning and development function in ensuring that this takes place in line with the overall business strategy. This must ensure that the ownership of leadership and management development programmes remains firmly with senior line managers in order to ensure that it is fully integrated with the business. Finally I will discuss ways of measuring the success, or otherwise, of various interventions to help ensure that they deliver recognizable value for the organization. Development of leaders and managers is a highly iterative process and this recognition can be the lever for further development in order to build organizational capability and ensure ongoing competitiveness.

Investigating the difference between leadership and management

The distinction between leaders and managers has been implicitly accepted in development literature since its beginning. Often discussed and reviewed, but never satisfactorily resolved, the underlying question of the difference between leadership and management and their overlap is a persisting debate. Mullins (2013: 375) notes that both leadership and management overlap and both qualities are required. 'It is one thing for a leader to propound a grand vision, but this is redundant unless the vision is managed so it becomes a real achievement'.

The debate is essentially between finding and developing individuals who are efficient in maintaining organizational direction and those who are effective in envisioning and driving an organization towards specific goals. Taking into account the variety of organizations and industries – nationally and internationally – identifying and differentiating managerial and leadership capabilities is problematic.

Leadership and management are both functions that guide and direct an organization. However, leadership is focused on providing overall guidance and strategic direction, very much like the captain sailing a ship – setting the course, taking overall control and guiding the ship to its destination. Management is a function which maintains control and ensures that all the resources are readily available, and all members of the ship and the ship's processes are capable of completing the journey. The roles complement one another, but also overlap – the captain is, in fact, responsible for both elements. In practice, differentiating between the two can be challenging.

The overlap between leadership and management can cause confusion in L&D as these roles have contrasting requirements, but in reality both tend to be a requirement of many roles. It is therefore incumbent on the L&D practitioner to support employees in identifying the difference between the two and understand when they are operating out of each role. The short diagnostic questionnaire below (Table 3.1) can be used to support employees in identifying the balance of activities in which they are involved and the appropriateness of that balance.

Kotter (1990) has been particularly insightful in understanding the difference between management and leadership. He noted that leadership is a practical active task which is a necessary complement to management: 'Each has its own function and characteristic activities. Both are necessary for success in today's business environment.'

Table 3.1 Quick diagnostic to identify if you are involved more with leadership or management tasks

Tick here if the description on this side describes you	What does this task involve?		Tick here if the description on this side describes you
	Does it involve efficient use of resources?	Does it involve designing effective systems or processes?	
	Is it mostly concerned with current team and production issues?	Does it involve future resources, team projects or other new innovations?	
	Are you focused on getting things done right?	Are you focused on ensuring that the organization is doing the right thing in the emerging economy?	
	Have you identified a better way of getting things done – perhaps cheaper, faster or easier?	Have you questioned the way things are done to ensure that they are aligned against what the business will need to stay competitive?	
	Is it primarily concerned with maintenance of existing organizational systems?	Is it primarily involved with predicting what will be needed in future systems and processes?	
	Are you dealing mostly with people within the organization or directly related to your own function?	Are you mostly dealing with people across the entire organization or external people?	

(Continued)

Table 3.1   *(Continued)*

Tick here if the description on this side describes you	What does this task involve?		Tick here if the description on this side describes you
	Are you focused on one part of the organization?	Are you focused on the whole organization?	
	Do you have authority over a group of people who recognize you are the decision maker?	Do you influence a large group of people, some of whom you don't know, through your behaviour and choices?	

Managers tend to focus primarily on the administration of processes, ensuring that systems and policies are implemented smoothly and managing the various complexities of day-to-day operations. This can happen at a range of levels from supervisor of basic processes through to implementation of highly complex global systems. Kotter notes that 'Management is about coping with complexity. Its practices and procedures are largely a response to the emergence of large, complex organizations in the 20th century (Kotter, 1990: 103). Certainly, the emergence of large multinational organizations has led to the development of a profession of managers. This is verified through the professional body, the Institute of Leadership and Management. They provide research and support for the ongoing development of leaders and managers and are a useful ongoing source of research as well as practical support.

In terms of development of both leaders and managers, 25 years ago Kotter noted that organizations in his opinion were over-managed and under-led, with a pressing need to develop their capacity to exercise leadership. In his research, he found that one factor differentiating successful organizations was a pro-active search for leadership talent, actively seeking out people with leadership potential and exposing them to career experiences designed to develop that potential. Indeed, with careful selection, nurturing, and encouragement, dozens of people can play important leadership roles in a business organization. He noted that while improving their ability to lead, companies should remember that strong leadership with weak management is no better, and is sometimes actually worse, than the reverse. The real challenge is to combine strong leadership and strong management and use each to balance the other.

The quick diagnostic in Table 3.1 uses a series of heuristics or rules of thumb to identify whether the activity taking place is primarily leadership or management focused. This can prove useful as an initial tool to support managers in identifying the extent to which they are focusing on the appropriate tasks, or perhaps whether they are approaching their tasks from the appropriate angle.

If your ticks are more to the left, then you are involved primarily in management activities. Are you taking enough of a leadership approach?

If your ticks are more to the right, then you are primarily involved in leadership-based activities. Are you ensuring that as well as starting activities you are making sure that activities are completed efficiently?

This rough and ready questionnaire should provide a source of reflection to enable you to identify the balance of leadership and management activities in your work – are they at an appropriate level? Do they match your role description? If not, should you adapt or could the role itself be adapted? How will you manage this situation?

Models of management

Management is a process conducted in organizations to enable them to survive, and hopefully thrive over the longer term. There have been many definitions of management which have been a focus of intense study for decades. There are many definitions of management, which take multiple perspectives, but are primarily complementary. This is in contrast to the leadership literature where varying perspectives frequently conflict.

Henri Fayol (1841–1925) revolutionized our understanding of management. While he spent his entire working life in one mining organization, his ideas have been applied across industries and it could be suggested that even at the present time his ideas constitute the foundation of our understanding of management and what it is to develop managers. Fayol's core process was the breaking down of the management task into specific principles of management. These are:

- *Division of work* – specializing specific tasks and sets of processes for efficiency.
- *Authority and responsibility* – a clarity around the role of the manager in giving clear orders and instructions, with sanctions.
- *Discipline* – ensuring that organizational requirements are met, through persuasion and tact as well as sanctions.
- *Unity of command* – orders should come from only one person to avoid confusion.
- *Unity of direction* – there should be a singular head and plan for a set of activities.
- *Subordination of individual interest to the general interest* – the needs of the business as a whole come before those of the individual.
- *Remuneration of personnel* – should be fair and appropriate both in amount and in the mode of payment.
- *Centralization* – there should be a central recognizable authority for the organization as a whole.
- *Scalar chain (line of authority)* – a clear chain of authority should be identifiable from the most junior to an ultimate authority.
- *Order* – there should be a place for everything and everything in its place.
- *Equity* – personnel should be treated with both kindness and justice.
- *Stability of tenure of personnel* – managers should remain in position for a significant period of time.
- *Initiative* – deciding on a plan and putting it into action.
- *Esprit de corps* – a sense of harmony among the personnel.

(Fayol, 1949/1916.)

These can be collapsed to the processes of forecasting, planning, organizing, commanding, coordinating and controlling. This list is typically thorough of Fayol and, although constrained by both location and time, these principles have played a key role in our understanding of management. The analysis that Fayol conducted was based on his personal experience rather than any strictly scientific or rigorous study and has some elements of overlap as well as a clear focus on direction solely from the top of the organization. His importance to the learning and development community stems additionally from his insistence that management theories could be taught and managers developed.

The most significant management theory that followed Fayol was that of Taylor, known as scientific management, or Taylorism. The focus here was on efficiency of process. His method included breaking and analysing workflow in order to break down tasks to smaller components and build efficiency. The methods of scientific management, whilst less popular after the 1930s, have influenced many approaches in management, notably Total Quality Management, which also focuses on building the efficiency of complex processes across large organizations. In terms of learning and development, Taylorism focuses on simplifying the task rather than developing the employee.

The approaches of Fayol and scientific management seek to apply a standard template or best practice approach across industry. They contrast with the current emphasis on the role of frontline managers. Purcell *et al*. (2003) identified the importance of the activities of line managers in engaging and enabling employees. In most cases, line managers implement the learning and development activities. Purcell *et al*. investigated the 'black box' of motivation – that is, they wanted to understand what line managers can do to support the motivation of employees. Their findings were that a combination of three factors are key in enabling both individual and team performance. These factors are:

- **Ability** – To identify the specific abilities that each employee has and to ensure that they are placed in an appropriate role and that development is available to allow them to perform well.

- **Motivation** – Providing the right levers to motivate employees to higher levels of performance, for example.

- **Opportunity** – To have the opportunity to develop and grow both within the role and also through moving into other roles, whether a sideways move or a promotion.

Deceptively simple, these factors provide a template for the design of L&D interventions, which are fully aligned with HR interventions and enable the organization to build performance. More recently, this model has been linked to the literature on employee engagement. Frontline managers are particularly important and there is a very good ACAS booklet called *Front Line Managers* (2014) which distils a number of ideas from the literature for practitioners use.

Brech in 1984 went on to suggest that management is the social process of planning, coordination, control and motivation. These approaches looked at the tasks that managers undertake in order to ensure the smooth running of a business. In the 1980s, Tom Peters took more of a process-based approach to identify management as the maintenance of organizational direction based on sound common sense, pride in the organization and enthusiasm for its works. In the 1990s, Graham Winch indicated that the primary challenges of management are coping with change and uncertainty and maintaining task completion despite ambiguity in the internal and external environments.

It is clear that management is partly the process of getting things done through people and partly the creative and energetic combination of scarce resources into effective and profitable activities, and the combination of the skill and talents of the individuals concerned with doing this.

Definitions and models of leadership

Leadership as a subject has been studied in depth over a long period of time and from a number of different perspectives. Each of these perspectives is of value in informing the beliefs and values of organizational managers and leaders, as well as their teams. For example, one early theory is that of the great man. This indicates that leaders are born, and when the circumstances require, these leaders will emerge. An example of this is Winston Churchill, and it is generally accepted that this, in practice, is at the core of all managerial and supervisory activities. In fact, from the perspective of distributed leadership, every single employee accrues some leadership to the extent that they have a choice in their work – more of that later. We should note that every manager and all of those in managerial positions have a leadership function. In fact, a distributed leadership perspective would indicate that every team member has their own leadership role to undertake.

Trait approach to leadership

This approach to leadership focuses on the individual characteristics of the leader. These characteristics include:

- demographic factors such as age, gender and education;
- interpersonal attributes such as honesty and self-confidence;
- task-related characteristics such as intelligence and conscientiousness.

Judge, Colbert and Ilies (2004: 547), in a major meta-analysis, found a moderate (.21 to .27) average correlation between intelligence and leadership. The correlations between leadership and extraversion (.31) and conscientiousness (.28) were higher. Other writers support this view, citing other key traits. For example, Kirkpatrick and Locke (1991) suggest there is evidence that drive, the desire to lead, honesty/integrity, self-confidence, cognitive ability (general intelligence) and knowledge of the business have all been shown to be distinguishing traits of leaders. However, these links are not particularly strong and there is no cause and effect relationship identified, simply co-relations where better leadership outcomes are related to, for example, extraversion. This approach also ignores the importance of the context in which leadership is enacted.

One specific approach here focuses on the mythic quality about leadership which is known as the Great Man theory. This indicates that 'cometh the hour, cometh the man – or that leaders will emerge when they are really needed. Winston Churchill is seen as a man who emerged as a strong and vital leader when the UK was in desperate need during World War 2. It is noteworthy that this refers only to male leadership, a topic we will pick up on later in this chapter.

Implications for L&D

The implication of this for L&D is that leaders are born, not made. Therefore, it is incumbent upon the organization to focus heavily on recruitment and ensure that the correct people are recruited. Once they are in the organization, employees can develop some specific technical skills and perhaps also enhance the natural capabilities that they already have, such as the knowledge of the business and, to a lesser extent, self-confidence. However, there is no real potential for development outside a fairly narrow range, as other attributes are traits that indicate whether someone has 'the right stuff' for leadership.

Whilst leaders do not consciously adhere to this belief, in fact, we can see from other means that this understanding of leadership is still very real in organizations today. The CIPD (McDowell *et al.*, 2015) indicated a need for shared leadership with less of a sharp focus on one individual as a figurehead. They noted that:

> Today's CEOs feel pressure to have and provide all the answers...
> (which they)...relate to a perceived tendency for others to 'hero worship' CEOs – overly attributing success to their individual performance.

That is, the 'great man' theory still applies with specific attributes identified that, here, are seen as very valuable and deserving of significant reward. This reward aims to retain the CEO, as finding a replacement would be very difficult, and in the majority of cases would be externally recruited rather than internally developed.

Style theories of leadership

The theories focus on leader behaviour instead of generic characteristics, ie it is what leaders do that matters, not who they are. Blake and Mouton developed a model based on work at Ohio State and Michigan Universities during the 1950s. This model focuses on the two core concerns of managers which combine to produce the grid below:

- A concern for production involves a focus on task completion.
- A concern for relationship focuses on building relationship and engagement among team members.

Blake and Mouton Managerial Grid

Blake and Mouton (1978) identified that there are a number of styles of leadership which can be used. They differ by the focus or concern of the leader. There are two primary areas of concern. The first is a concern for production – that is a focus on the task itself with consideration of issues such as timescale and quality of results. The second concern is a concern for people – that is a focus on the relationships within the team and the satisfaction that employees derive from the workplace. These two concerns are not necessarily exclusive and their combinations lead to a range of characteristic styles of leadership. Each of these styles may be suited to specific leadership scenarios.

Five styles of leadership

- **Impoverished** – in which minimum effort is expended to get the required tasks completed and to sustain a sense of membership and relationship among team members. This leadership style is not likely to be effective.
- **Country Club** – this leadership style is strongly focused on relationships, leading to a comfortable, friendly organization and work tempo. This style may suit a professional services organization in which professionals are self-starters.
- **Middle of the road** – here adequate performance levels are enabled by balancing task and morale.
- **Produce or perish** – a highly focused and efficient approach, largely operations-led.
- **Team leader** – this style ensures high standards of work and task completion which is accomplished by committed team members.

Implications for L&D

These theories clearly indicate that behaviours can be taught. A helpful self-diagnostic questionnaire is available which can be used to support current and developing leaders in identifying their own levels of concern for production and relationship. This provides a clear indication that the L&D professional has a role to play in developing the leaders of the future.

Contingency theories of leadership

Contingency theories of leadership reject the idea that there is one best way of leading and instead suggest that effective leadership depends, or is contingent upon, the situation that is being addressed. The situational factors that could be addressed are wide and include the type of task that is being undertaken, the nature of the followers (eg their levels of motivation, their capabilities, etc.), the organizational culture, the national culture, etc. Each of these situational factors moderates, or has an impact on the effectiveness of the leader and their choice of behaviours.

There are a number of leadership models based on contingency theory. Their underlying assumption is that for a leader to be effective there must be an appropriate fit between the leader's behaviour and style and the conditions in the situation. What works in one situation may not work in another.

This indicates that there are some leadership styles that could cause positive harm and subdue performance levels. This can be seen in an organization where a new senior manager is recruited who doesn't 'fit' in some way and organizational performance suffers as a result.

Fiedler's contingency model

Fiedler's model was the first to link leadership style with organizational situation. The model consists of two main elements:

- The *preferred leadership style*, which is identified from a 'least-preferred co-worker' scale (LPC). His scale asks leaders to identify the person that they least like to work with, from all the people that they have ever worked with, and then rate that person on a number of items, including pleasant–unpleasant, insincere–sincere, open–guarded, boring–interesting. A high score indicates a motivation to a build relationship, while a low score indicates a motivation to focus on the task.

- The *situation* in which the leader will work which is categorized in terms of leader–team relations, the degree to which the task is structured, and the position of power of the leader.

Whilst this model provides a greater range of characteristics to consider in terms of leadership, it is in some ways overly simplistic for academic research but overly complex for practical use. In particular, the LPC score does not appear to provide an intuitively clear link with leadership styles.

Path–goal theory

This contingency theory focuses on how a leader enables subordinates to achieve organizational goals through a consideration of the actions that a leader can take as well as the characteristics of the work environment. Hewstone, Stroebe and Jonas (2011) note that it focuses on the leader's capacity to influence the employee's perception of the goal and discusses five types of behaviours to enable goal achievement:

- **Clarifying behaviours** – reduces ambiguity about the task and reinforces the link between task achievement and reward.

- **Work facilitation behaviour** – manages resources, removes roadblocks and ensures that employees have the required skills and are delegated to effectively.

- **Participative behaviour** – consults and discusses with employees to raise self-confidence of employees.

- **Supportive behaviour** – friendly, supportive behaviour to increase employees' engagement with the group.

- **Achievement orientation behaviour** – sets challenging goals, focuses on excellence and builds levels of effort among employees.

This model is one of the first to consider follower characteristics and their perceptions of the task at hand.

Implications for L&D

Contingency models suggest that it is important for leaders to understand their own style of leadership and also take care to think through the situation in which they are leading. These models suggest that style is relatively fixed and that leaders should focus on changing the situation in order to adapt it to their own style. The key to leadership capability here appears to lie primarily in good relations with followers, so leaders should pay particular attention to building positive team relationships. L&D's focus is therefore on self-awareness, developing an understanding of group interactions as well as enhancing people skills. It can also require a closer link with OD as it may be appropriate to place a leader into a situation that matches their strengths. The path-goal theory provides a structure for developing skills in leading a group.

Leader–member exchange

Leader–member exchange theories of leadership differ from previous theories in that they focus on the one-to-one relationship between a leader and a subordinate. This relationship is known as a dyad. A single leader will have as many dyads as their span of control. That is, they have one dyad per direct report. This allows consideration of each relationship and recognition that leaders treat different people differently. Those who are in favour will be likely to receive better treatment, perhaps being put forward for interesting projects, or allowed to work from home more frequently, etc. However, those who are somewhat out of favour may have less access to 'perks' such as a change of work pattern or a more beneficial shift.

The relationships between leaders and followers take a typical route:

1 *Role taking* – in which the relationship is established and the leader assesses the capabilities of the follower.

2 *Role making* – in which, through a focus on getting on with the job, the leader informally assigns the new follower to an in-group or an out-group. This in-group is the set of favoured employees who are often quite similar to the leader and receive more of the leader's attention. The out-group is composed of those less favoured individuals who may have criticized or betrayed the leader in some way and who have restricted access to the leader and fewer opportunities.

3 *Routinization* – during this stage, choices for how each dyad is treated are reinforced and routines are established, such as asking either the leader or a team member for advice, putting our ideas forward for an in-group member or holding onto them for an out-group member.

This approach to leadership reflects organizational reality. It is a descriptive theory which also has been linked to group and leader performance levels. Martin *et al.* (2016) conducted a meta-analysis of previous research into LMX (leader-member exchange) leadership quality and work performance. A meta-analysis combines the results of many previous studies and is generally considered to be a very robust approach that helps us to identify real results. What they found is that there is a clear relationship between LMX and improvement in both task achievement and organizational citizenship. They also found that LMX leadership approaches reduce counterproductive performance. This is organisationally deviant behaviour that undermines the leader and the organisation – the flip side of this is that low LMX relationship – i.e. those in which the follower is assigned to the out-group, do tend to be related to higher levels of counterproductive performance.

CASE STUDY

As an intern, Jas has worked hard to build relationships and develop into playing a full part in his department. The organization is an IT services company that Jas has been with for six months., and he is soon to finish and return to complete his degree in business management at BPP university. However, Jas has recently had a change of manager. His last manager was very friendly and he and Jas got on well; Jas became his trusted sidekick and spent a lot of his time on interesting projects supporting his manager in specific tasks. His new manager is much more process driven and Jas has been stuck with boring tasks – he feels that he has much less chance to develop; it is almost as if his new manager dislikes him. His previous manager had discussed the possibility of being offered a role on graduation, but when he raised this with the new manager he was simply passed onto HR who told him to apply as an external in his final year. Jas feels a little lost and cannot believe the difference between the two managers. He is not sure he wants to come back to this business after all.

As a L&D professional, how can you spot this type of issue in your organization? What interventions could you use to ensure that managers are developed for consistent values and attitudes across the business?

Implications for L&D

Martin *et al.* (2016: 103) suggest that 'leadership training that focuses on improving the quality of relationship between leader and follower is likely to have benefits for follower performance ... (in particular) ... through enhancing the follower's job satisfaction, trust, work motivation and empowerment.' They go on to note that the perspective between leaders and followers differs, so that interventions should support leaders in understanding the different perspectives of various team members, in particular appreciating different biases in judgement of leaders and followers as well as understanding the factors that can enhance performance. This should be combined with interventions around strong relationship-building skills.

Martin *et al.* (2016) suggest that organization design should also be engaged in order to support leaders in developing high-LMX relationships with all their followers through smaller group sizes as well as increasing the leader's time and resources and constructing fair and robust performance management and reward systems.

Transactional and transformational leadership

These styles of leadership have been a focus of research for a number of years.

- *Transactional leadership* is based on the transaction between leader and follower as an exchange of resources available. These can include time and skills on the part of the employee and rewards such as praise and interesting work on the part of the leader. Transactional leadership is based within the bureaucratic structure of the organization and is a legitimate authority. The emphasis of this style of leadership is on the clarification of goals and objectives to link work tasks and outcomes, for example organizational punishments and rewards. There is an appeal to the self-interest of followers with a recognition of mutual dependence and an exchange process, ie if you complete task 'x' then I will give you reward 'y'.

- *Transformational leadership*, by contrast, focuses on generating mutual goals by seeking higher levels of motivation and commitment among followers. The emphasis here is on the leader generating a vision for the team. This generates a sense of admiration and loyalty among the followers with the leader being perceived as charismatic or inspirational. There is an emphasis on high ethical values, co-operation and freedom of choice for the followers.

Bass (1985) as reported by Hewstone, Stroebe and Jonas (2011) has identified four sub-dimensions of transformational leadership:

1 *Idealized influence* – the behaviour of the leader is admirable, eg. role-modelling, conviction, etc., which enables followers to start to identify with the leader.

2 *Inspirational motivation* – the vision is articulated in a way that has the capacity to motivate followers to commit to it.

3 *Intellectual stimulation* – leaders encourage creativity in their followers.

4 *Individualized stimulation* – each follower is led according to their individual needs.

Breevart *et al.* (2013) carried out a 34-day diary study of the impact of both transactional and transformational leadership on cadets on board a naval vessel. They found that followers were more engaged when led through a transformational style and that this led to a more favourable work environment in which cadets were more autonomous and provided more support for one another. This shows the daily impact of transformational approaches to leadership.

Implications for L&D

Bass (1999) notes that leaders will demonstrate both transformational and transactional leadership styles and indicates that both can be developed in leaders. Avolio and Bass (1991) have produced a Multifactor Leadership Questionnaire which can be used to assess the degree to which participants use transactional or transformational leadership. This enables both their own self-awareness as well as organizational understanding of their approach to leadership.

Amazon has had a fair amount of negative press concerning its leadership capability. The *New York Times* reported on more than 100 testimonies from employees of Amazon across the business which described a very tough and uncompromising workforce, driven by a list of leadership principles (Kantor and Streitfeld, 2015). Whilst these have driven high performance levels, the article questions the cost of this performance in terms of a negative impact on the lives of employees. It includes 100 testimonials of employees who were treated callously, even during times of personal crisis. The article reports an unyielding, hard culture which is continuously reinforced by Jeff Bezos, who monitors a continuous stream of data reporting on performance levels. One specific example quotes an employee who 'didn't sleep for four days straight' due to workload, corroborating the organizational myth that 'Amazon is where overachievers go to feel bad about themselves'. Another employee, who had a particularly good performance record and needed to take care of her elderly father who had cancer, stated, 'When you're not able to give your absolute all, 80 hours a week, they see it as a major weakness'. These factors lead to reported high levels of employee turnover, which may reinforce the organizational myth of exceptional strength.

Jeff Bezos responded very quickly to this article in a memo to all employees, stating, 'The article doesn't describe the Amazon I know or the caring Amazonians I work with every day', and went on to instruct employees to raise any such cases with HR (Lewis, 2015). The speed of his response may raise questions about his willingness as a leader to ponder over new information as well as the flexibility and adaptability of the culture he has created.

As an HR specialist interested in developing leadership skills within Amazon, this article is particularly revealing. It guides the options that are available for the L&D practitioner.

The 'Amazon' model of leadership? There is an explicit model supported by the organization, focusing on strong, decisive leadership which is willing to be unpopular in the service of customer satisfaction. The implicit model follows this closely, but, according to the article, without a willingness to dig deep to understand the reality within the organization.

- What is the leadership model in your organization?

- How effective is that model in all parts of the organization?

- What are the organizational needs that provide the scaffolding for leadership and management skills?

Different approaches to developing leaders and managers

Roffey Park, in their 2016 annual review of the management agenda (Lucy *et al.*, 2016), asked almost 1,000 managers, from across a range of functions, a simple question – *what are the main people challenges your organization is facing now?* More than 80 per cent of respondents indicated that developing appropriate leadership and management styles was their single biggest people challenge. This is a consistent finding from across industry – that the identification and development of managers and leaders is a core task of the organization. That task is generally delegated to the HR function, specifically L&D. However, ownership of leadership development belongs firmly with the main line leadership, from the C-suite downwards.

Additionally, Roffey Park identified that 25 per cent of HR managers questioned did not believe that their organization had the required leadership and management capability to deliver their strategic objectives. Lack of appropriate leadership to inspire and motivate for change is also a key concern for respondents. When asked about the current skill gaps in leadership, the creation of learning culture and supporting the development of employees were identified by 55 per cent of HR managers.

The impact of this survey is to indicate the real need for development of both leaders and managers, and there are a number of different approaches that can be taken. They should be chosen with reference to the culture, pace of work, specific needs, topic, budget, etc.

Informal vs formal interventions

Approaches to developing leaders and managers may be formal, informal or a mix of the two. Formal approaches indicate that the organization has a clear strategy for development with a tightly constructed implementation plan. Interventions here may include lunchtime listen and learn sessions in which specific topics are taught over the lunch hour, formal training sessions of a couple of hours up to a couple of weeks, or studying for formal qualifications such as the ACCA for finance professionals.

Informal learning indicates that the manager or leader is directing the learning themselves and that they are managing their learning with the support of the organization. This can include methods such as job rotation, for example, where graduates experience a series of different functions in their first two years. It may also include secondments in which the manager 'swaps' jobs with another manger either in-house or externally. This has been of use for head teachers who are able to experience a new way of doing things in a new school, while being supported by a coach. It may also involve the development of a special project, perhaps a stretch project in which a manager has been involved in order to engage them with a new area such as working in a new culture. These are generally complemented with either coaching or mentoring to support the manager in identifying and building on the learning garnered during the experience.

Coaching and mentoring are examples of interventions that are used across industry. They may be undertaken both formally and informally over a range of time periods, and are discussed in depth in a later chapter.

Approaches to developing leadership and management skills can vary. There are a number of tools available and their use varies according to the specific context in which they are being applied.

Action learning

Action learning is a method in which both individuals and the organization itself are developed through small group work in which real-life problems are addressed. Typically the group consists of five to eight managers who voluntarily meet together on a regular but infrequent basis (perhaps every six weeks) and discuss a specific knotty challenge that needs to be addressed. The group members each mentor, question, challenge and support one another, identifying specific activities that may resolve the challenge. Over the course of the six weeks, each member puts the advice received into practice to try to resolve the issue. The feedback provides learning, often on an individual as well as an organizational level.

CASE STUDY

A high-tech manufacturing organization holds a permanent action learning group. Individual mangers are invited into the group, which is considered a matter of prestige. There, they present a specific business issue that has been intractable and work with others on their business issues. Each member of the group has nine months as a member and they come from all areas of the business. Over the nine months, they build trusting relationships with one another and also, more often than not, resolve the business issue. Another benefit which is often unexpected is the enhanced self-awareness and understanding of group processes having experienced the feedback and challenge inherent in this process.

Could action learning groups be useful in your organization? Do you have previous experience of these groups? Who are the stakeholders who need to be consulted as part of this intervention? What are the key factors for success in your organization?

Digital approaches to leadership and management development

One of the primary developments in L&D has been, in common with all areas, the use of digital approaches, making use of online and computer facilities. The CMI, in a recent survey, identified that 97 per cent of managers spend at least one day a year on digital learning.

The CMI identify a number of key trends in the use of digital learning to lead. These are:

- *70:20:10 – informal and experiential*, as part of both experiential and informal learning in the 70:20:10 model. Currently primarily used to deliver e-learning, there is considerable potential for further interactive uses of digital learning, eg via social media sites such as yammer.

- *Opening up learning.* The use of MOOCs – massive open online courses – which can deliver specific 'capsules' of knowledge to large numbers of individuals, often at no cost to the learner.

- *Knowing as finding.* The expertise of the manager is based on their capacity to find out what they need to know, rather than knowing it already. The L&D function therefore needs to curate appropriate and high-quality content for the managers to sift through.

- *Instant skills.* The use of online resources to find instant skills at the point of need. These could include 'how to measure a social marketing tool'. Again, the importance of integration with a wider L&D offering as well as curating high-quality resources is key here to ensure depth of management capability.

- *Blog, tweet, speak, learn.* The use of social media for learning through discussion and peer mentoring. This is identified as particularly relevant with 'trusted' groups, such as on LinkedIn.

- *Don't tell me what to learn or when to learn it.* The use of digital resources is led by the learner at their own pace and at times of their own choosing.

- *Let technology do the work.* Digital resources can be used to enable learning of many types, including 360° feedback, etc.

- *Nibbling, grazing and gourmet dinners.* The quantity of learning carried out at any one time seems to have shrunk from what the CMI refer to as a 'gourmet meal' of up to a week away, down to 'grazing' for specific information.

These trends can be capitalized on by an organization but do require flexible and agile approaches within L&D. This reinforces the need for L&D to see themselves as supporters of the business, providing the resources required to enable the organization to maximize its competitiveness through its people.

The use of digital as a tool is now ubiquitous across industry – however, the use of an online approach does not always indicate that learning has actually taken place. Digital learning needs to be carefully integrated into the broader L&D offering to ensure that it is used effectively and to its fullest extent.

Appreciative enquiry

Appreciative enquiry is a process which is used across organizations both for development of individuals as well as groups, and as a tool for organization design and development. The key to appreciative enquiry is a process in which the first questions to be investigated assess what is going well. This is in sharp contrast to the majority of interventions which take a remedial perspective to work out what is going wrong in an organization and mend it. This approach is limited to a focus on what is going wrong with specific instances and only addresses discrete specific issues. Appreciative enquiry, by contrast, asks questions around the culture and style of the organization and reinforces successes, building self-confidence in the organization. Focus groups and one-to-one discussions are held to identify what the organization is doing well. These build a picture of the capability of the organization and can develop both an appreciation of that as well as a clear pathway to develop those capabilities specifically within the culture and meaning of that specific organization.

Appreciative enquiry consists of five key steps which provide a logical sequence that is adaptable to the requirements of specific organizations. Each step can be carried out with a range of participants, across all levels of the organization. This flexibility has increased the popularity of appreciative inquiry. Indeed, Bushe and Kassam (2005) have indicated that its popularity has outstripped evidence of its efficacy.

1 *Identify the main focus of the enquiry*. Careful identification of the specific area of consideration is important here – this early investigative stage may be quite broad, but have a clear overall focus.

2 *Discover what is going really well in this area*. This stage focuses on gathering information through interviews, focus groups, etc. to identify successes across the area of focus. These should involve all employees and will demonstrate what each one means by success.

3 *Dreaming about what might be*. Given the organizational mission and values, combined with the capabilities identified, this stage encourages imagination to identify where the organization could possibly go – what it could develop into, customers it could delight, new services it could provide, etc.

4 *Designing*. Co-constructing the future in a way that captures what might be – here, the focus moves from what could be, to how it could be brought about. With frequent reference to the successes, the team designs potential structures and processes to enable the dream of what might be.

5 *Delivering the dream.* In this stage, the choices and options identified earlier are brought into reality and the changes identified
are implemented, as far as is practicable. The co-creation stage is
referred to frequently and agreement is sought for the implementation of the design.

Use of competency frameworks

Competency frameworks provide bundles of behaviours, skills and
knowledge which identify the key capabilities of an organization.
Typically identified through some form of job analysis, they provide
a coherent framework for many elements of HR practice, typically at
a point of assessment such as selection and appraisal. They can also
be useful as a structure for learning and development interventions.
Where they are defined at different levels for an organization they
can also support succession planning and the full range of leadership
interventions. There is a fuller discussion of competency frameworks
in Chapter 2.

Assessment and development centres

These are events with multiple participants, multiple assessors and
multiple exercises. The difference between the two is that assessment
centres have some form of assessment for selection as their heart.
This is often selection onto high-potential programmes and can
lead to anxiety in participants, some competitiveness and a strong
desire to prove themselves which often interferes with performance.
Development centres, on the other hand, involve assessment for development, ie their purpose is to help participants to develop. Where they
are supported by a programme of interventions they can be particularly effective as a leadership development tool. Further detail about
assessment and development centres can be found in Chapter 2.

Management self-development

One approach to developing managers and leaders is to accept that
they are their own experts. This approach, derived from a humanistic

approach, also recognizes the complexity of the role of leaders and managers as well as expecting them to have a drive for their own development and self-improvement. Therefore, the L&D function can act as a support in enabling managers and leaders to develop themselves. This typically happens within clear organizational guidelines, linked to the performance management system for example, or the use of coaching or mentoring with development centres to support enhanced self-awareness.

The CIPD (McDowell *et al.*, 2015: 24) notes that there is a lack of a coaching culture in the C-suite and they argues that 'executives should be offered coaching and development in coaching skills, then in turn coach or mentor others. This should help to create a culture of continuous learning and reflection, where constructive challenge is encouraged, even of those in most senior positions.'

Canon Europe have adopted a self-development approach for managers with the use of an online development hub. For leaders and managers this is supplemented with a World Café-style approach to support knowledge sharing, experience and peer-to-peer mentoring (Matthews, 2016).

World Café process

The World Café is an intervention that allows large groups of managers and leaders to discuss key issues. A large function room is set up with multiple sets of small tables. Each table hosts one specific question of importance or interest to the organization. The World Café is a structured development process which facilitates open conversation and dialogue through a series of questions that are discussed in a fairly short time period. There are usually between four and six participants per table, ensuring that everyone has a chance to be involved in the conversation. The length of the discussion is relatively short, usually around 30–45 minutes. This allows a series of free conversations in which everyone is involved and promotes the exchange of knowledge and understanding. The outcome is an enhanced understanding of different perspectives across the organization, better relationships across this population and a shared understanding of variations across the organization alongside a reinforcement of the organizational culture. These benefits rely upon the effective implementation of the method, in particular taking care about the questions and how they are posed.

Feed forward interviews

These are designed to help individuals to understand the types of behaviours and skills they have that enable them to perform well and to think about ways to use these behaviours and skills in other contexts to make further improvements in the future.

The key steps in a feedforward interview are:

1 Encourage the participant to think of a success story in their career; an event or project that they are proud of.

2 Through the use of coaching techniques, uncover the key behaviours, skills, knowledge and other attributes that led to the success. Identify in particular how they engaged with challenges and identify any themes from their stories. It may be necessary to discuss more than one story to pull out the key themes of their individual contribution and capabilities.

3 Extrapolate the past into the future – what are the core strengths that they can use in future projects? How have they successfully negotiated challenges? What could future successes look and feel like?

The role of the learning and development function

The primary role of the L&D function is to facilitate the strategic development of the organization through enhancing and growing the capability of leadership and management within the organization. However, this is not necessarily through direct processes, but may be through raising the line management skills of managers themselves. These skills can include coaching and mentoring in combination with performance management and learning needs analysis.

In an interview with HR Grapevine (Di Lieto, 2016), Benny Higgins, CEO of Tesco Bank, stated:

> It's wrong to assume that it's the job of HR to develop people, it's not; it's the job of HR to support the business in developing people... HR is there to make sure those leaders, and those individuals, have the right level of support.

He goes on to indicate that L&D professionals need to operate in a strategic way to focus on the core organizational capabilities: 'They've got to work out... how they can be part of developing that DNA that produces the right kind of organization and sustains it in the right manner.'

This can include elements such as defining the organizational meaning of leadership and engaging stakeholders in understanding and embodying that definition. The primary focus on organizational success with a keen business eye is an essential requirement for efficient delivery of service to the organization. The L&D function can therefore be considered as a business partner with a particular focus on the management of change as well as organizational development as key elements within their role.

Gubbins and Garavan (2009) identify that competitive advantage for organizations depends on the knowledge and skills present in the organization. For the L&D function this means a business partner approach, which requires intimacy with the business model for the organization as well as a deep understanding of the product range, brands and services as appropriate. This is necessary for the L&D professional to be recognized as an equal partner across the business. This can lead to a significant degree of complexity, especially, as Gubbins and Garavan (2009) note, in multinational corporations where there is a need to maintain consistency across business units which may be quite divergent in their location, function, culture, etc.

They view the role of the L&D function as changing from providing activities through a centralized role to focus on results-based and strategically integrated activities which impact the bottom line of the organization. The role becomes one of transformational professional, providing a service 'aimed at helping the organization to achieve its strategic goals through change and development interventions... operating in strategic partnership roles... it results in more commitment and a positive attitude towards training and development' (Gubbins and Garavan, 2009: 255).

The L&D professional must therefore focus on building long-term strategic relationships across the business, generating social capital through strong cross-functional relationships. In practical terms, this is translated into a focus on relationship building for all members of the L&D function as well as ensuring that all interventions contribute to the overarching strategic goals. In addition, this element of keeping their finger on the pulse helps ensure that proposed interventions are more likely to meet with a positive response as they are so embedded within the culture, needs and strategic objectives of the organization.

CASE STUDY

XPT, a software design house, has made significant advances in security of peer-to-peer lending protocols. This has led to it being acquired by a multinational organization. It is recognized for its innovation, which the acquirer is unwilling to interfere with. Therefore, the L&D business partner was engaged early in the acquisition negotiations to explore congruence between both the culture and the leadership definition in both organizations. Through a series of investigatory meetings she identified the core areas of overlap and mapped out areas of difference. This mapping exercise was used as part of the transformation process which successfully retained the degree of innovation whilst transitioning the organization as a whole.

When you are designing interventions, what resources do you have to help ensure that the interventions are closely tied into the organization's capabilities? How can you ensure that you are focusing on current and emerging capabilities that will build sustainable success for your organization?

Core questions for L&D professionals to ask when designing a strategy

- What do we mean by 'leadership' and 'management' in this organization?

- What is the culture of our organization – or what shift in culture do we want our L&D strategy to help us achieve?

- What are the best methods of developing individuals in the leadership and management skills and behaviours needed at key transition points in the leadership pipeline?

- How can we evaluate our L&D effectively, in terms both of whether training and learning needs are accurately identified and of the impact of that activity on the business and on individuals?

(Beard and Irvine, 2005.)

These questions provide a guide to some of the core thinking that needs to precede a learning needs analysis. This thinking takes place at an organizational level and should help to ensure that the L&D strategy is integrated both horizontally and vertically.

- Horizontal integration ensures that L&D strategy is consistent with other processes across the organization, in particular OD and HR practices. Core challenges here include the equality of current HR processes as well as historical 'remnants' and reputations. Also, a silo mentality can pit the HR, OD and L&D teams against one another. This is very likely to lead to a failure to build organizational success.

- Vertical integration ensures that the L&D strategy builds organizational capability at all levels from owners, through the C-suite, to contributors. A challenge here is any lack of joined-up thinking across the organization, which can lead to specific parts of the organization focusing on their own short-term benefits rather than the best outcome for the whole wider organization.

Development of L&D strategy

The L&D strategy should be completely aligned with the organizational mission and vision. An exploration of organizational values is also of use here; even where they are clearly stated, it can be advantageous to ratify their currency prior to setting a long-term L&D strategy. The business plan and core business objectives should be placed at the core of the L&D strategic plan, accompanied by a future-facing review of the environment in which the business is operating. This includes a

PESTLEE analysis which considers the Political, Economic, Sociological, Technological, Legal, Environmental and Ethical drivers in the environment. These are factors which the organization will have to respond to and should seek to predict and understand. For example, a current sociological trend toward health, freshness and organic food is a key concern for a food manufacturer and as such should be integrated within the L&D strategy, for example in the use of materials, locations, etc.

The PESTLEE analysis should be complemented by a SWOT analysis. This identifies the strengths and weakness of the organization in relation to its market position and the environment, and goes onto identify specific opportunities and threats to the business. These opportunities and threats are the key to populating the L&D strategy. Strengths are likely to be the primary capabilities and resources which need to be built upon, whilst Threats will include the development needs that the organization must consider.

At this point, the overall strategy and key development areas for the organization as a whole have been identified. Further work is needed to check that these are accurate and to identify any further significant development needs, for example graduate development programmes or supervisory skills for junior managers. The strategy needs to be converted to a practical plan which will feed into the budget cycle and provide a practical outline template for delivery of the strategy, given resource constraints.

Learning needs analysis

A learning needs analysis takes the L&D strategy and applies it at a local level. The needs of a group of managers and leaders are considered both as a group and individually. This can be carried out in a number of ways, including reviewing learning needs identified at appraisal, interviewing a cross section of senior managers to identify what they see as the key areas for development in the leadership and management group. Also, ensure that they can identify what they and their direct reports will need to develop in order to achieve the business targets. It is also useful to review achievement against current business metrics, considering elements such as customer complaints, employee engagement metrics, financial indicators, etc.

CASE STUDY

At Apple, a case study approach is used to teach decision-making strategies and practices specific to Apple. Lashinsky (2011) notes that Steve Jobs recruited Joel Podolny, former dean of the Yale School of Management, to lead a new Apple University. Following orders from Jobs, Podolny hired a team of business professors to write 'a series of internal case studies about significant decisions in Apple's recent history' similar to the kind of case studies created by the top business schools but for an internal Apple audience only. These cases are taught by top executives and cover subjects such as decisions around manufacturing and the success of Apple's stores, in order to 'expose the next layer of management to the executive team's thought process'.

How to ensure the ownership and success of leadership and management development programmes

The underlying question of what makes an effective leader is very difficult to answer, in part because it is also difficult to identify what good leaders do and in particular what part of their performance is due to them and what part is due to their context, team, business cycle, organization life cycles, fashion, or even, perhaps, luck. Therefore, the goalposts for measuring success are vague at best and are rarely defined. Because of this, much management development practice tends to lack a convincing evidence base. Most research is conducted on in-company groups and is primarily qualitative, with the result that it is difficult to generalize or apply to different businesses.

Additionally, research has tended to focus on top managers and has not really fully addressed middle- and first-line levels of the leadership pipeline. In addition, much of the practice in leadership and management development tends to be based on a range of current models which are more fashionable than evidence based. These can tend to be damaging, as they negatively impact stakeholder confidence and can prejudice decision makers against new initiatives. In practice, sometimes leadership and management development interventions that can be used as an instrument of control, for example as a reward or as a punishment. This confuses their purpose and makes any objective evaluation even more problematic.

Indicators of success for leadership and management interventions

It is often tempting to consider indicators of success as only coming from objective, research-based methods. However, sometimes we can look at the fruits of our labours and recognize that they show the effectiveness of our practice in themselves. For example:

- **Individual performance evidence** – as the individual employee performance improves measurably, so this reflects on their development. On a case-by-case basis it is possible to try to tease out exactly which interventions were more helpful.

- **Effective succession** – one of the key roles of learning and development is to provide a clear succession for key roles in the organization. Where this has been effective it demonstrates not only sound practice in learning and development, but also good strategic planning which predicted the need for successors and the potential of the current incumbent.

- **Retention of key employees** – it is a truism that employees leave their manager rather than the business, if this is the case we can see that retention implies some degree of management capability. Where managers are poor, turnover tends to increase. This is particularly the case for key employees as they can more easily move to new roles due to the value of their skills and experience.

- **Value-added indicators** – where the L&D team have a clear idea of the key levers for the organization they are able to provide interventions against those. An example of this may be where customer satisfaction has been found to drive sales and so an extensive intervention in customer sales is implemented. This is followed by a significant increase in sales. The value-added indicators have demonstrated the effectiveness of the learning experience.

- **Participant satisfaction indicators** – almost every L&D intervention has some kind of happy sheet on which participants indicate what they found useful/helpful/challenging/fun/boring, etc. Their satisfaction is an indicator of a positive learning experience. This initial experience is important as it enables a more open attitude to learning the knowledge, skills or attitudes involved in the learning intervention.

CASE STUDY

Frances was the L&D business partner for a medium-sized light manufacturing business. In her appraisal she was asked how effective her programmes had been over the previous 12 months. She struggled, as she hadn't carried out any specific evaluation activities. She started to get a bit downhearted but her boss stopped her and pointed out that senior managers who had taken part in her new mentoring programme felt more in touch with the day-to-day reality in the business and high-potential junior managers had been retained more frequently. Her self-managed learning sets had built closer relationships between disparate parts of the organization, which meant that there was an ease of communication. She was tasked with building on this by setting up an evaluation programme to identify the key elements of the interventions that were building this success.

Ensuring ownership

Leadership and management development can become the plaything of the C-suite. They can also become the 'property' of the HR team. However, to be truly effective they need to become the property of all leaders and managers. There are some core stages in ensuring that this happens:

- **Identifying key stakeholders** – a stakeholder is anyone with a legitimate interest in the leadership and management development programme. Some of the key stakeholders are the customers of those interventions, eg line managers, C-suite, suppliers and customers. Understanding who the key stakeholders are and communicating to them about the various interventions as appropriate is a key way to ensure that they have some ownership of the process.

- **Involving and ensuring contributions of key stakeholders** – as well as communicating with key stakeholders it is possible to build a sense of ownership by collaborating with them in building the success of the programme, for example asking for their input in initial outline stages, encouraging participants to introduce the next cohort of participants to the programme, or to take part in evaluation, taking a clear steer from top managers in the design and purpose of the intervention, discussing budgetary requirements and their specific requirements with senior managers, etc. This essentially follows the practice of respecting the needs, wants and desires of the key stakeholders and meeting as many of them as is practicable.

- **Individualized interventions** – ownership is generated when participants recognize that the intervention is for them and is adapted to their specific needs. Therefore, interventions like coaching, which are by their very nature highly individualized, have a higher level of ownership than, for example, appraisal training.

- **Demonstrating and communicating achievement of success indicators** – it is natural for people to be attracted to success and to steer away from any form of failure, hence the difficulty in encouraging managers to reflect on both their weaker as well as their stronger attributes. By sharing the successes a sense of ownership and a desire to be part of the project can be effectively built up.

Leadership and management are discretionary activities. This means that they are carried out according to the preference of the individual, within their own setting. Therefore managers and leaders can have very different ways of achieving their goals depending on their age, gender, nationality, personality, experience, discipline, education, etc. The impact of this for leadership and management development is that the goalpost for success can be ambiguous – we are aiming to support excellent performance, at some point in the future, for currently unknowable tasks with a highly heterogenous group of mature and experienced individuals who vary in their willingness to receive what we offer.

The CIPD (McDowell *et al.*, 2015: 4) recognizes that 'CEO reward is rarely sufficiently adjusted to reflect a decline in company performance', perhaps supporting the dialogue that the need for the leader is enhanced by poor performance but also cutting across the link between reward and performance which is the basis of much reward policy. This reflects a contradiction in our understanding of leadership and management. However, the CIPD indicates that it reflects 'high levels of CEO influence on organizational decision making… (and)… by-product of social interactions and power balances'. That is, what sort of leader is being rewarded. This is reflected in the LMX theory of leadership – where LMX refers to leader-member exchange.

Leadership and management development programmes are embedded within an organization's culture and perception of itself. They support the development of those individuals they are also reporting to, particularly where they have a responsibility for C-suite development. As a result of this, the metrics of success are very close to the activity and stakeholder management is even more crucial. However, accessing and understanding the true requirements of the stakeholders and what they regard as success can be problematic.

A discussion of pay is appropriate to our consideration of the nature of leadership and management as it is a concrete indicator of what an organization really believes that leadership is for. Within L&D this is essential, as we are developing leaders and managers primarily for organizational success. Certainly, there is an expressed need for the development of leaders. For example, the Aberdeen Group in September 2015 reported a survey in which 36 per cent of respondents identified the need to develop a stronger leadership bench as a top priority for their organization.

The CIPD (2015) considers three primary requirements of CEOs from a reward perspective. This sheds light on what the organization truly values and has implications for leadership and management development, as indicated in Table 3.2 below.

Table 3.2

Perspective on CEO reward	Definition of perspective	Implication for L&D
Profit-driven Transactors	It is important that CEOs generate high profit and that a short-term perspective creates wealth for shareholders	• Strong commercial focus • L&D resources pointed towards profit generating and cost-cutting interventions • Evaluation of L&D will be on the extent to which it supports profit generation • Longer term capability development is less valued • Personal insight and growth is not seen as a valid subject
Long-term Nurturers	CEOs need to nurture and support their organizations, with a clear focus on results in the long term to create stakeholder value	• The results of L&D will be seen over a longer term • The customers for L&D are all stakeholders • Value is perceived as a range of metrics including elements such as employee engagement, reputation, CSR, etc.
CEO Behaviourists	Behaviour matters more than results to create meaning and purpose for the organization	• L&D is a key factor in the war for talent • L&D supports retention of employees • Longer-term success of the organization is built through capability in a broad range of arenas including self-insight, engagement, relationship building etc.

Conclusion

In this chapter we have discussed the distinction between leadership and management. The distinction is important but unclear. In practice it co-exists within a number of people, particularly in lean organizations where individual contributors are required to both manage processes for which they are responsible as well as enact distributed leadership. There is a plethora of different approaches and theories concerning leadership and management, many of which overlap and represent different theoretical perspectives or contexts. The extent to which they provide a useful resource for the L&D professional also varies.

References

ACAS (2014) Frontline Managers [online] http://www.acas.org.uk/media/pdf/j/4/Front-line-managers-advisory-booklet.pdf

Avolio, B J and Bass, B M (1991) *The Full Range of Leadership Development: Basic and advanced manuals*, Bass, Avolio, & Associates, Binghamton, NY

Bass, B M (1999) Two decades of research and development in transformational leadership *European Journal of Work and Organizational Psychology*, **8** (1) pp. 9–32

Beard, C and Irvine, D (2005) Management training and development: problems, paradoxes and perspectives', in *Human Resource Development*, 2nd edn, ed J P Wilson, Kogan Page, London pp 380-403

Blake, R R and Mouton, J S (1978) *The New Managerial Grid*, Gulf Publishing Company, Houston

Breevart, K ,Bakker, A, Hetland, J, Demerouti, E, Olsen, O K and Espevik, R (2013) Daily transactional and transformational leadership and daily employee engagement, *Journal of Organisational and Occupational Psychology*, **87** pp. 138–57

Bushe, G and Kassam, A (2005) When Is Appreciative Inquiry Transformational? A meta-case analysis, *The Journal of Applied Behavioural Science*, **41** (2), pp. 161–81

Di Lieto, C (2016) Tesco Bank's CEO, Benny Higgins, says 'It's not the job of HR to develop people', *HRGrapevine* [online] http://www.hrgrapevine.com/markets/hr/article/2016-02-22-tesco-banks-ceo-benny-higgins-says-its-not-the-job-of-hr-to-develop-people

Fayol, H (1949) *General and Industrial Management*, trans Constance Storts, Pitman, London. Original work published 1916

Goffee, R and Jones, G (2000) Why should anyone be led by you? *Harvard Business Review*, **78** (5), pp 62–70

Gubbins, C and Garavan, T N (2009) Understanding the HRD role in MNCs: the imperatives of social capital and networking, *Human Resource Development Review*, 8 (2), pp. 245–75

Hewstone, M, Stroebe, W and Jonas, K (2011) *Introduction to Social Psychology: A European perspective*, BPS Blackwell

House, R J (2004) *Culture, Leadership, and Organizations: The GLOBE study of 62 societies*, Sage Publications

Hutchinson, S and Purcell, J (2003) *Bringing Policies to Life: The vital role of front line managers*, Chartered Institute of Personnel and Development, London

Judge, T, Colbert, A and Ilies, R (2004) Intelligence and leadership: A quantitative review and test of theoretical propositions, *Journal of Applied Psychology*, 89 (3), pp. 542–52, copyright 2004 by the American Psychological Association 2004

Kantor, J and Streitfeld, D (15 August, 2015) Inside Amazon: Wrestling big ideas in a bruising workplace, *New York Times*

Kirkpatrick, Shelley A and Locke, Edwin A (1991) Leadership: Do traits matter? *The Executive*, 5 (2), pp. 48–60

Kotter, J P (1990) What leaders really do, *Harvard Business Review*, 68 (3), pp. 103–11

Lashinsky, A (2011) How Apple works: Inside the world's biggest startup, *Forbes Magazine* 9 May 2011 [online] http://fortune.com/2011/05/09/inside-apple/

Lewis, G (18 August 2015) Amazon boss responds to allegations of 'shockingly callous management practices' *CIPD* [online] http://www.cipd.co.uk/pm/peoplemanagement/b/weblog/archive/2015/08/18/amazon-boss-responds-to-allegations-of-shockingly-callous-management-practices.aspx

Lucy, D, Porkavoos, M, Sinclair, A and Hatcher, C (2016) The Management Agenda 2016, *Roffey Park* [online] https://www.roffeypark.com/research-insights/the-management-agenda-2016/

Martin, E, Guillaume, Y, Thomas, G, Lee, A. and Epitropaki, O. (2016) Leader-Member Exchange (LMX) and performance: A meta-analytic review, *Personnel Psychology*, 69, pp. 67–121

Matthews, J (2016) Five minutes with Caroline Price, senior vice president of human resources at Canon Europe, *HRGrapevine* [online] http://www.hrgrapevine.com/markets/hr/article/2016-02-11-five-minutes-with-caroline-price-senior-vice-president-of-human-resources-at-canon-europe

McDowell, A, Whysall, Z, Hadjuk, P and Johnson, D (2015) The power and pitfalls of executive reward: A behavioural perspective, *CIPD* [online] https://www.cipd.co.uk/Images/the-power-pitfalls-executive-reward-behavioural-perspective_2015_tcm18-8900.pdf

Mullins, L J (2013) *Management and Organisational Behaviour,* 10th edn, Pearson, Harlow

Purcell, J, Kinnie, N, Hutchinson, S, Rayton, B and Swart, J (2003) *Understanding the People and Performance Link: Unlocking the black box*, Chartered Institute of Personnel and Development, London

Spillane, R and Martin, J (2005) *Personality and Performance: Foundations for managerial psychology,* UNSW Press, Sydney

Using
facilitation skills

04

Introduction

Facilitation is used in many ways in the workplace and facilitation skills are needed by individuals in a number of roles. A facilitator may, for example, help a work group to address a task effectively. This may be the case when a group comes together to develop a strategy, to plan a restructure or to address an outstanding workplace problem. In other cases, the facilitator's role may be more directly focused on supporting learning. Sometimes this will be in a group or team context and the focus of learning may be helping the group or team to work together more effectively. This is commonly the case in team-building workshops, for example. Group facilitation may also be part of a leadership or other professional development programme where participants learn to work together and in doing so develop interpersonal skills which they can apply back in the workplace.

Learning may also be facilitated in an individual context and may be used in consultancy, using Schein's model of process consultancy, which was introduced in Chapter 1. Individual support can also take the form of coaching or mentoring, both covered in Chapter 5, and both practised widely in organizations.

Facilitation is a core skill for learning and development professionals in all these areas. However, it is also an important skill for many other members of the organization. Leaders and managers in particular are expected to support learning for individuals, groups and teams, whether as coaches, mentors, group or team leaders or simply as line managers. They may also use facilitation skills in chairing meetings or gaining team and group agreement or commitment to a particular course of action.

This chapter will look at the role of the facilitator in supporting learning in both professional development and task-focused contexts. You will read about the ideas about learning which underpin facilitation and how it can be used to support learning. Because facilitated learning draws heavily on reflection on experience, you will also look closely at reflective and experiential learning, both of which were introduced in Chapter 1 of this book. You will read about ways of helping groups and teams to work more effectively and about methods and techniques which can help to make your facilitation more effective. Finally, you will be encouraged to think about how to apply these ideas to your own learning as you develop your skills as a facilitator.

The role of facilitation in supporting learning

In helping individuals or groups to learn, the facilitator creates the conditions in which they are able to take control of their learning and supports them in developing the skills they need to manage their own learning effectively. In an age characterized by continuous change, individuals and organizations need to continuously develop new skills, new knowledge and new understanding. For many it is a condition of their continuing employment that they meet this requirement and for many organizations it is a condition of their continuing success that they are able to do so.

Only a small amount of this continuous learning, however, will come from formal training courses where those with expert skills (such as trainers) pass these on to learners. Far more important is self-managed learning, in which the individual takes responsibility for his or her learning. Sometimes, too, this learning will happen in groups or teams, so that there can be shared learning. In either case, the learning itself, just like the process of learning, may be highly personal to the learner or learners and may include new understandings peculiar to their context.

In this approach, learners need to be highly skilled in self-managed learning and particularly in drawing learning from reflection on experience. Encouraging and supporting the development of these skills is an important part of the facilitator's role. This means that the facilitator too needs well-developed skills in reflective practice and experiential learning and to be able to model good practice in both. Where the facilitator of learning is a manager or leader, these skills can be modelled in the workplace as well as in individual sessions.

Ideas about learning which underpin facilitation

At the heart of facilitation is the idea that real learning is directed by and is the responsibility of the learner or learners. This is a central tenet of person-centred learning, an idea associated with the work of Carl Rogers. This seemed radical and controversial as it gained popularity in the 1960s, but it is widely accepted now and has produced a revolution in thinking about how to help people to learn. It is an approach to learning now well established in adult and tertiary education, in professional development and in workplace learning.

The idea of constructivist approaches to learning was introduced in Chapter 1 of this book. This is the idea that knowledge and understanding are created by and personal to the learner, so that the content of what is learned cannot be prescribed. This poses a major challenge for teachers, university lecturers and trainers – but not for facilitators who recognize that their role is to support the process of learner-led learning for individuals and groups.

Barnett (2000), writing about the role of university lecturers, pointed out that in this new world of learning their distinctive skill is now about challenging the quality of learners' thinking. In the workplace, trainers' roles have also changed. While some have moved to more strategic roles as human resource development specialists (as outlined in Chapter 1) others have become facilitators of learning in groups and teams and many also support individual learning as coaches or mentors.

It is not the purpose of this chapter to argue that all learning must be learner-led and facilitated. There are times when teacher- or trainer-led learning is still the best option and there is debate about what the balance should be between trainer-led and learner-led learning and concerns about when and how facilitated learning should be used.

There are also sometimes concerns that, used unskilfully, facilitated learning can leave learners without the support and guidance they need. This underlines the need for facilitators to assess carefully the needs of their learners and to judge the level of support and direction they need.

The remainder of this section will look more closely at person-centred learning and at learning from reflection and reflective practice.

Person-centred learning

Carl Rogers argued that traditional approaches to teaching are simply irrelevant in a fast-changing world (Rogers, 1961). He advocated an approach to learning in which the needs of the whole person are taken into account in the learning process and challenged traditional ideas about teaching which emphasized, for example, the importance of structuring learning for the students and assessing their learning in relation to the objectives set by the teacher. Rogers said that nothing of real value could be taught by one person to another. Instead, he thought that the responsibility for learning should be handed to the learner and that support for this learning should be provided by a facilitator. With this approach, he argued, the individual would be encouraged to achieve his or her potential in a way that was simply not possible through traditional teaching.

Rogers suggested that the ability to create a genuine relationship with the learner was central to the role of the facilitator. This meant being able to relate openly and honestly to the learner as a whole person. He called this 'realness' (Rogers, 1983:121) and regarded it as one of the 'core conditions for facilitative practice designed to motivate people to learn' (Reynolds, Caley and Mason, 2002:37). The other two core conditions Rogers identified were empathetic understanding and acceptance. By empathetic understanding he meant the ability to see the learning process from the perspective of the student, arguing that when students feel understood, rather than judged, they are better able to focus on learning. He described what he meant by acceptance like this:

> it is prizing the learner, prizing her opinions, her feelings, her person.
> It is caring for the learner, but it is a non-progressive caring. It is an acceptance of this other individual as a separate person, having worth in her own right (Rogers, 1983:124).

Rogers' person-centred approach to learning has been very influential in thinking about learning and facilitation. At its heart is the idea that real learning is learning from experience, or experiential learning. However, while Rogers himself was dismissive of the value of one person teaching (or training) another, in fact the skills of teaching and training remain very important in some situations. What the balance should be between teacher-led and student-led learning remains a subject of discussion and controversy, particularly in schools and universities. In the workplace, however, it is clear that learner-led learning has an important role to play, as argued at the start of this chapter, and the skills of the facilitator (and coach and mentor) are fundamentally important for learning and development professionals.

Carl Rogers was a psychologist by training and drew on his experience, particularly as a therapist, in his writing about education. It remains true that many ideas about helping people to learn which influence practice in facilitation, coaching and mentoring are drawn from psychology.

Applying these ideas to your practice

Think about a time when you have learned something important and when you were helped in this learning by someone else. Make some notes about what you learned, and the contribution of the person who helped you to learn.

Feedback

It is quite possible that you learned significantly from simply being told something or being given helpful information. This can be a good and useful way of learning. However, you may have learned through skilful questioning which helped you to think more clearly about the issues; or you may have received feedback which raised your awareness of behaviours about which you had previously been less aware.

The next section of this chapter will look at the importance of reflection on experience. Supporting this reflection is an important part of the role of the facilitator and you may find it helpful to spend some time thinking about your own experience of learning or being helped to learn in this way, before you read any further.

Reflective learning

Learning from experience (experiential learning) is at the heart of person-centred learning, and much of the facilitator's work is about supporting reflection on experience and helping individuals to draw the learning from it. You practised both reflection and experiential learning in the last reflective exercise. Reflecting on experience may have seemed straightforward, but most people need to develop the skills of learning in this way and to practise them. You were introduced to reflective learning in Chapter 1, where you read about the stages of Kolb's learning cycle. You also read about Schön's argument that reflective learning is an important element in professional development which prepares individuals for the reality of workplace practice with all its ambiguities and uncertainties. In this section, you will develop a deeper understanding of reflective practice so that you can support its use in facilitating learning.

What is reflective practice?

The idea of reflective practice is not new, and indeed can be traced back to the thinking of the 18th-century Enlightenment. Reflection was then seen as a route to social change and it was believed that:

> human beings have the capacity to reflect rationally on their own
> actions and to use the understanding thus derived as a basis for personal
> change which is an important element in social change (Hunt, 2005 in
> Harrison, 2009:121).

Reflection is still regarded as a route to personal change, and this idea is now firmly embedded in approaches to organizational and professional learning. This personal change is often seen, for example, as an important part of the change process in organizations and as an important contributor to continuous organizational learning (Senge, 2006).

Moon (2004:82) defines reflection as:

> a form of mental processing – like a form of thinking – that we use to
> fulfil a purpose or to achieve some anticipated outcome, or we may
> simply 'be reflective' and then an outcome can be unexpected. Reflection
> is applied to relatively complicated ill-structured ideas for which there is

not an obvious solution and is largely based on the further processing of knowledge and understanding that we already possess.

This is a helpful definition which emphasizes the value of reflection in managing complex and ambiguous situations. However, the skill with which individuals will manage this process will vary, and personal reflection can vary from being relatively superficial to being much more insightful; learners will also vary considerably in their willingness to address the ambiguity and complexity at the heart of reflection. The extent to which learning can be drawn from reflection depends on the level of reflection the learner is able to achieve.

Gray (2007) draws an important distinction between reflection on personal experience and critical reflection. In the latter, the learner considers not only the experience which is the subject of the reflection but also the assumptions which underpin those reflections. He also introduces the idea of critical self-reflection, which means thinking about and challenging 'the way one has posed problems and one's orientation to perceiving, believing and acting' (Gray, 2007:9).

Both critical and self-critical reflection can lead to profound changes in understanding and Gray is far from alone in pointing to the importance of challenging the assumptions which underpin

---

Descriptive writing – this simply reports what happened and does not explore the reasons behind it. This does not demonstrate reflection.

Descriptive reflection – here there is description of events, but there is also some exploration of the reason behind them. This may take the form of providing justification for them ('I did this because...'). There is also some recognition of other perspectives or possible perspectives.

Dialogic reflection – at this level the learner demonstrates the ability to view experience from a broader perspective, exploring different possible perspectives for what has happened.

Critical reflection – demonstrates an understanding of a variety of perspectives and recognizes that these may be influenced by different historical and/or socio-political contexts.

Levels of reflective learning: adapted from Hatton and Smith (1995).

our thinking if deep reflection and learning is to be achieved. Other writers who have pointed to the importance of challenging the perspectives informing reflection include, for example, Hatton and Smith (1995), who offer a framework for assessing the levels of reflective learning.

Single- and double-loop learning

Argyris and Schön have also emphasized the importance of challenging assumptions and perspectives, if learning is to be effective. They have drawn a distinction between single-loop and double-loop learning (Argyris and Schön, 1992). Single-loop learning is based on simple reflection on practice and produces learning which is informed by previous experience and values. By contrast, double-loop learning involves questioning the assumptions and values which underpinned the action or experiences that are the subject of reflection or review. Schön's reflection-in-action, which you read about in Chapter 1, describes the process of reflecting on practice in the moment (Schön, 1983). This, by its nature, requires the learner to question and challenge personal assumptions, perspectives and even motivations. Knowles *et al.* (2015) observe that the most effective learners practise both double-loop learning and reflection-in-action.

Developing skills in reflective practice

The skills of reflective practice may come very easily to some learners while others, as already noted, find them much harder to develop. This can lead to confusion and even frustration for students who would much prefer more directive guidance from those helping them to learn. The difficulties this causes can be compounded when facilitators fail to understand the problems learners are experiencing. Moon (2004) observes that those who introduce reflective practice to students are likely to understand reflection well, and may not easily understand why others do not. It is also worth remembering that understanding reflective practice may be particularly difficult for those educated in a culture where there is no well-established tradition of facilitated learning or reflective practice.

In this section, you will look at ways to help others to develop reflective skills and by doing so to take responsibility for their own practice.

Building reflective skills

The descriptive reflection which constitutes the second stage of Hatton and Smith's levels (already described) is relatively accessible to learners and may be sufficient for some purposes, such as the review of performance in a task. Once learners are able to work at this level, they can be encouraged to move towards reflection at a deeper level. They will make progress towards this deeper reflection if they are encouraged to recognize that there can be significant differences in the way different individuals see the same event. Further depth can be added if they are encouraged to recognize that each of us can look at our own experiences from different perspectives and that these perspectives can vary over time (Moon, 2004).

A facilitator may work with individuals in a group to encourage these shifts in perspective. This can be achieved through skilful questioning about what happened, and about the assumptions and frames of reference that lie behind the way events have been related and interpreted. A coach or mentor can play the same role, as can a coaching supervisor or a critical friend with well-developed skills in reflective practice.

Sometimes it can help to encourage the recording of reflections, for example in a learning portfolio or a learning log. This is a widespread practice in professional development and this reflective writing is often assessed. The levels of learning outlined by Hatton and Smith (1995) and introduced earlier in this chapter may be used for this purpose. Moon (2004) points to the opportunity this provides for second-order reflection. This happens when the author of the reflective writing completes a review of this writing and reflects on any assumptions which underpin it.

Raelin (2002) identified five skills which can support reflection: being, speaking, disclosing, testing and probing. They are worth studying closely because they are important skills for any facilitator of learning and are in many ways the staples of his or her toolkit. Note particularly Raelin's emphasis on the importance of 'being', that is

Table 4.1   Raelin's skills of reflective practice (adapted from Raelin, 2002)

Reflective skill	Practising this skill means
Being	Being present in a way that helps to create and support a reflective climate. This includes suspending judgement while experiences and situations are explored and discussed.
Speaking	Giving expression to shared understanding within the group of what is happening within it, and the meaning of shared experiences.
Disclosing	Expressing personal responses. Individuals may make disclosures which may help others to understand them better or they may express their personal feelings.
Testing	Asks open questions to help the group to understand its behaviours and the thinking which underpins them.
Probing	Questions individual members of the group in order to understand better their suggestions or actions; does so in a non-judgmental way.

behaving in a way that is supportive of reflective practice. Another way of putting this might be to say that the facilitator should offer a presence which supports reflective practice. Raelin suggests that important behaviours in supporting reflection include '…empathy and open-hearted acceptance… deep interest and curiosity… invite questions… pause, reflect, contemplate' (Raelin, 2002:70).

In a learning group devoted to reflective practice these behaviours will be as important in members of the group as in the facilitator. They are also important skills in supporting reflective practice in the workplace.

Cultural perspectives on reflection

The value placed on reflection in learning and development in the UK and North America is relatively recent, and has produced a revolution in thinking about learning, as already noted. Although these new ideas are probably more firmly embedded in tertiary, adult and workplace learning than in schools, they have nonetheless influenced the curriculum at all levels. This means that ideas about reflective learning (and self-managed learning) are reasonably accessible to most learners educated in these cultures. This is not always the case in other countries, however, and it cannot be automatically assumed that the same learning processes can be easily rolled out in organizations which span different cultures. The problems this can cause are illustrated in the following case. While the focus of this study is a university programme of study, the learning from it has clear relevance to workplace learning in an international context.

A study carried out by Fenton-O'Creevy and van Mourik (2016) explored the challenges faced by Japanese students studying an online MBA programme at the Open University Business School. This is a programme of study which emphasizes reflective and experiential learning (as well as other postgraduate study skills such as critical thinking). It is in the nature of online learning that students typically remain in their own country and in their own social contexts; they are at the same time participating in a programme of study based on a very different set of assumptions. This study illustrates the confusion this can cause for learners who may not recognize or understand the cultural assumptions underpinning the learning tasks they are being asked to complete.

In the case of experiential learning, for example, there is an underpinning assumption that there is value in questioning your own beliefs and those of others, including teachers. By contrast, educational practice in Japan places a much stronger emphasis on being respectful of teachers and the expert knowledge they possess, and questioning is only valued after the student has fully mastered the ideas and knowledge they offer. Two comments from students in this research project illustrate the gulf between their previous educational experiences in Japan and their MBA studies in a UK University:

'In Japanese university, our class style, there's no debate or discussion. Just learning from the teacher's guide and writing down the report.'

'So all the exams I took... in my student period had a right answer: one right answer.'

Writers on facilitation

This section introduces the work of writers on facilitation whose ideas may help you to decide how you want to develop your own practice as a facilitator.

Casey, Roberts and Salaman (1992) offer an introduction to the practice of group facilitation, emphasizing the role of the facilitator in helping the group to learn. They emphasize the importance of carefully measured contributions by facilitators so that they contribute effectively to this learning. Heron's model of facilitation (Heron, 1999) goes into much more depth about the range of options the facilitator has in the way he or she interacts with the group and the different purposes interventions can serve. The section on Burnard (2002) is taken from his writing on professional development for nurses. It introduces the role of the facilitator in encouraging participants to question and challenge assumptions. He emphasizes how difficult this can be for the facilitator. You will see that each of these writings introduces new levels of complexity for the facilitator. When you are facilitating you will need to be aware of your own skill levels and you will read more about how to assess and develop these later in this chapter.

Casey, Roberts and Salaman

Casey, Roberts and Salaman (1992) emphasize that the role of the facilitator is to help members of the group to learn, both about the way the group is working together and about themselves and their contributions to its effectiveness. The role of the facilitator, therefore, is to help group members to become more aware of processes within the group and of the effects of their own behaviours and interactions with others. In doing so, he or she enables members of the group to take responsibility for their own learning. It follows that the facilitator's role is not to tell members of the group what they should learn, but to help them to make sense themselves of what is happening and to draw learning from it. The process of learning in group facilitation is thus a joint and collaborative exercise, to which both the facilitator and the members of the group contribute.

Casey, Roberts and Salaman identify three steps in the process of group facilitation: taking in what is happening; making sense of this data; and making judgements on the basis of this sense-making about how and when to intervene.

In taking in what is happening, the authors emphasize the importance of noticing both what is happening in the group and also what is happening for the facilitator. They call this 'taking in from the group' and 'taking in from self' and note that the most effective interventions seem to be drawn from awareness in both these dimensions at the same time. Taking in what is happening in the group means noticing behaviours, interactions and interventions. These can include what is said and what is not said, verbal and non-verbal interactions and the more general mood of the group. Awareness of self is rather different and the authors suggest that facilitators pay attention to their own emotions, feelings and even physical sensations.

Making sense of the data taken in from the group and self is challenging and requires the constant exercise of judgement. In interpreting data from the group, the facilitator will draw on personal experience of working in and with groups as well as theories from personal reading. You will read about a number of theories in this book which will help you to make sense of what you see in groups. Obvious examples include Tuckman's theory of group formation (introduced in Chapter 1) and Belbin's theory of team roles, both of which you will read about later in this chapter. Making sense of data from self depends on knowing yourself and your reactions and recognizing what they mean. Good self-knowledge, for most of us, depends on determined reflection and self-challenge in questioning our own assumptions and reactions so we can better understand ourselves. This is often achieved through personal development work in groups, but cannot be easily or quickly done.

Casey, Roberts and Salaman caution against going too far in ascribing meaning to what is observed. They distinguish between making sense of what is happening (looking for meaning and possibilities) and going further by offering interpretations or explanations of what is noted. Since no facilitator is infallible, interpretations can be wrong and they argue that a more cautious approach can lead to better-founded interventions. The boundary between 'making sense' and 'interpreting' is uncertain, however, and the authors recognize that where it lies is a matter for the facilitator's judgement – and may sometimes be misjudged.

The third step in this model is to decide whether or not to use the understanding from steps 1 and 2 to make an intervention and, if so, what this intervention should be. All interventions are intended to promote learning, either about the group or what is happening for individuals within it, and to enable change and growth to take place. This means raising group members' awareness of what is happening within the group, not by telling them what is happening but by helping them to perceive it for themselves.

The facilitator may offer the group insights from what he or she has taken in (from self or the group) and the sense made of these, without interpretation or detailed explanation. The facilitator may also offer relevant theories which the group members may find helpful in making their own sense of the data they are receiving, either from their own observations or from the facilitator's interventions. The authors observe of the facilitator that:

> He/she must find a way to stimulate awareness in others by sharing his/her insights (and the supporting theories) but stopping short of depriving others of the opportunity to work it out for themselves (Casey, Roberts and Salaman, 1992:12).

John Heron

Heron (1999:1) describes a facilitator as someone who 'has the role of empowering participants to learn in an experiential group' and who is voluntarily accepted by the group in this role. He identifies a wide range of contexts in which a facilitator may work, including therapy, personal development, interpersonal skills or management training, adult learning or higher education. His model of facilitation, which is widely used and referenced, makes clear the variety of styles a facilitator can use. Heron identifies that the facilitator can operate in three quite distinct ways which he calls 'modes' (Heron 1999:7–8). These are:

- **Hierarchical** – the facilitator makes decisions for the group about how its learning will be managed.
- **Co-operative** – the facilitator works collaboratively with the group to make decisions about how its learning will be managed. Responsibility is shared and decisions will be negotiated.

- **Autonomous** – the group takes responsibility for decisions about its learning. The facilitator does not intervene but is still present and may provide support where needed.

It would be quite natural for a facilitator to work in hierarchical and directive mode with a newly formed group whose members might be inexperienced in group work or group learning. As the group matures, learners can be expected to take on more responsibility, so that the facilitator can move to the collaborative and autonomous modes. It is possible, where the group comprises skilled and experienced learners, for the facilitator to work in autonomous mode with a newly formed group. This is high risk, though, unless he or she really knows the learners and their abilities.

In any case, the judgement about which mode to use is important, and can be difficult. This is compounded by the fact that facilitators will often have a distinct preference for one mode over another, and may linger too long in the wrong mode. Where the wrong decision is made, there can be significant damage to the learning process. For example, too much hierarchy may hamper the development of self-managed learning skills and cause resentment but too much co-operation may also hamper progress to autonomous self-directed learning. Where autonomy is over-used, the group's work may be chaotic and unproductive – and even damaging to the development of individual members.

Dimensions of facilitation

In addition to the three styles, or modes, of facilitation, Heron identifies six aspects, or dimensions, of the facilitator's role:

- **Planning** – organizing the group's activities so that it can achieve learning.
- **Meaning** – the sense individuals make of their experiences and interactions within the group.
- **Confronting** – raising awareness of group behaviours and processes which interfere with learning (such as avoiding behaviours and resistance). It is likely to involve challenge.
- **Feeling** – managing feelings and emotions within the group.

- **Structuring** – shaping and structuring the group's learning.
- **Valuing** – creating a supportive learning environment in which individuals feel valued and in which members of the group express respect and support for each other.

Heron argues that each of these six dimensions of facilitation would be practised in each of the three modes, but that their expression would be different – for full details of this model, see Heron (1999). This model is a reminder of the complexity of facilitation: it is a skill which takes considerable time and practice to develop.

Philip Burnard

Burnard (2002) identified the potential role of the facilitator in helping learners to develop their critical thinking skills through reflective and experiential learning. This means helping them to question and challenge received ideas and to develop new perspectives and understandings (as previously discussed in this chapter).

In this approach, the facilitator is critical of the student's ideas and assumptions (although not of the student personally.) However, the student may in turn challenge the assumptions and ideas of the facilitator, who must be willing to demonstrate the same ability to challenge personal assumptions and beliefs as is expected of the student.

In this model of facilitation, the facilitator makes no claim to special status and may take turns in leading the process of shared learning. Burnard emphasizes how challenging it can be to facilitate this sort of learning. He observes:

> Setting out to engage in an experiential learning session of this sort is something of an act of faith. There is no way of knowing beforehand how such a session will end. Either students or facilitator, or both, may change their ideas as a result of the session. The facilitator who practises in this way 'lives on the edge' and is prepared to take risks both with herself and with her students in order to move thinking and feeling forward (Burnard, 2002:53).

The quote above is taken from Burnard's handbook for nurses and other healthcare professionals on developing the interpersonal skills they need to be effective in a caring role. The approach it describes would not usually be used in a task-focused group where the facilitator might not want to 'take risks' in quite the same way. However, this account provides a helpful insight into an approach to facilitating learning which, used skilfully, can produce profound learning for participants. The modelling of equality in the learning process which Burnard describes can also produce cultural shifts in the organization. This can be important where, for example, there is a recognized need to challenge assumptions about the importance of hierarchy.

Facilitation skills

This section will introduce some of the facilitation skills you would need in working with groups and teams. However, to develop more advanced skills you are likely to need to undertake substantial training which includes working within groups and reflecting on your experiences there. This could be done with the support of a coach, mentor or supervisor, for example. Working in groups can produce strong emotions, particularly where the group is encouraged to focus on process rather than task issues, and the facilitator (or facilitators) may need well-developed skills and experience to create a safe learning environment for the group (and the facilitators). Where the focus of the group's work is on task issues, the facilitator's role is likely to be less challenging and, perhaps, correspondingly less rewarding.

Schwarz (2002:50) draws a useful distinction between 'basic' and 'developmental' facilitation. In the former, the group is focused on a specific task-related problem, such as developing a strategy or writing a communication plan, for example. In this case, the facilitator's role is to help the group to work together effectively to address the task, but does not focus on helping the members of the group to learn how to work well together more generally. In developmental facilitation, by contrast, the facilitator is helping the group both to address the problem and to learn to work better as a group. In the latter case, very much more advanced skills and experience will be needed to produce a good result.

When facilitation is used to support personal development, as is often the case in interpersonal skills or leadership development training, for example, the facilitator will need considerable skill to ensure that a safe learning environment is created for all participants. These groups will often be co-facilitated, so that there is additional resource available to support the group and also so that facilitators can support each other. They will typically spend a great deal of time discussing their experiences of the group and its members, as well as their plans for future interactions with the group.

Preparing to facilitate

Before you facilitate any event or programme you will first need to be clear about its objective or objectives. You may be an internal facilitator with the organization (perhaps a member of the learning and development department) or you may be external to the organization and brought in as a consultant. In either case, you will need to agree with your client what you are expected to achieve and within what timeframe. You may also agree how you will measure the success of the event or programme.

The client may not be part of the group you will be working with – you may for example be invited to take on the work by a member of the HR or learning and development department. In this case, you may find that you also need to have preparatory conversations with at least some of those who will be participating in the event to make sure that you have a good understanding of the issues to be addressed. This can be very helpful in preparing for team-building workshops, for example, or when you are facilitating problem-solving workshops or sessions. In these cases, you will need to have a good understanding of the issues to be addressed. You may well find that some of the issues you uncover at this stage are not those originally identified by the client, and so you may need to revisit discussions about the objectives for the session and how it is to be handled.

In addition, in this early stage of contracting with the client, all parties should have a common understanding of what can be achieved and should be in agreement about the part each will play in achieving agreed objectives. Without this common understanding you may run into serious difficulties in your subsequent practice.

Advance information

Advance information to participants may include an outline of the purpose of the event as well as details of the time, venue and (if relevant) the dress code. This can also be an opportunity to provide some information about yourself. This can include an outline of your skills and experience, how you work and what participants can expect in working with you.

The physical environment

The decisions you make about the physical environment will depend in part on the nature of the event you are planning to run. Typically, working and learning groups will not be larger than about 12 participants – this is about the largest number of people who can be expected to work together productively. You may be asked to facilitate larger groups but in this case you will probably decide to make use of sub-groups.

In deciding on the physical layout, the first important point to make is that you should avoid a classroom-style configuration and ensure that seating is arranged to support group learning. Where the group is small enough to work as a single group, the room should be set up so that all participants can see and hear each other. The facilitator will also need to see and be seen, hear and be heard. Ideally there will be plenty of room for individuals to move around. It is also important to think about whether sub-group work will be needed and if so how this will be accommodated – ideally separate rooms would be available for this purpose.

One obvious room layout is the horseshoe (Figure 4.1). One advantage of this layout is that it allows the facilitator to sit slightly apart from the group and this can make it easier to change roles. For example, the facilitator can easily stand back from the group when his or her contribution is not needed, or conversely can move closer to the group or to individuals within the group, depending on the circumstances.

Figure 4.1   A horseshoe-style arrangement

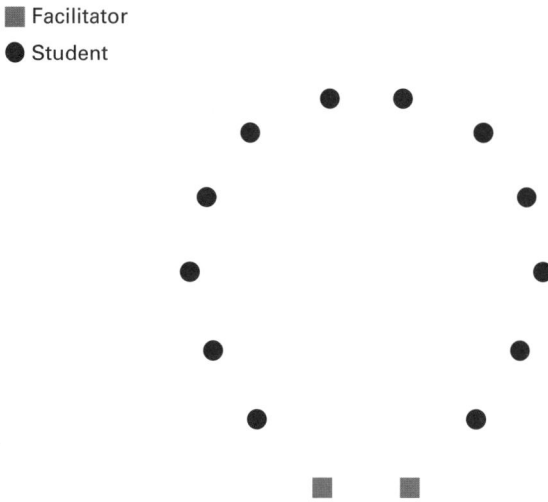

Alternatively, participants and the facilitator may be seated in a circle, in which case the facilitator will be presented rather more as being simply one of the group. Both these configurations allow participants a clear view of each other and of the facilitator (and vice versa) so that body language is clearly visible, and this can be helpful in developmental facilitation. If you are asked to facilitate a working group in a task, however, you may need to seat them around a table so that notes can be taken easily. You may also be asked to facilitate virtual groups, where participants are in many locations. Here your main concerns are likely to include ensuring that the technology is working well and, if a video link is not available, that all participants have supplied photographs. You should also make sure you are familiar with the technology being used, or at least that you have access to support if you need it. You will read more about facilitation in a virtual environment later in this chapter.

If you are asked to facilitate a large event, such as a conference for example, you might choose to seat participants around a series of circular tables. In this case, you might ask participants to work in sub-groups at their tables, rather than in one single large group. In the case of a large virtual conference you could ask participants to work in sub-groups in their individual locations, where this is possible. You may have less control of how rooms are configured in this case, but it makes sense, where possible, to encourage seating arrangements which make discussion easier.

Whatever the size of the event, it will be important that the venue is free of distractions such as noise or poor lighting; a good supply of refreshments can help events to run smoothly. On the day of the event, you should arrive early and check the room and any equipment you intend to use; if the event runs over several days you should do this every day.

Preparing yourself

As well as being fully briefed on the purpose of the event, you will facilitate better if you are mentally prepared. This means being free of personal distractions and able to be fully present with the group so that you can observe and respond to behaviours and activities there. Your presence – the way you present yourself to the group – will affect the way members of the group feel and behave. Usually an open and friendly presence will help the group to be productive. Your physical presence is important too, so you should plan to be free of any other work interruptions so that you are fully available, both in the sessions you are facilitating and, if needed, to talk to participants during breaks.

Opening group sessions

Many facilitators will personally welcome every participant in the group. Whether you do this or not, you should certainly make sure you know each participant's name (unless you are facilitating an exceptionally large group). You should also take care to introduce yourself so that the group has a good understanding of who you are and how you can contribute to their work. This is an important part of your building rapport with the group. When working with a group of around 12 participants you might ask each member of the group to introduce themselves. You might also use an icebreaker early in the first meeting to help the group members to get to know each other and feel comfortable in each other's company. In choosing your icebreaker you should take care to respond sensitively to the expectations of the group. Some at least may be feeling anxious or reticent and may appreciate a gentle start to the session. It may be enough simply to ask participants to introduce themselves – if you do this it is helpful to indicate what information you would like them to give. This could be their name and role and perhaps also an outline of what they want to achieve from their time with the group.

Paired introductions

This is a simple way of starting a group session. Simply allow six minutes for participants to work in pairs, each introducing themselves to each other. Each then takes on the task of introducing the other to the group. To keep this exercise reasonably short you could limit each introduction to two minutes.

Cocktail party

Ask participants to stand up and come to the centre of the room. Each participant's task is to introduce themselves to each other member of the group and to find out some simple information – perhaps their name, role and purpose in attending the event. For a group of 12 participants you will need to allow about 25 minutes.

It is the briskness and structure of this exercise which makes it unthreatening, even for those who feel shy or unconfident, and it usually seems to be fun for participants. Of course, this only works where the physical layout of the room provides an opportunity for participants to mingle. It is unlikely to work if they are seated boardroom style around a table.

True or false?

Ask participants to work in small groups, ideally of three or four people. Each person writes on a piece of paper one unusual fact about themselves which is true and two which are not. The other members of the group then try to identify which statement is true and which are not. This is an amusing way to enable individuals to get to know a small number of other members of the group. It is a useful icebreaker in a large group (for example at a conference) where individuals may welcome an opportunity to start building relationships.

Ground rules

It is also often very helpful, at the start of a meeting (or the first meeting in a programme), to discuss and agree ground rules with the group about how the members of the group will work with each other and how they will work with the facilitator. In developmental facilitation (using Schwarz's definition already outlined) this can be a good way to start exploring process issues within the group. In basic facilitation, where the group has more of a task focus, it can still be very helpful to devote some time to exploring how the group and facilitator will work together. This can be recorded (for example on a flip chart) as a summary of the group's agreement with each other. Content may include, for example, a commitment to be respectful of each other, to listen to each other's contributions and (particularly in a developmental group) to treat all disclosures within the group as confidential. You can also deal with very practical issues here, such as how the group will manage telephony. It is not always realistic to ask that phones be turned off, but you may be able to agree only to take calls during breaks. The agreed ground rules in a developmental learning group may be much more detailed than those needed for a work group focused on a specific task. In the former case, the process of coming to agreement can itself provide an opportunity for the facilitator to start learning about the way the group is working together and this can become quite a protracted process. For a task-focused work group this would probably not be a good use of time. In some cases, where the group is likely to be able to work effectively, this stage may be omitted. However, where participants have difficulty working together it can be very valuable to agree some basic ground rules, which can prevent tensions and problems later.

If you record the group's agreed rules on a flip chart, take care to record accurately what is said and agreed using the group's own words where possible. If you impose your own ideas or language the participants are less likely to feel a sense of ownership of the rules and may not feel much need to be bound by them. You can of course challenge, ask for clarification, question the thinking behind contributions and give feedback on them. In a developmental learning group, you may also give feedback on the behaviours you see in the group as it works towards agreement. If you conclude that you must be directive about the ground rules, be open about this and about the reasons why you think this is necessary.

The agenda

It can also be helpful to agree the purpose of the session at the start. This can take the form of simply asking each group member to say what they hope to get out of it. This can be combined with introductions as suggested above and often the facilitator will write on a flip chart each individual's hopes for what they will achieve. They can then form an agenda the group can refer back to in its time together.

It is quite possible that there are hidden agendas in the group: there may be hostilities between individuals, for example, or there may be issues related to membership of other work groups. These may not be openly expressed at the start of the session (it is probably unlikely that they would be) but you may pick up clues that help you to surface issues which, if they are not addressed, may later create obstacles to progress.

Working with groups

Facilitators may be asked to work with learning groups and work groups, including cross-departmental and inter-organizational groups. Groups can be an important source of learning and members of the group may create together new understandings or perspectives which individuals could not reach alone. This is particularly true in professional development, such as leadership development, where the richness of different perspectives can be a strong support to individual learning and growth.

To facilitate learning in groups, the facilitator needs to understand group dynamics. You were introduced to some ideas about helping groups to develop in Chapter 1, including Tuckman's theory of group development and Schein's analysis of group formation. This section will look in more depth at the dynamics you will need to consider when working with groups and some of the skills you will need. Much of this section is also relevant to working with teams, and you will read more about teams later in this chapter.

Distinguishing between task and process

In your work as a facilitator you will need to draw a distinction between task and process skills. This is an important distinction for both leaders and managers since, to be effective, they need the skills to be able to deal both with task (or production) issues and process (or people) issues. In your work with any group you will need to keep this distinction in mind and to be clear about when you are helping the group to complete the task they have been set and when you are helping them to understand the way they are working together in addressing the task (these are process issues). For some members of the group this distinction will be obvious while for others the focus on achieving the task may seem so important that they may be perplexed if they are asked to spend time considering process issues.

Where your role as a facilitator is primarily to help a group to complete a task it will be important that you notice and manage process issues so that they do not compromise the outcome of the group's work. However, you will also need to pay attention to task issues so that the group achieves its objectives. If you have been asked to facilitate a working group producing a specified outcome such as a strategy, for example, you will not be thanked if this is not achieved. It can be very helpful in this case to check regularly with the group on how well they feel the task is progressing. In developmental facilitation, however (where your main focus is to help the group to learn to work together effectively and/or to develop personal effectiveness skills), attention to process issues will be your most important focus and concern. You will need to watch carefully for behaviours which may compromise effective group working. You will also need to plan interventions which help the members of the group to become more aware of these behaviours and to learn how to manage them for themselves. This can include giving feedback on behaviours which are helpful and those which hinder, and it is a key skill for a facilitator to be able to do this in a way that does not alienate the group. You will read more about giving feedback later in this chapter.

Applying these ideas to your practice

Spend some time thinking about an occasion when you have been part of a group in which the behaviours of individual members of the group made it difficult to achieve a task effectively. This might be a work group with a joint task or a group outside work, such as a group of friends or family planning a holiday or other joint venture. Try to also identify individual behaviours which helped the group to achieve its task effectively.

Feedback

You may have identified helpful behaviours which are explicitly task focused. These may include organizing and planning, for example, and can be very important in achieving a good outcome; their absence can usually be expected to hinder progress. However, you may also have identified behaviours which demonstrate concern for people (or lack of it) and these too can also help or hinder considerably. Helpful behaviours here include taking account of the needs and interests of other members of the group and this may be demonstrated by attentive listening, thoughtful questioning to clarify thinking, and supporting and encouraging others. Conversely, unhelpful behaviours might include ignoring or overriding others' contributions (perhaps demonstrated by interrupting or over-talking).

In addition to noticing behaviours which focus on task and people, you will also need to notice the dynamics of what happens within the group. We will turn to these next.

Supporting the group and its members

Being part of a group, particularly a newly formed group, can be a stressful experience. You read in Chapter 1 about the challenges individuals may face when they join a group or team. These include uncertainties about the role they should adopt in the group, the amount of influence they can or should expect to have and even whether other members of the group will like them (Schein, 1988). There may also be stressful times for individuals during the life of the group – and this is particularly common in developmental groups. For this reason, when the facilitator offers challenges to individuals, this should be accompanied by support. This is in recognition of how hard it can be for individuals to have to question their own behaviours, attitudes or assumptions.

There may be times when individuals withdraw from the group, either physically or simply by ceasing to participate in discussion. This can be because the experience is upsetting or feels unmanageable. When this happens, the facilitator may need to provide support to help the individual to re-join the group.

Managing conflict within the group

You read in Chapter 1 about the likelihood of conflict in the early stages of group formation, as group members explore how to work together, often challenging each other and the boundaries of the task they face (Tuckman, 1965). For these reasons, the facilitator may choose to be rather more directive and supportive in the early stages of group formation and then later in the process to step back and enable the group to manage itself. In developmental facilitation, however, where members of the group are learning how to work together effectively, there can be opportunities to learn from this conflict.

Sometimes discontent, for example in the storming phase of group formation, can be expressed in attacks on the facilitator by other members of the group, or blame may be placed on someone or something external to the group – such as the organization for example. Burnard (2002) points out that this blaming of others can be a way for the group to avoid taking responsibility itself for the issues it faces. The facilitator may choose an intervention which helps the group to become more aware of its behaviours and to develop a better understanding of approaches to recognizing and managing conflict.

The expression of blame can be powerful and challenging, both for the facilitator and for individual members of the group. This can particularly be the case when individuals claim to be speaking for the whole group. It can be helpful to ask group participants only to speak for themselves, so that their contributions begin 'I think...' or 'I feel...'. This is sometimes referred to as 'speaking for I' and the group may agree to include this as part of the group contract when the group comes together.

Encouraging self-awareness within the group

Where the facilitator's role is help the group to learn to work better as a group it will be important to help them to develop their self-awareness. This will also be important where group members are working together to improve their leadership skills, for example. This is a skill which individuals will often be helped to develop through their participation in facilitated group work and which will be important in helping them to be effective in the workplace, whether in leadership roles or in working with groups and teams. It is likely that there will be significant variation within the group in the self-awareness individuals have at the start. Those with high levels of self-awareness may have a good understanding of their own strengths and weaknesses and of the impact of their behaviours on others. Those with lower levels of self-awareness, conversely, may simply not realize the impact of their behaviours on others and may have a limited understanding of how others see them.

There are a number of ways in which individuals can be helped to become more aware of the impact of their behaviours on others. This may be achieved by using 360-degree feedback, which allows each to receive anonymous feedback from colleagues who are peers, senior to them and junior to them (this process was explained in Chapter 2). Tests which try to measure aspects of personality may also be used. Feedback may also be given within the learning group, and this will usually be done by inviting each participant to offer feedback to every other member of the group. This needs to be preceded, however, by careful guidance to group members on how to give and receive feedback. It is also good practice to ask participants to offer positive feedback in each case as well as areas for development.

Guidance to group members about how to give feedback effectively could include the following:

- Remember that the purpose of feedback is to help the recipient to be aware of the impact of his or her behaviours and to understand how to work most effectively with others. It follows that there is no place in feedback for expressing ill-feeling or blame.

- It is very helpful, in giving feedback, to be specific about the behaviour or behaviours you are commenting on and their effect on you. For example, 'you started to talk about something quite different as soon as I finished speaking and I felt that my contribution had been ignored'.

- Only give as much feedback as the recipient can be expected to deal with. Giving too much feedback can be counter-productive and may produce a defensive response.

- Try to give feedback about behaviours which have had a positive impact on you as well as those which have not. The goal in giving feedback will always be to raise awareness of strengths to be encouraged as well as areas for development. It is also often the case that giving positive feedback can make it easier for the recipient to hear and respond to less positive feedback.

- Only give feedback the recipient can act on. This is why it is important to focus on behaviours rather than attributes (such as being tall, for example) which cannot be changed. For the same reason, feedback needs to be given soon after the event it relates to. Feedback given much later (as sometimes happens in annual appraisals, for example) cannot really be addressed and is not helpful.

Guidance to group members on how to receive feedback effectively could include the following:

- Make sure you have understood the feedback you have been offered. If necessary, ask questions to clarify your understanding.

- Try not to be defensive, even if the feedback seems unfair. This means not explaining yourself or defending yourself, since these can both be barriers to understanding.

- Having made sure you understand the feedback, consider whether it is helpful to you and whether you can make use of it. If you cannot, you can put it aside and take no further action.

- It is much easier to consider feedback carefully when it is given professionally, as already described. Even when it is given badly, however, you may be able to draw some learning from it, so it is worth giving it your consideration.

Giving and receiving feedback well are important workplace skills and fundamental to continuous learning and development. In practising these skills, therefore, participants in facilitated learning programmes are developing important skills which will help them to be effective in the workplace. Facilitators should also be able to model these skills in giving feedback both to the group and to individuals. Equally, facilitators may be offered feedback by the group or individuals and should always demonstrate a commitment to listening closely to what is being said to them and ensuring they understand it.

Next steps

It is often helpful to plan time to agree the next steps, either for the group as a whole or for individuals within it. In a task-focused group, you may have identified actions that need to be taken during the group discussions. If so, this is the time to summarize them and to confirm who is responsible for each. If there is further work for the group to do, this is also the time to agree what the next steps will be.

In a development group, you might set time aside for individual action planning. This is a time for each participant to reflect on the programme and to make sure the most important learning has been captured. This might take the form of individual reflection or working in pairs or small groups – or you might decide to allow individuals to decide what works best for them. The output of this activity should be some form of record of learning and some commitment, perhaps in the form of an action plan, to deciding what to do differently as a consequence of this learning. Without this, new realizations or understandings can be forgotten surprisingly quickly.

Closing a facilitated group session

At the end of a group session it is important to make sure that all issues raised during the session have been dealt with and that where necessary individuals (or the group as a whole) have been supported and helped to move forward. This may sometimes mean dealing with issues outside the group, for example in a one-to-one session.

It is also important to give the group a sense of closure, and this can take a variety of forms. A simple way of closing a session can be to look back over the outcomes individuals identified for themselves at the start. If you recorded these on a flip chart, you can close by referring back to them and checking to what extent they were met. Hopefully you will have been watching them as the session progressed and trying to make sure they were addressed. Alternatively, you might ask each participant to offer a statement of what they have learned and what they will do next. These statements may be task focused or (in developmental groups) may be powerful statements of personal learning. In this case, the statements might be expressed in poems or pictures, for example.

Where you have facilitated a series of sessions, perhaps over a period of days or weeks, you may prefer to finish with a more comprehensive review of the learning that has been achieved over the time the group has spent together. This provides an opportunity for participants to reflect back on their experiences of the sessions and draw out as much learning as possible from these. The case study below shows how this can work in practice.

CASE STUDY

The aim of this professional development session was to help participants to develop the interpersonal skills they needed to work effectively in groups and teams. It had lasted four days and the group had worked together intensively throughout. At the start of the week they had completed a complex work-related task, working to a tight deadline so that they had to balance the challenges of completing the task with those of working well as a group. After completing the task, each was given feedback by every other member of the group on their contribution to the task and on how others had experienced working with them.

The group was then introduced to a number of psychometric instruments and given feedback on their individual and group profiles (these had all been completed by participants in advance of the programme). Each instrument was selected to help raise awareness of a different aspect of group or team working.

Each participant had a personal coaching session in which they had the opportunity to discuss and review all feedback received up to that point. This included 360-degree feedback (collected from peers and junior and senior colleagues) which had been collected before the start of the programme.

Group members were given time to work together in small groups and to share their learning and new insights. This was an opportunity for each to help others and to be helped in turn. Each was asked to complete, as a result of this exercise, a plan setting out how this new learning would change workplace practice and how the personal development started in this programme would be continued.

This was a demanding learning experience and for some participants it was at times challenging and even emotional. The final review session was therefore an important opportunity for each to share their final reflections on their learning and to prepare to return to the workplace.

In this final session, one of the facilitators reminded participants of their journey through the week, recapping what had been covered in each session and some of the key moments. This was intended to give them time to remember and to reflect again on their experiences during the programme. The facilitator then led a discussion in which the group shared their perspectives of their experience, identifying where they felt that they had learned something really important and also where they had struggled to find learning.

Finally, the session closed with each participant asked to say what had been their most important learning from the week and to identify one change they were committed to make as a result of this learning on their return to the workplace.

Working with virtual groups and teams

Virtual groups and teams may be drawn from different parts of the same organization (which may be geographically dispersed) or from different organizations with similar aims. They are likely to use information technology to communicate and this may include internet or intranet tools which enable face-to-face communication or discussion forums. These may or may not be complemented by meetings in person, and so the ability to work effectively in virtual environments is increasingly important, both for facilitators and for participants.

There are some obvious advantages to virtual working, which largely mirror those of online learning (introduced in Chapter 2). For example, travel time and disruption to working patterns is reduced and these are great benefits for geographically dispersed organizations. Additional benefits can include (depending on the technology used) the ability to record meetings and to share documents easily online. Online presentations can be given, and written chat facilities may be available to complement oral discussion.

There are also some obvious challenges, however, including the difficulties of communicating well in virtual meetings and discussions. Where the group or team has a global reach and draws members from different cultures and nationalities there can be additional challenges. These include managing a range of languages and different values and beliefs, not to mention dealing with different time zones. The importance of the facilitator being skilled in using the relevant technology was emphasized earlier in the chapter but it is important to be prepared for the fact that participants too may need guidance and support in using it.

This section will look more closely at some of these challenges and at the skills facilitators need to deal with them.

Building a sense of community

It is helpful to pay particular attention to relationship building in the early stages of a virtual meeting or group session. This can include spending extra time on introductions if participants have never met before – it can be very disconcerting for participants if they are uncertain of the identity of those present. This can be done by self-introductions in the usual way.

A complementary icebreaker might involve participants indicating their location on an online map. This is particularly useful if participants are spread around the world and provides an opportunity to remind everyone of the different time zones participants are working in.

It can help considerably if an opportunity can be provided for the group to meet face to face at an early stage of community building, but of course this is not always possible.

Supporting effective communication

Communication is often hampered in virtual environments by the fact that the physical signals provided by facial expressions and body language are often harder to read – this can be true even when video is available. This can make it hard to spot emotional responses, which can show when tensions are beginning to emerge or when individuals begin to respond emotionally. It is also very easy for participants to speak over each other, not recognizing that others wish to speak, or to speak at great length, not recognizing that others are disengaged.

It can be helpful, in agreeing ground rules, to tackle the question of how participants' contributions will be managed – particularly in a large group. You might, for example, suggest that voting buttons (where these are available) are used to signal when an individual wishes to speak. This risks compromising the flow of the discussion, but it does help the facilitator to know who wants to speak and to make sure everyone gets a chance to contribute.

In any case, the facilitator will need to pay close attention to monitoring participants' reactions, for example by noticing when individuals are not commenting or contributing while at the same time managing those who are speaking too much, without giving offence. It is important to pay attention to ensuring that all members of the group are encouraged and enabled to participate throughout. However, there can be a significant challenge in paying attention to both verbal contributions and written 'chat' contributions (where these are available) and it can be very helpful to have a co-facilitator to help to monitor these sources of information.

Virtual groups and teams may communicate through asynchronous tools such as discussion forums and these will often have a facilitator to guide and support contributors. In this environment, it is easy for participants to feel isolated and it is an important part of the facilitator's role to create a sense of community and to encourage the involvement of all participants. They should be asked to provide photos of themselves as well as the usual self-introductions. Each should be acknowledged personally, either by the facilitator or by other members of the group, and participants may need to be reminded of the importance of responding to others' posts as well as making their own contributions.

As in all facilitated learning it is important to hand over responsibility for the discussion to the group. However, the facilitator must commit to a regular presence and will also need to monitor all contributions.

In this case, the ground rules for the group (all of which apply to the facilitator as well as participants) might include the following reminders:

- to respond to others' posts as well as making personal contributions, even if only to acknowledge or agree with them;
- to treat all posts as confidential, although confidential organizational information should normally not be posted;
- to check carefully that messages posted cannot be misinterpreted as being rude or sarcastic;
- to use humour with great care, since it can easily cause unintended offence.

It is worth setting out clearly how posts which seem to contravene the guidelines will be dealt with. The facilitator might, for example, commit to removing posts which seem unprofessional and to discussing with the contributor what the next steps should be.

Teams

This section will deal with teams, which are a particular form of group. Teams are ubiquitous within organizations and there is a considerable demand for facilitated team-building and team-development workshops to develop shared understandings of how to work together well and of how the individuals who constitute a team can best contribute to it.

To work effectively with teams you will need a good understanding of team dynamics. These include the group dynamics which you read about in the previous section, but you will read in this section about issues peculiar to teams. You will also read a case study which illustrates how you might work with a team in practice.

What is a team?

A team is distinguished from other groups by the fact that its members are jointly accountable for performance and are dependent on each other to achieve results. An effective team is characterized by a sense among its members of belonging and of shared identity (even though individual team members may also belong to other teams). Leadership in a team is typically shared. Even where there is a team leader, he or she will involve team members in decisions about common goals and ways of working. This contrasts with the situation in work groups where the manager is more likely to work with individual members of the group to agree their goals. Teams can take a variety of forms, including executive teams at the top of an organization, project teams formed to carry through a particular project, advisory teams and work teams (Thomson and Arney, 2015). Some teams are explicitly self-managed, with no formal leadership role at all.

Helping teams to work effectively

In working with teams you may need to address any of the group dynamics issues already discussed. However, there is another important area to address, which is peculiar to team dynamics. This concerns the way team members work together and relates to the role each person adopts in the team and interpersonal relationships within the team.

Belbin's team roles

One useful way of helping teams to improve the way their members work together is to encourage them to think about the role each plays and how they contribute to the team through these roles. A team role inventory, often used for this purpose, was developed by Belbin while working with executive teams at Henley Management College (now part of the University of Reading). Belbin was curious to discover why some teams performed much better than others and discovered that team success was not produced by putting the most intelligent individuals together. Instead, he identified that in the best-performing

Table 4.2 Belbin's Team Roles (adapted from Belbin, 2004)

Co-ordinator (previously known as chairman)	Marshalls the team's resources, recognizing team members' strengths and weaknesses and identifying how to use individuals to best effect.
Implementer (previously known as company worker)	A good organizer, willing to put the company's interests first and to take on tasks which may not be enjoyable, simply because they need to be done.
Plant	Creative and innovative: has an ability to contribute new ideas and ways of thinking about issues facing the team.
Completer-finisher	Pays attention to detail and is able to plan ahead so that all aspects have been considered. Makes sure that all tasks are seen through to completion.
Monitor-evaluator	Serious-minded and able to make sound judgements based on analysis of all relevant factors.
Shaper	Brings energy to moving the team forward and can significantly shape its activities and outcomes.
Team worker	Pays attention to people issues in the team, promoting harmony and helping to reduce conflict and tension between other team members.
Resource investigator	Finds and makes good use of resources outside the group, including useful networks and contacts.
Specialist	Contributes specialist knowledge and skills.

teams, members worked in complementary roles. Moreover, he identified that eight quite distinct roles needed to be covered (and later he added a ninth role).

Belbin's self-perception inventory is intended to enable members of a team to identify which roles they can best take on (and those to which they are not suited). Belbin argued that individuals can exercise some choice in the roles they adopt, although this is limited by personal qualities, so that all roles are accessible to some and not others. Using this inventory to raise awareness among team members of the roles they best play in teams and therefore the contributions they best make can be valuable in itself. However, once team members have completed these it also becomes possible to look at a profile of the whole team. At this point it may become obvious that one or more roles – such as completer–finisher or plant, for example – is not being covered. This can help to explain weaknesses in the team's performance and it may be that one or more new team members are needed to change and improve the team's performance.

If you want to complete the Belbin questionnaire for yourself, you can try it out (for a fee) on the Belbin website (www.belbin.com) which also provides details of training in its use. You will also find fuller details of the team roles and the strengths and weaknesses of each.

Myers-Briggs Type Indicator and Firo-B

There are a number of other instruments which may be used to help raise awareness of the qualities each team member brings to the team's joint endeavours. Like Belbin's team roles inventory they can also be used to provide a profile of the team as a whole, illuminating the strengths and areas for improvement and shedding light on relationships within the team.

The Myers-Briggs Type Indicator (MBTI) is widely used for this purpose. It is also often used in coaching and leadership development, for example to support self-awareness and personal development. The MBTI explores personal preferences against four dimensions. From these, 16 distinct personality types can be identified, each with its signature preferences in behaviour and propensities to work in particular ways with each of the other types. The value of the MBTI lies in developing understanding of the differences between individuals, expressed for example in behaviours, ways of communicating, organizing and relating to others. This understanding can contribute to improved relationships in the workplace as well as improved self-understanding and self-management.

The Fundamental Interpersonal Relations Orientation (Firo-B) instrument can also help to raise awareness of personal behaviours and is particularly useful for illuminating behaviours and relationship patterns in groups. Developed by Schutz and introduced in 1958, this test assesses how each individual approaches the key elements of relationship building: inclusion (interaction with others); control (either controlling others or being controlled); and affection (willingness to develop closeness with others).

Neither MBTI nor Firo-B should be used without training; they should only be administered and feedback given by those licensed to use them. There are of course other instruments which you can use in team development. However, you will only want to use those which are well enough researched to demonstrate that they are valid (ie they measure what they claim to measure) and reliable (ie they measure consistently each time they are administered). These are unlikely to be available to users without training.

The following case study shows how MBTI and Firo-B can be used in team development.

There were five members of the senior management team: Peter (the CEO), Mark (his deputy), Sarah, Andrew and David. Ian had arranged the workshop, with Peter's agreement, in an effort to help the team to work more effectively. The difficulties he had identified included tensions between members of the team and a sense that they were seen in the wider organization as disunited and failing to pull together.

Before the workshop, all participants were asked to complete MBTI and Firo-B questionnaires. The facilitators also met with Ian (as the sponsor for the intervention) to find out more about the issues which seemed to be facing the team and what he hoped to achieve from the workshop.

On the day of the workshop, the group met with the facilitators for informal introductions over coffee. The group then sat in a small horseshoe configuration with the two facilitators. The workshop began with participants being asked to say a bit about their hopes and expectations for the workshop. This formed the agenda, which was recorded on a flip chart and left on display. The issues recorded there included those already flagged up to the facilitators before the workshop.

With the permission of all group members the MBTI and Firo-B profiles of group members were shared. Each instrument was explained to the group before each set of profiles was displayed, so that participants could understand the significance of the insights offered.

One striking piece of learning from the MBTI profiles was the strong introvert preference of the CEO. An important insight, both for him and for his colleagues, was the effort it cost him to be as outgoing as his role required him to be. Peter resolved to develop strategies to enable him to manage the need to be more outgoing than he would ideally want to be. His colleagues (all strongly extravert) developed a better understanding of Peter, having previously felt puzzled by behaviour they found less sociable than they had expected.

Further exploration of the team's MBTI and Firo-B profiles helped them to gain insights into the needs of other team members and their ability to contribute to the team. The agenda items agreed at the start of the workshop were explored in the context of better mutual understanding. At the close of the session, participants agreed that they had a better understanding of each other and were able to identify specific ways to improve their work together as a team.

This is an anonymized version of a team-building workshop co-facilitated by the author.

It is also possible to offer 360-degree feedback for teams. This type of feedback is widely used in individual personal development, where it provides an opportunity to receive feedback from senior and junior colleagues as well as peers (this was covered in Chapter 2). In teams, 360-degree development feedback can come from those inside and outside the organization who have an interest in its performance. The insights this can generate can be very helpful in enabling the team to make judgements about its effectiveness and about areas where performance improvements may be needed.

Managing your own development as a facilitator

Facilitation can be challenging work and developing your skills will take time. As in coaching and mentoring, which you will read about in Chapter 5, you will benefit from having support mechanisms to help you to develop your skills and to reflect on and learn from the dilemmas and challenges you will certainly face in working with groups. This can include finding someone to support you in your reflective practice; this could be a coach, mentor or supervisor, or simply a more experienced colleague. It can also help to be part of

Figure 4.2 A sample skills development form

What do I want to learn?	What shall I do to achieve this?	Who or what can help me?	How will I know I have succeeded?	Keep a note here of what you have learned and any reflections on your learning

a learning group yourself in which you can reflect with others on the processes within the group and receive feedback on your own behaviours and impact on others. This experience can be particularly helpful if you work with developmental groups. To prepare for this work you should expect to work intensively on understanding your own presence and the impact of your behaviour on others.

The skills you will need to develop to be effective as a facilitator have already been outlined in this chapter, including the reflective skills you will need to practise. As in all other areas of your skills development these can be part of your planned continuous professional development and an example of a skills development form you might use for this purpose is provided in Figure 4.2.

Applying these ideas to your practice

Choose an area in which you would like to develop your facilitation skills. Write an objective for this learning and a plan for meeting this objective.

When you have carried out your planned learning, write a reflective account of what you have learned.

Feedback

You may find it helpful to discuss your plans with a colleague, mentor or manager. You may also benefit from developing your facilitation skills in the context of a group where you can receive feedback on your progress and support in your continuing development. Because facilitation can be challenging, even for experienced facilitators, it can be helpful to ensure that you have continuing support for your development. This can be in the form of membership of a developmental group, as already noted, or by working with a more experienced facilitator who provides mentoring or supervision.

Conclusion

There has been a profound change in thinking about approaches to supporting learning and this has led to a move away from teacher- and trainer-led learning to a strong emphasis on the importance of learners taking responsibility for managing their own learning. This self-managed learning depends on well-developed skills in reflective practice. An important part of the role of learning and development professionals in this new world is to help learners to learn how to manage their learning and to facilitate learning in groups and teams.

There are a number of models of facilitation which offer approaches to working as a facilitator with group and teams.

This chapter has included an overview of writing about facilitation by Casey, Roberts and Salaman, Heron, and Burnard. Casey, Roberts and Salaman emphasize the importance of the facilitator noticing both what is happening in the group and what the facilitator is experiencing, and of drawing on both in making judgements about how and when to intervene. Interventions must be carefully judged so that they do not deprive members of the group of the opportunity to develop their own learning and understanding from their experiences. Heron outlines the variety of ways in which the facilitator may work with the group and the variety of roles he or she may carry out. This can mean working in hierarchical or co-operative mode, or (in autonomous mode) letting the group take responsibility for its own learning. Burnard emphasized the role of the facilitator in encouraging participants to think critically about their learning and discussed the challenges this can offer the facilitator.

Facilitation can be used in a range of contexts, including therapy and counselling, for example. In this chapter, the emphasis has been on workplace learning. Here there is an important distinction between facilitating groups and teams in dealing with tasks (basic facilitation) and developmental facilitation in which the aim is to both to address the task and to learn how to work better as a group. In the first case, the facilitator helps the group to work effectively together on the task in hand. In the second, the facilitator helps the group to develop an improved awareness of their own behaviours and impact on others. This can help the group to work more effectively in future tasks and can also contribute to personal development for individual members of the group.

Facilitators need a well-developed understanding of the dynamics of groups and teams and of the differences between them. This includes being able to recognize and manage the processes of group formation and some of the common obstacles to group and team performance, such as hidden agendas and conflicts between participants. There are a range of instruments such as Belbin's team roles inventory, the Myers-Briggs Type Indicator and Firo-B which can help the members of groups and teams to understand their interactions with each other and to use this understanding to improve their performance when working together.

In developing your own skills as a facilitator, you will benefit from support for your own reflective practice from a critical friend, a supervisor, coach or mentor, or from peers. It can be very helpful to work in a learning group which provides opportunities to reflect on practice and to receive feedback on personal behaviours and your impact within the group. As in all other areas it can also be helpful to develop your own plan for skill development as part of your continuing professional development.

Reflective questions

What should the balance be, in the workplace, between self-managed learning and trainer-led learning?

How can you distinguish between the learning which individuals can and should take responsibility for and the learning which should be provided for them in trainer-led form?

When facilitating task-focused group work, there may well be obstructive behaviours within the group. How much responsibility does the facilitator have for challenging these behaviours?

How can you introduce the idea of self-managed learning to those whose education so far has not given them any understanding of the value of this or of reflective learning?

How can you help those who are strongly focused on task issues to understand the value of managing process issues as well – particularly when those individuals are in senior roles?

References

Argyris, C and Schön, D A (1992) *On Organizational Learning*, Blackwell, Cambridge MA

Barnett, R (2000) University knowledge in an age of supercomplexity, *Higher Education*, **40** (4), pp. 409–22

Belbin, R M (2004) *Management Teams: Why they succeed or fail*, 2nd edn, Elsevier, Oxford

Blake, R R and Mouton, J S (1978) *The New Managerial Grid*, Gulf Publishing Company, Houston

Burnard, P (2002) *Learning Human Skills: An experiential and reflective guide for nurses and health care professionals*, 4th edn, Butterworth-Heinemann, GB

Casey, D, Roberts, P and Salaman, G (1992) Facilitating learning in groups, *Leadership and Organization Development Journal*, **13** (4), pp. 8–13

Fenton-O'Creevy, M and van Mourik, C (2016) 'I understood the words but I didn't know what they meant': Japanese online MBA students' experiences of British assessment practices, *Open Learning: The Journal of Open, Distance and e-Learning*, DOI: 10.1080/02680513-2016.1177503

Gray, D E (2007) Facilitating management learning: developing critical reflection through reflective tools, *Management Learning*, **38** (5), pp. 495–517

Harrison, R (2009) *Learning and Development*, 5th edn, CIPD, London

Hatton, N and Smith, D (1995) Reflection in teacher education – towards definition and implementation, *Teaching and Teacher Education*, **11** (1), pp. 33–49

Heron, J (1999) *The Complete Facilitator's Handbook*, Kogan Page, London

Knowles, M S, Holton III, E F and Swanson, R A (2015) The Adult Learner: The definitive classic in adult education and human resource development, 8th edition, Routledge, Abingdon

Moon, J A (2004) A Handbook of Reflective and Experiential Learning, Routledge, Abingdon

Raelin, J A (2002) 'I don't have time to think!' versus the art of reflective practices, *Reflections*, **4** (1), pp 66–79

Reynolds, J R, Caley, L and Mason, R (2002) *How do people learn?* CIPD, London

Rogers, C R (1961) *On Becoming a Person*, Constable, London

Rogers, C R (1969) *Freedom to Learn*, Charles E Merrill Publishing Company, Columbus Ohio

Rogers, C R (1983) *Freedom to Learn for the 1980s*, Charles E Merrill Publishing Company, Columbus Ohio

Schein, E H (1988) *Process Consultation Volume 1: Its role in organization development*, 2nd edn, Addison Wesley, MA

Schön, D A (1983) *The Reflective Practitioner: How professionals think in action*, Basic Books, New York

Senge, P M (2006) *The Fifth Discipline: The art and practice of the learning organization*, revised edn, Random House, London

Schwarz, R (2002) *The Skilled Facilitator: A comprehensive resource for consultants, facilitators, managers, trainers and coaches*, Jossey-Bass, San Francisco

Thomson, R and Arney, E (2015) *Managing People: A practical guide for front-line managers*, Routledge, Abingdon

Tuckman, B W (1965) Developmental sequence in small groups, *Psychological Bulletin*, **63** (6), pp. 384–99

Implementing coaching and mentoring   05

Introduction

Coaching and mentoring are both widely used and their popularity shows no sign of abating. They are often used to support individual change and skill development and coaching, particularly, is widely used to support strategic change programmes. In this case, there may be a large number of coaching interventions happening at the same time in the organization and at all levels, right up to board level. Learning and development professionals will often have the task of designing and managing these coaching interventions.

Both coaching and mentoring can make an important contribution to talent management and development programmes by supporting skill development and (particularly in the case of mentoring) by helping individuals to prepare for promotion and adjust to new roles. Both can also support retention by enhancing the value of the development opportunities provided to employees and demonstrating the value employers place on them.

Coaching and mentoring skills are at a premium in most organizations. Line managers and leaders are expected to develop these skills so that they can support a culture of continuous learning in which individual employees are able to take responsibility for and manage their own personal development. Learning and development professionals too need to be able to draw on these skills to provide coaching and mentoring support at all levels of the organization. They also need to understand how these skills can be used to contribute to organizational learning, to talent management and development, to cultural change and to change management.

This chapter will explore what is meant by the terms 'coaching' and 'mentoring', the similarities and differences between them and the different types of coaching and mentoring. There is an outline of some basic skills used in both and guidance on how to develop these and prepare for a coaching or mentoring session. This chapter will also cover some of the ways in which coaching and mentoring interventions are used, such as in supporting change and cultural change, and will discuss the management of these interventions.

Throughout the text there are comments from two experienced practitioners. Janet Turner has worked as a senior HR professional in multinational IT companies and in those roles has been coached, has coached others and has been responsible for selecting and appointing coaches. Elizabeth Walmsley is an experienced executive coach who has also worked as a CEO and as a non-executive director. Their comments are presented in boxes labelled 'practitioner viewpoint'.

What do we mean by coaching and mentoring?

Both coaching and mentoring are words that can be used in a variety of ways and there is disagreement about the definition of each (Garvey, 2004). Both are methods of facilitating and supporting learning. Clutterbuck (2008:8) comments that both 'work on the quality of the learner's thinking' and that advice is only offered when the learner does not have the resources he or she needs to make progress. They draw on very similar skills, including goal setting, being able to listen attentively and being able to ask questions skilfully.

Coaching and mentoring are both used to support individuals in managing their own learning, and both are important aids to the shift from training to learning which you read about in Chapter 1 of this book. Much of their appeal for organizations is that they can support continuous self-managed learning; they can provide support for individuals in finding ways to respond to fast-changing environments, including planned organizational change and the changes that follow from promotion or moving to a new role. In the case of coaching, particularly, it can also be used to support team development; team coaching will be discussed later in this chapter.

Underpinning both coaching and mentoring lies an idea about learning and development which you met in Chapter 1 of this book. This is constructivism, the idea that understanding and knowledge are created by the learners themselves, and that helping people to learn is about helping them to identify and create new understandings for themselves. This contrasts with the idea that learning is best achieved when an expert shares his or her knowledge with others – a more traditional and, to some, a more comfortable model of learning. As you will see, it does tend to be assumed that mentors will have greater experience or expertise than those they mentor, and the mentoring relationship often involves the sharing of insights and understandings by the mentor. However, this is in the context of a relationship in which the mentor is supporting self-managed learning as described above.

One of the challenges of both coaching and mentoring is to build a relationship in which learning can best be achieved. You have already read in Chapter 4 how a facilitator must judge when and how to intervene to support learning; this may be through questioning or through challenge and the skill of the coach or mentor is to judge when each is appropriate.

While coaching and mentoring share many similarities, there are also many differences, one of which has already been suggested. The distinction between the two is not clear cut, however, and it is worth spending some time considering how to distinguish between them and identifying in which circumstances each is most appropriate. You will probably also already know that coaching takes many forms, and trying to distinguish between these can be difficult. In the next section you will explore the differences between coaching and mentoring and also between different types of both.

Differences between coaching and mentoring

In some ways it is easier to recognize the similarities between coaching and mentoring than the differences between them. Both are ways of supporting self-managed learning; in other words they leave the ownership of personal development with the learner. Both draw on the same sorts of skills to achieve this, as noted above. Clutterbuck (2008) identifies that the similarities between coaching and mentoring can include the following:

- both draw on the experience of the helper;
- both can take place over long or short periods of time;
- both can involve goal setting by or for the learner;
- both support the learner in making transitions;
- both support personal growth.

There are, however, two distinguishing characteristics of mentoring which can help to differentiate it from coaching. The first is that in a mentoring relationship the helper (the mentor) will normally have more experience than the person being helped. The mentoring relationship is normally, to some degree at least, intended to involve sharing some of the learning from that experience. Secondly, mentoring relationships can be very long term while coaching relationships, by contrast, are usually for a defined and limited term. Neither of these differences is absolute, however. For example, coaches are sometimes employed because they have relevant experience; this may be experience of the organization or sector, or of working at a senior level. There is considerable debate among coaches about

---

Practitioner viewpoint

The role of coach should not be seen as simply building on the learning and experience of the coachee. The coach may not be sharing expertise directly (as in a training environment) but is certainly drawing on it in appropriate situations. This is particularly the case in fast-changing environments or where the coachee needs to get up to speed quickly in a new role. The coach may then help by offering new perspectives, bringing in new ideas, offering new networks and challenging the status quo to provide a wider framework of learning.

Elizabeth Walmsley, executive coach.

how important relevant experience is, with some coaches arguing that it is the skill of supporting learning that really matters. For this reason, many successful coaches have backgrounds in psychotherapy or sports coaching, rather than in business, while others are able to draw on their experience as senior leaders or managers. Others, however, emphasize the value of the experience a coach may bring, complementing the creation of knowledge and understanding of the learner.

While mentoring relationships are typically long term, in practice, some, such as induction mentoring relationships, can be for a limited and defined duration. Conversely, while coaching relationships are usually expected to be for defined and often quite short periods, they can sometimes be long term and undefined – this can be the case in executive coaching for example.

In practice, as is probably clear by now, there are overlaps between coaching and mentoring practice and it is hard to draw a firm distinction between them. However, while the terms are used interchangeably at times (CIPD, 2015) there are differences. The CIPD argues that mentoring is 'a distinct intervention using coaching skills but with different timescales and agendas' (CIPD, 2011:4) and that organizations see mentoring as 'a distinct approach to building capability using basic coaching skills and techniques on a wider canvas' (CIPD, 2011:15).

Some of the sections in the rest of this chapter will refer only to coaching, although what you read in them will be directly relevant to mentoring. This is particularly the case where coaching skills are discussed, as these cannot really be distinguished from mentoring skills (as noted above).

Different types of coaching

There are many different types of coaching, and as a learning and development practitioner you will need to be able to distinguish between them. This will help you to identify which sort of coaching best suits your organization's needs and to make judgements about how coaching is to be delivered. Sometimes distinctions are drawn on the basis of who is delivering the coaching (as in peer coaching and line manager coaching, for example) and sometimes on the basis of the content of the coaching (as in executive coaching). It is also common to distinguish between external and internal coaching.

This section will help you to understand these different types of coaching and, where relevant, the strengths and weaknesses of each and factors to take into account when choosing between them.

Executive coaching

Executive coaching is normally provided for senior managers who are expected to move into major leadership roles. It may also be provided for those who have taken on a new role and need support in learning how to be effective in it, or for senior managers who need support in leading others through change (or managing their own altered roles in an organizational change programme). It can be an important way of helping to retain valued employees, both by demonstrating the value the organization places on them and by supporting their career development. In organization-wide change programmes, executive coaching may be provided to the senior team to help them to develop and model the new behaviours and learning now expected throughout the organization.

Since the focus of executive coaching is often leadership skills and/or personal effectiveness, this type of coaching can often have a strong personal development focus. It can therefore be very helpful for the coach to have skills in understanding and supporting personal development, and many coaches who work in this area may have a background in facilitating leadership or personal development programmes or even psychotherapy. Where the focus is on helping the individual being coached (coachee) to deal with real work issues it can be very helpful for the coach to have significant experience of working at a senior level, perhaps even at a more senior level than the coachee. In addition, where coaching is being provided for senior managers to support a programme of change, the coach will need a good understanding of change management issues and probably of organization development (OD) more widely.

Inevitably, executive coaches will not have all these skills to the same degree, and typically some coaches will offer more (sometimes much more) in one area than others. When selecting coaches, whether internal or external, it is important to have a good understanding of the skills they offer and to be clear how well these match the needs of the coachee and the organization. It is quite common for executive coaching to be provided by external coaches who are bought in simply for this purpose.

Line manager coaching

It is the line manager, more than anyone else in an organization, who influences the way individuals feel about their work. A skilful line manager can encourage employees to feel engaged in their work and motivated to contribute extra and discretionary effort, and this can have an important impact on employees' and the organization's performance (Purcell and Hutchinson, 2007). Managers who use coaching skills in their discussions and other interventions with their staff can make an important contribution to motivating and engaging them.

There are, however, some limits to a manager's role in coaching his or her own staff, and where a specific and time-limited coaching intervention is needed, the line manager may not be the best person to deliver it. This is partly because of concerns about confidentiality. As you will see later in this chapter, all coaching relationships depend on some degree of confidentiality, which needs to be discussed and agreed between coach and coachee. A line manager, though, cannot easily offer this and cannot ignore, as a line manager, what has been learned as a coach. There can also be conflicts of interest between the line manager role and the coach role simply because in the former role the manager has objectives to achieve and will have a view about how the coachee can best contribute to these, and this inevitably compromises the independence a coach should be able to offer.

Similarly, a coach and coachee will always agree a contract at the start of a coaching relationship, but this cannot supersede the existing relationship between line manager and direct report, which is already in place by virtue of their existing relationship. For all these reasons, some would argue that managers cannot take on the role of coach for their own reports (Arney, 2006). Others, however, take a different view and argue that, difficult as it is for line managers to combine both roles, the benefits of managers using coaching skills in their discussions with their staff make the challenge worthwhile (Pemberton, 2006).

Practitioner viewpoint

It is difficult for line managers to be coaches in the purest sense because they cannot play the role as neutrally as an external coach can – they have to wear two hats. In addition, time constraints and other pressures on senior managers can affect their availability and ability to meet the coachee's needs. That said, there is great value in managers developing coaching skills because the models and processes can help to strengthen their overall ability as a manager. Through coaching they can develop skills which can be used on a regular basis and as a matter of course to develop the ability of those around them.

Janet Turner, senior HR professional.

There is no dispute about the fact that line managers do need to develop coaching skills. They may well be coaches for members of staff in the organization whom they do not line manage, and organizations' preference for internal rather than external coaches has been

---

Practitioner viewpoint

Coaching relationships need to be characterized by trust and confidentiality and both present a challenge for the line manager who is also the performance manager charged with pursuing the organization's agenda. Performance issues often arise specifically because individuals experience difficulties in the line relationship. So while the line manager should be encouraged to adopt and develop a coaching style they should also recognize that they may be unable to offer all the confidentiality or objectivity necessary for behavioural change.

Elizabeth Walmsley, executive coach.

reported by the CIPD (2015). Line managers who are skilled coaches can use these coaching skills to support their staff in their learning and development, and to encourage continuous and self-managed learning. In other words, line managers can use coaching skills in their line manager role without taking on the distinctive role of coach for those who report to them.

Internal and external coaches

Internal coaching is provided by employees of the organization, whether they are employed full-time as coaches or combine coaching with another role, such as line manager. External coaches are external practitioners who are brought into the organization for specific coaching contracts or interventions. They may be (and often are) freelance coaches or they may be employed by a specialist coaching organization.

There are some clear advantages in using internal coaches. They know the organization and may be able to understand and empathize quickly with the challenges facing those they are coaching. They are often able to offer much more flexibility than external coaches, and can sometimes be available quite quickly to discuss important incidents and developments (Pemberton, 2006). There can also be a wider benefit for the organization in investing in coaching skills for its employees to create a cadre of internal coaches. This can pay dividends when the organization judges that it wants to create a coaching culture, for example (you will read more about coaching cultures later in this chapter). On the other hand, it can be difficult to ensure that coachees feel confident that their coaching sessions are fully confidential, even where internal coaches make a firm commitment never to gossip about coaching sessions. Where internal coaches are also line managers (even if not coaching their own direct reports) there can be conflicts of interest, as with line manager coaching.

External coaches can also offer considerable advantages in some cases. They can be particularly valuable where an external perspective is needed, where the coach is expected to challenge the coachee, or where specialist coaching skills are needed. They can also provide greater confidentiality and objectivity. For all these reasons they are often used in executive coaching. Where external coaches are used regularly by the same organization they can develop a good understanding of its culture.

***

Practitioner viewpoint

There can also be considerable benefits in bringing external coaches together to identify systemic issues or to identify variations in perspectives or practice in different parts of the organization. While internal coaches can be brought together in the same way they are less likely to bring the independent perspective external coaches can offer.

Elizabeth Walmsley, executive coach

***

There can be higher costs associated with hiring external coaches. When planning for their use, both recruitment costs and the payment of fees need to be considered. There may also be costs associated with providing training for external coaches. This is particularly the case if they are being asked to contribute to a major coach programme where the sponsor expects coaches to work to common objectives and perhaps also expects common models of coaching to be used.

The CIPD's annual learning and development survey report for 2015 stated that coaching by line managers or peers (both important forms of internal coaching) is significantly more popular than using external coaches, with 32 per cent of respondents reporting it as one of their three most commonly used learning and development practices and 40 per cent that it was one of their most effective practices (CIPD, 2015). Most (65 per cent) also said that they expected coaching by line managers or peers to increase in the organization in the next two years.

Mentoring

Mentoring is not categorized in quite the same way as coaching. For example, there is little discussion of 'executive mentoring', although those taking on very senior roles may benefit from mentoring support, whether provided internally or by an experienced manager from another organization. It is also quite common for senior managers to mentor those preparing for senior roles. This can be a valuable way of providing exposure to the perspectives of those at more senior levels of the organization and can be an important element of a talent development programme for those identified as having high potential. Mentoring can also be used in this way as part of positive action programmes provided for those in groups under-represented in particular roles or at senior levels in the organization. Since mentors are not commonly drawn from outside the organization there is little debate about the respective merits of 'internal' and 'external' mentoring. Four useful terms to be aware of, however, are 'developmental mentoring', 'sponsorship mentoring', 'reverse mentoring' and 'peer mentoring'.

Developmental and sponsorship mentoring

Clutterbuck (2014) distinguishes between two quite distinct models of mentoring. In the sponsorship mentoring model, developed in the United States, the individual being mentored is expected to benefit from the greater status of the mentor and may be seen as his or her protégé. In this model the mentor takes a leading role and gives advice and guidance. In the developmental model, commonly found in Europe, there is a much stronger emphasis on supporting self-managed learning in the individual being mentored and he or she is expected to take a proactive role in identifying the issues to be addressed and the ways in which they will be addressed.

While the distinction between these models seems clear-cut, in practice there can be some mixing of the two. Thus, even where the mentoring relationship is identified as being developmental, it is not uncommon for the mentor to sometimes give advice and guidance.

Clutterbuck (2014) also points out that it is not uncommon for developmental mentoring to lead to relationships which involve some degree of sponsorship, at least at an informal level. However, the extent to which this is regarded as acceptable is likely to vary between organizations and cultures.

Reverse mentoring

Reverse mentoring is so called because the mentor may be junior to, or younger than, the mentee while also having higher skill levels in a specific area. This can often be the case where more junior (and/or younger) staff have very well-developed digital literacy skills and can provide valuable support through mentoring arrangements to support older or more senior staff in developing their own skills. In this case, a member of staff who may in some ways be less experienced than the mentee takes on a mentoring role because he or she has greater experience or skill in the specific area that is the subject of mentoring.

Reverse mentoring can also be used to help senior managers to develop an understanding of diversity issues (Clutterbuck, 2014), providing an opportunity to learn directly from mentees' experience. There may be other areas too where reverse mentoring can enable those at senior levels in the organization to learn from those working at more junior levels. Those working in customer facing roles, for example, may have valuable experiences to share on customer behaviours and expectations.

There is another important potential benefit in reverse mentoring. Senior managers may find it uncomfortable to seek to learn from those who are junior to them or to admit to a need to learn in areas as important as IT, diversity or customer relations. Where they are willing to do this, however, they can become powerful ambassadors and role models for a culture of continuous learning. For those who take on the role of reverse mentor there is recognition of the value of their skills and experience and this can contribute to engagement and retention. The experience of working with more senior managers can also help to develop their understanding of senior roles and perspectives and in this way can support talent development.

Peer mentoring

In peer mentoring, as in reverse mentoring, the mentor will often bring greater experience in a specific area to the relationship, although this is not associated with greater status in the organization. Used in this way, peer mentoring can provide an opportunity to spread experience and learning within the organization in a cost-effective way. For example, the author, who is a senior fellow of the Higher Education Academy, is a peer mentor for colleagues preparing their own applications for senior fellowship. Peer mentoring can also work in cross-organizational contexts, for example where the CEO of an organization provides support for a newly appointed peer in a similar role elsewhere.

Peer learning can also be used in cases where there is no obvious difference between the experience of each party. Clutterbuck (2014:91) comments that in this case the relationship may be established informally and that 'both parties simply recognize the value the other person can provide in offering support, counsel and a different perspective on the issues they face'.

Coaching skills

This section will introduce the basic coaching skills of setting goals, attentive listening and skilful questioning. You will read about how to prepare for a coaching session. This includes agreeing a contract at the start of a coaching programme which involves not only the coach and coachee but also any other relevant stakeholders. You will also learn about the boundaries of your role as a coach, how to prepare for a coaching session and how to manage your own well-being in coaching relationships. Finally, you will be introduced to one widely used coaching model, the GROW model.

Coaching skills are widely used in mentoring and mentors will need to develop an understanding of all the areas covered in this section. However, they are referred to as coaching skills throughout. This recognizes that practice varies between organizations and each will make judgements about how to draw on the coaching skills outlined here to prepare mentors for their roles.

Setting goals

Coaching conversations should be purposeful: it makes sense to agree the outcomes the coachee seeks to achieve from each coaching session (or series of coaching sessions). Identifying the goals for a coaching conversation or session will be the first step in the GROW coaching model introduced later in this chapter. However, it is important to be aware that setting goals too early may lead to the wrong goals being chosen, and sticking rigidly to goals once agreed can mean that important issues are missed.

Pemberton (2006) points out that the coachee may need the coach's help to think through the issues they face and advocates postponing goal setting until this has happened. Whenever goals are set, it is worth remembering that they can and should be revisited, either during a coaching session or over a series of sessions. As in facilitation, the presenting issues may not be the real issues, whether the coachee realizes this or not, and the coach will need to be alert to evidence that there are other unrecognized issues to be addressed.

While the agenda for learning through coaching is owned by coachees, it is an important part of the coaches' role to help them to think through how their personal goals fit into the wider organizational context. It may be helpful to encourage individuals to seek feedback from workplace colleagues about the goals chosen so that the coaching sessions can have maximum impact and effectiveness.

Listening and asking questions

Listening

Both listening and asking questions are fundamentally important skills in coaching. Both can help you to understand the issues brought to coaching sessions by those you are seeking to help. They can also help those being coached to develop a better understanding of these issues for themselves and a greater awareness of their own potential to deal with them. As in all facilitated learning, the purpose of listening and asking questions is to help the learner to develop the insights and understanding to manage his or her own learning. At the root of both listening and asking questions there must be a genuine desire on the part of the coach to understand the issues the coachee is facing, and to help him or her to find ways of dealing with them that really work.

Listening, in coaching, means more than simply hearing; it means listening in a way that enables you to understand what the individual is saying from his or her perspective. It also means demonstrating that you are listening, and you can do this in a number of ways, both verbal and non-verbal. Non-verbal techniques include offering eye contact and sympathetic body language, while verbal techniques include summarizing or paraphrasing what has been said. This can help you to check that you have understood what has been said and demonstrates that you have listened.

Non-verbal ways to support listening also include:

- Posture – you should always aim for a relaxed and 'open' posture. This means for example that your arms are relaxed and not crossed.

- Mirroring – often you will find, when you are listening intently, that you unconsciously reflect back to the speaker his or her facial expressions or body language, and this can convey a sense of empathy. Conscious mirroring can also encourage better communication, but needs to be done carefully.

- Eye contact – as the listener you should offer eye contact, leaving the speaker the choice of whether to look at you or not. Try to do this sensitively; intense eye contact can feel intimidating and may (sometimes) be culturally unacceptable.

- Silence – sometimes silence is a helpful part of a conversation. If the subject is difficult the speaker (and the listener) may need time to gather thoughts or to reflect. Try to be comfortable with silence and not rush in to fill natural pauses in the conversation.

When you listen attentively you will encourage your coachee to say more, which may include talking about feelings and emotions. This may mean that the individual being coached becomes emotional, and it is important that you are able to respond supportively to this. You may find that it helps to allow the coachee to express their feelings (these may be of anger, sadness or anxiety, for example). It is usually helpful to avoid responding emotionally yourself, although this can be challenging if the emotions seem to be directed at you.

Applying these ideas to your practice

Try to identify someone you regard as a good listener. This could be a friend, a colleague or a relative, for example. Watch carefully how he or she behaves when listening, and look for examples of posture, mirroring, eye contact and use of silence. If you can find more than one or even several listeners to observe, try to compare how each listener uses these techniques.

When you feel that you have a good understanding of how these techniques can work, try to find a situation in which you can try them out for yourself.

Feedback

You may find at first that you feel uncomfortable when you use these techniques. With practice, however, you should be able to use them fluently and unselfconsciously to improve your listening skills. You may find it helpful to observe yourself listening on a video recording. Alternatively, you could ask a trusted friend or colleague to observe and offer feedback (guidance on giving and receiving feedback was covered in Chapter 4).

Verbal ways to support attentive listening

- Encouraging responses – small and encouraging interventions can help the speaker feel you are listening and engaged.

- Reflecting – this means repeating back to the speaker what has been said, sometimes by repeating the speaker's own words. This is simply acknowledging what has been said and noting its importance without commenting on it.

- Paraphrasing – paraphrasing means repeating what the speaker has said in your own words and can be a good way of checking your understanding as well as demonstrating that you have listened and understood.

- Summarizing – another useful way of checking your understanding. By summarizing what you have heard you can provide the coachee with an opportunity to correct your understanding or to

Applying these ideas to your practice

As in the last reflective exercise, find one or more good listeners to observe. This time look for examples of reflecting, summarizing and paraphrasing. When you feel confident that you understand what is meant by each of these techniques, try to find a situation where you can try them out for yourself.

Feedback

You may be tempted to try to combine this exercise with the last one. However, each of these sets of techniques is so important, and so hard to do well, that you will probably benefit from working on each separately.

As in the last exercise, you will probably find it helpful to observe your own practice either by arranging to be video recorded or by seeking feedback from an observer.

give you additional information. Sometimes a skilful summary can also help the coachee to gain new insights into a situation.

The techniques outlined above and which you have practised in these reflective activities should demonstrate to the coachee that: you are willing to listen (through open and attentive postures and eye contact); that you have understood what has been said (through paraphrasing and summarizing); and that you are able to empathize with his or her feelings (mirroring helps here). Hawkins and Smith (2013:10) identify these as three levels of listening which they call, respectively, 'attending', 'accurate listening' and 'empathetic listening'. They identify a fourth level which they call 'generative empathetic listening'. In this the listener uses intuition to understand and reflect back what is heard, helping the coachee to develop an enhanced understanding of what he or she has said.

Asking questions

Skilful questioning can help the coachee to think through more clearly the issues he or she is facing, to become more aware of the range of issues to be considered, and even to promote self-awareness.

Three types of question which you might expect to use in coaching are:

- open questions;
- closed questions;
- probing questions.

Open questions allow the coachee to decide for themselves what they will tell you. Good examples of open questions you might use in coaching include:

'How are you feeling?'

'What would you like to discuss?'

Closed questions are often used to clarify, for example in trying to be clear what exactly has happened. The answer may simply be 'yes' or 'no'. Examples you might use in coaching include:

'Was that your own idea?'

'Did you explain how you felt?'

Probing questions are used to find out more, for example if you feel that you have not heard the whole story. Examples you might use in coaching include:

'What happened next...?'

'I'd like to go back to something you said earlier... Could you tell me more about...?'

This simple classification of questioning can be helpful in raising awareness of the types of question used in coaching. However, there is more to be said about how questions can be used to support the coachee's thinking. Used well, they can help the coachee to identify what he or she already knows, to develop solutions to problems for him or herself and even to develop self-awareness.

When questions are used like this, they strongly support attentive listening: the coach uses questions to identify and follow up the clues which the coachee gives to his ideas, perceptions and interests. Downey (2002) also argues that the coach should note where the coachee's interest lies and should ask questions which follow that interest. In the following case study, notice how the coach uses short open questions to encourage the coachee to explore the issue concerning him.

CASE STUDY

John is on secondment to a public sector organization (referred to here as PSO) from a large multinational company (referred to as MNC). He has been given six coaching sessions to help him to work effectively in his new organization and to use his experience there to support his career development. This is an excerpt from the third session in this series.

> *John*: A new job has come up in my department here at PSO, as Head of Information Management, and I am very keen to apply for it.
>
> *Coach*: Can you tell me a bit more about that?
>
> *John*: I would really love to take on this role. It would make me part of the senior management team here at PSO and I'd like to achieve that.
>
> *Coach*: Is there anything to stop you applying? (Short open question.)
>
> *John*: I'm afraid that if I do I will offend MNC and that will damage my prospects for a successful return there.
>
> *Coach*: It sounds as if you're not sure yet where you want to develop your career. (Reflecting back.)
>
> *John*: That's true. I am really torn at the moment and I don't know where I see my career going from this point. I did wonder whether I might be able to apply for this new role on a temporary basis as part of my secondment, but I don't know whether that is possible.
>
> *Coach*: How could you find out whether that is an option?

By the end of the session John has agreed that one of his actions will be to establish with his manager in PSO whether it is feasible for him to apply for this promotion on a temporary basis and as part of his secondment. He and his coach have also agreed that at their next session they will talk more about how John sees his future career developing when his secondment ends.

Preparing to coach

Before you start any coaching you will need to be clear about its purpose. This may concern organizational objectives related to change, or the career development of the coachee, for example, and will normally be set out in a coaching contract. You will also need to have thought through a number of issues related to your coaching practice, such as the boundaries of your competence and any ethical issues you may face. Finally, you will need to be prepared for each individual coaching session, and this includes being mentally prepared and in a fit emotional state to practise. All these issues will be explored in the following section.

Developing a coaching contract

In most coaching interventions there will be a three-way contract between the organization, the coach and the coachee. The organization which sponsors the sessions will have its own objectives for them and it is part of the purpose of the coach to deliver these. The individual being coached will also have his or her own objectives, which hopefully (and ideally) will align well with those of the organization. However, in practice this sort of tri-partite contracting can be a challenge and there can be tensions between what the organization wants to achieve and what the individual wants to achieve in a first coaching session.

Applying these ideas to your practice

Spend some time now thinking about what sorts of information you might expect a coach to keep confidential if you were being coached. How might your discussions with your coach be constrained if you felt that your comments might be repeated or reported back to the organizational sponsor of this coaching?

Feedback

Most of us would think very carefully about what we said if we thought it might be repeated, and much coaching (and mentoring) depends on open discussion of the issues. On the other hand, complete confidentiality is not really possible, for the reasons given in this chapter. A full and honest discussion of the limits of confidentiality at the start of a series of coaching sessions is most likely to enable the coachee to speak openly to the coach while also recognizing where the boundaries of confidentiality lie.

In agreeing your initial contract with a coachee you will need to address the difficult issue of confidentiality. You will certainly want to (and should) offer to respect the confidences offered to you in the coaching sessions. You might undertake for example never to gossip about your coachee and not to repeat what has been said to you in an attributable way. However, there are two very large caveats to make here. Your coachee must understand that you cannot keep confidential information about criminal activity, about serious concerns about the coachee's welfare, or about behaviour which may be damaging to the organization. You will also need to reserve the right to talk about the content of each coaching session, albeit in anonymized form, when you discuss your experience of coaching with your supervisor (you will read about coaching supervision later in this chapter).

Ethics

A number of ethical issues have already been raised in this chapter. Your approach to contracting and dealing with issues of confidentiality, and your recognition of the boundaries of your competence, for example, are all rooted in an ethical approach to coaching and mentoring.

As a coach or mentor you will want to think through the ethics of your practice. A helpful way to do this is to review the code of ethics provide by a coaching association. For example, the European Mentoring and Coaching Council (EMCC) and the Association for Coaching have produced a local Code of Ethics for coaches and mentors (AC and EMCC, 2016). This sets out good practice and standards of conduct for coaches and mentors, covering areas such as contracting, integrity, confidentiality, supervision and continuing professional development. It also emphasizes the importance of recognizing equality and diversity, of being inclusionary and of respecting individual differences.

Both coaching and mentoring can play an important role in programmes to support the career development of those in groups under-represented at senior levels in the organization and this makes an understanding of diversity issues a particularly important skill area for both. More generally, coaches should be expected to make a strong commitment to continuing professional development, including taking part in supervision of their practice – both are covered later in this chapter. This commitment to constantly improving practice is an important element of an ethical approach to coaching.

Preparing for a coaching session

Every coaching session will require you to find some time to prepare. This is partly about practical issues: you will need to read any notes from earlier sessions and perhaps from discussions with the sponsor. You will also need to ensure that the coaching session takes place, if possible, in an environment where you will not be disturbed (in the session itself you can avoid potential distractions by switching off your mobile phone and asking your coachee to do the same).

Just as importantly, however, you will need to prepare yourself for the session. Throughout the coaching session you will need to be aware of how your own feelings may be impacting on the conversation. If you are calm, relaxed and receptive, your coachee is likely to respond very differently than if faced with a tense, anxious or irritated coach.

The impact you can have simply by virtue of your mood or feelings is sometimes referred to as your 'presence'. In coaching, as in many areas of leadership and management, your presence can make an important difference to your effectiveness, and negative feelings such as anxiety, nervousness or stress may make it difficult to attend fully to your client.

Simply monitoring your feelings as you prepare for a coaching session can raise your self-awareness, and this alone may help you to manage your feelings. Otherwise, you may find it helpful to explore techniques such as mindfulness which can help you to set aside negative emotions and focus fully on your client.

The coaching session

There are many ways of managing a coaching session and experienced coaches will often develop their own signature models and frameworks for doing so. In this section you will read about one very popular and widely used model, the GROW model, which can help you to structure your coaching sessions effectively. This model, described more fully in Whitmore (2002), provides a straightforward and easily remembered framework and has the added benefit of supporting a reflective approach to learning by mirroring Kolb's learning cycle, which you read about in Chapter 1 (O'Connor and Lages, 2007).

GROW is an acronym: Goals, Reality, Options, What (will you do). It describes a structure in which each of the four elements is followed, usually sequentially. You may find, however, that the reality of coaching is less neat than this and the process of discussion less linear. GROW may therefore be seen as a framework to build on, one which you can vary as your experience develops.

Goals

In the GROW model the first stage in a coaching session is to agree the purpose or the goal or goals of the session. Downey (2002) points out that this will mean first identifying the topic to be explored in the session and certainly you cannot easily identify goals without agreeing the general area to be discussed. The goals you agree with the coachee should identify what he or she wants to achieve in the session. You might move towards identifying it with questions like:

What would you like to discuss in this session? (Topic)

What would you like to achieve by the end of the session? (Goal)

Ulrich (2008) argues that these goals should be aligned with organizational goals, and certainly they should be compatible with the contract agreed with the sponsor, as noted above.

Reality

Once the goals have been agreed, your next task as coach is to help your coachee to recognize and understand the reality of the situation to be addressed. Your questions and the quality of your listening will be important here in helping your coachee to see clearly the issue or issues to be dealt with. This can be challenging in itself, particularly if the coachee experiences strong emotions in thinking about these issues. Your task as coach is to support non-judgemental assessment of the reality to be addressed, so that the best options for action can be identified.

The following example illustrates how this could work in practice. Notice how the coach is monitoring the coachee's responses, when she seems upset, even though this is not explicitly acknowledged in the questions asked. The coach is calm and attentive throughout.

CASE STUDY

This is the third of six coaching sessions provided for Sara by her employer, to support her development as a manager. She has recently moved to a new role in a high-profile and rather pressurized office.

Sara: I simply can't see how I can succeed in this role. My manager seems to really dislike me.

Coach (noticing that Sara seems tense and agitated): What makes you say that?

Sara: He criticizes and undermines me. Nothing I do is right.

Coach (noticing that Sara is becoming tearful): Can you give me an example of when this has happened?

Sara (taking a deep breath and steadying herself): He shouted at me last week and told me that a report I had written was not good enough.

Coach (noticing that Sara is rather calmer now): Tell me a bit more about that incident.

Sara: This was a paper on options for reducing expenditure in our department. The deadline was very short and I worked very late to complete it. To be honest I wasn't absolutely sure what he wanted – and now it is being rewritten by someone else.

Coach: Did you ask for feedback about what was wrong with the report?

Sara: No, I was too upset to do that.

Coach: Have there been any other incidents like that?

Sara: No, just that one.

Coach: Has anything else happened to make you think your manager dislikes you?

Sara: He hasn't been welcoming or friendly. He has disagreed with me in front of my staff and he has never given me any positive feedback on my work, although he constantly corrects my written work.

Coach: Do you ever see him behaving like this in other contexts or with other people?

Sara: I suppose he's never really very friendly or outgoing. I hadn't really thought about that. Perhaps I am not the only person he treats like this.

Options

In this part of the coaching session the coachee is encouraged to identify options for dealing with the issue or issues now identified. The emphasis here is on encouraging him or her to identify a number of possible options for action before deciding what to do next. This may take some time, and questions which encourage and clarify will help, as will attentive listening.

You should avoid making judgements at this stage about the options being identified, and discourage your coachee from doing so. The emphasis should be on exploring possibilities and generating options. This could even include a short brainstorm, as in the following case study.

CASE STUDY

This case study is part of a coaching session in which Andrew and his coach are working on the goal of finding a way to reduce the stress of his long daily commute to work. Andrew feels that the commute is damaging both his health and his effectiveness at work but has ruled out the options of changing jobs or moving house, at least in the short term. In exploring reality he identified that the most challenging part of the commute was the car journey between his home and the railway station and finding a car parking space.

Coach: Let's brainstorm some options for dealing with this, and this time I will join in. How else might you get to the station?

Andrew: I could take a bus… or a taxi.

Coach: You could car share.

Andrew: I could travel earlier to avoid traffic… I could stay nearer the station overnight.

Coach: Could you walk?

Andrew: No! It's 15 miles! But perhaps I could ask to work at home one day each week…

What will you do next?

For the coaching session to be useful the coachee will need to move on from listing options to evaluating their likely value and selecting which can best form the basis for action. Again, your role as coach is to support and clarify – and challenge if necessary. Once one or more actions have been identified it is worth spending some time exploring how they will be carried out and by when. This action planning can be an important help in encouraging the coachee to make a commitment to action. The responsibility for action remains with the employee, although you will probably want to make a note to check on progress at your next coaching session.

Advantages and disadvantages of the GROW model

The GROW model can help you to be purposeful and focused in your coaching but also runs the risk of being rather restrictive if you stick to it too rigidly. It is worth remembering that stages can be revisited or even reordered, and don't have to be followed in a strictly linear way. Used well, it is a useful model to know and can support effective coaching.

The GROW model also supports reflection on experience. Exploration of Reality, for example, encourages reflection on the current situation and related experiences while the Options and What (will you do) sections encourage the learner to think about what might be done to address the issues being discussed and to make plans to try out one or more of the options identified. O'Connor and Lages (2007) point out that this neatly follows the stages of Kolb's reflective cycle with the stages mapping onto the cycle as shown in Figure 5.1.

Figure 5.1 Reflective practice and the GROW model

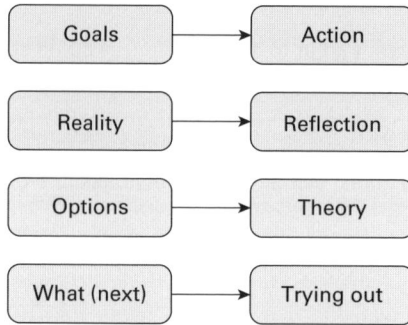

Supervision

Both coaching and mentoring can be challenging and even, at times, emotionally draining. Both coaches and mentors need opportunities to reflect on their practice and, at times, to seek support in talking through difficult issues. This can be provided through supervision, as it is in counselling and other helping professions. The importance of this supervision in coaching practice is widely recognized, although Hawkins (2008) found that it was much less widely practised. Where internal coaching programmes are developed, it is important to include provision for it. Mentors also need opportunities to reflect on their practice and should receive support in addressing difficult issues and developing their personal mentoring styles. Supervision of mentoring practice, however, is not common.

Supervision can make an important contribution to supporting coach (and mentor) welfare, for the reasons already given. It can also make an important contribution to supporting coaches and mentors in developing their skills. It provides an opportunity to reflect on practice with the support of an experienced practitioner, to explore dilemmas and uncertainties and to develop new insights and understandings. In this way, it can play an important role in supporting continuing professional development.

Supervision can make an important contribution to both quality enhancement and quality assurance. Quality is enhanced by the support that supervision can provide to improved practice and continuing professional development (CPD). Supervisors can also support ethical practice by giving feedback on boundary management and professional practice, both important contributions to quality assurance. Where supervision is provided by the organization it can also help to ensure that coaching and mentoring practices support the sponsor's standards and objectives (CIPD, 2006:3).

Supervision can be provided in a variety of ways. It can take the form of 1:1 reflective conversations or can be provided through groups, which can either be composed of peers or led by a single supervisor. In any of these cases supervision can be provided face to face or virtually, whether by telephone or through online forums, for example.

Managing your development as a coach or mentor

In developing your practice as a coach or mentor you will need to find ways both of learning more about coaching and mentoring and of practising your skills. This might be in the workplace, or you might choose another organizational setting to which you have access, such as a voluntary organization or organized social group to which you belong. As in all your continuing skill development you will find it helpful to plan your development, framing objectives which specify what you particularly want to learn and how you will do this. You will find it helpful to reflect on your practice and to find ways to keep improving it and you may find it helpful to record these reflections. They are likely to be richer if you can find a coach or mentor to support your reflections on your learning – this could be a peer for example. You may also find it helpful to seek feedback from a trusted colleague or adviser.

In planning the development of your learning about coaching and/ or mentoring you will find it helpful both to plan and to keep a record of your learning. You may already be in the habit of doing this, for example as a member of a professional body such as the Chartered Institute of Personnel and Development (CIPD).

In planning your learning objectives you should try to specify what you want to achieve, how you propose to do this and how you will know whether you have succeeded. You may also find it helpful to think through who can support you in your learning (and what barriers you may have to overcome). A possible template for planning and recording your continuing professional development (CPD) was offered in Chapter 4 (Figure 4.1). You can, though, use any template you choose.

Reflection on practice is likely to be an important part of your learning about development of coaching and mentoring skills. You read about reflective practice in Chapter 1, where you were introduced to two reflective models, developed by Kolb and Pedler *et al*. In reflecting on your own practice, you may find it helpful to refer back to these models and use them to help you think about your practice and ways of shaping your future learning.

Applying these ideas to your practice

Choose an area in which you would like to develop your coaching and/or mentoring skills. Write an objective for this learning and a plan for meeting this objective.

When you have carried out your planned learning, write a reflective account of what you have learned.

Feedback

You are likely to find continuing professional development much easier if you are able to work with others, both in developing your plans and in reflecting on your learning from them. You may be able to find support at work, if your manager supports your development of coaching or mentoring skills, or through a professional association such as the CIPD or alternatively a coaching association (examples were provided earlier in this chapter in the section on ethics). You could also try to find a colleague or friend who can give you feedback either on your reflections or your practice.

Coaching and mentoring interventions

Coaching and mentoring can be used in a wide variety of ways in organizations. Both can be used as interventions to support individuals, for example when moving into new roles. They can also be used to improve good performance for individuals (this is often the purpose of executive coaching) or to address poor performance. In addition, coaching and mentoring can be used to support larger initiatives such as managing change, managing cultural change or developing leadership capability. This section will consider some of the factors to take into account when introducing coaching interventions for these purposes.

Coaching for change and cultural change

When transformational change is sought in organizations it often has the purpose of creating greater employee engagement and more agile working, in both cases in pursuit of competitive advantage. This often means considerable cultural change and coaching can have an important role here in helping individuals to develop the skills they need in the new order. Both change and cultural change can make demands on leaders in the organization which are challenging in themselves and may require leaders to develop new skills, and coaching can make an important contribution to building leadership capability in the wider organization.

Some go further and argue that there is a case for building a 'coaching culture'. This would incorporate the skills of coaching, such as skilful listening and questioning, to provide mutual support in continuous learning, clear thinking and personal growth. Clutterbuck and Megginson (2005:19) define a coaching culture as one in which coaching is 'the predominant style of managing and working together, and where a commitment to grow the organization is embedded in a parallel commitment to grow the people in the organization'. They quote Sherman and Freas (2004:90), who identify the benefits of this coaching culture as: 'more candour, less denial, richer communication of talent, and disciplined leaders who show compassion for people'.

Managing a coaching or mentoring intervention

If the benefits of coaching and mentoring are to be fully delivered, their use has to be thought through and planned. Any large-scale programme should be seen as a strategic intervention and managed as such. This means that the objectives of the programme will need to be aligned with the organization's learning and development strategy, resourcing issues thought through and the wider issues of sustainability and measurement of outcomes considered.

Table 5.1 suggests some questions that need to be asked in each of these areas.

Table 5.1 Planning a coaching or mentoring programme

	Question	**Why?**
Planning	What are the objectives of the programme and how do they align with the organization's learning and development objectives?	Investment in coaching and mentoring will yield the best results if it supports wider strategic objectives.
Sustainability	Who are the key stakeholders in the proposed programme and how are they likely to react?	Once you have identified the stakeholders who may support or challenge the programme you can choose strategies to draw on their support or to reduce their opposition.
	Who will sponsor this programme?	Influential sponsors can encourage others to support the programme.
	How well does the organization's approach to learning and development support coaching/ mentoring?	A supportive learning and development culture will improve outcomes. If necessary, you may also need to consider further measures to embed coaching in the organization.
Resourcing	What coaching competencies exist within the organization?	This will help to determine whether you buy in coaching skills, whether in the form of external coaches, coach training, coaching supervisors or supervision training.
Evaluation	How will the success of the coaching intervention be measured?	This will demonstrate the value to the organization and to individuals of the investment in coaching.

Planning

Strategic approaches to HRD were covered in Chapter 2 of this book and the importance of aligning the objectives of a coaching intervention with wider strategic objectives has already been noted. Any coaching intervention should also be designed to meet identified learning or talent development needs and methods of identifying these were also covered in Chapter 2.

A first step in strategic planning is to consider the organization's internal and external contexts. The organization's structure is an important part of the former and will have an important effect on the design of a coaching intervention. The CIPD (2007, in Open University, 2016) points out that in a centralized structure where consistency is highly valued, a more formal and standardized approach may be needed. In this case, teams of internal coaches may be trained to follow common processes and practices. External coaches might be used in this model to support internal coaches in developing their skills and to coach individuals in key roles. These individuals might include board members, for example, who might be expected to model commitment to learning through coaching and to supporting others' learning through coaching (this can be a powerful support to the development of these skills in the wider organization). By contrast, in a decentralized structure where there are different styles of working, the introduction of coaching might take a variety of forms with less central control. In this case, decisions about how and when to use coaching might be made at a local level (CIPD, 2007 in Open University, 2016).

Practitioner viewpoint

Learning and development professionals will frequently be involved in multiple coaching interventions as part of a wider learning and development programme. This means that it is important to ensure that all parties are aware of the different elements and interventions taking place so that development is complementary and not contradictory.

Elizabeth Walmsley, executive coach.

The recruitment, management and support of coaches who are contributing to a change programme will be an important part of the role of the learning and development department. Resourcing is covered later in this chapter but it is worth noting here that their contribution needs to be planned and managed so that their contributions are in synergy with each other and are also congruent with and support other elements of the programme.

Sustainability

However well planned the coaching intervention, its impact will be limited unless attention is paid to creating support structures and removing obstacles. Careful consideration of stakeholder perspectives can support sustainability and a well-placed sponsor or sponsors can also help. The culture of the organization can also be an important help or hindrance to the effectiveness and sustainability of a coaching intervention.

Stakeholder analysis is an important part of the strategic planning process. This usually consists of an assessment of who has most interest in the planned activity and who has the most power to influence outcomes for good or for ill. Those who have most interest and most power need the closest attention, whether to secure their support or to reduce their potential opposition. This may mean explaining the purpose of what is planned and seeking to understand stakeholder perspectives and identify how their expectations can be met or potential objections addressed.

These stakeholders may be within the organization or outside it. Internal stakeholders may include line managers, senior managers up to and including board level, budget holders, those who will be coached and those who will be expected to develop coaching skills.

External stakeholders may include customers, shareholders, clients, and (in the case of public services) tax payers and service users. The CIPD (2012:11) emphasizes the importance of being outward looking and of making sure that the focus is not simply on those who deliver and receive coaching. They observe that:

> often the coaching world can be internally focused and insular, focusing on a narrow group of stakeholders – primarily a select band

of executive coaches, or those who define themselves as such, and, secondly, those who receive coaching.

Where one or more senior members of the organization are committed to supporting coaching their sponsorship can help to encourage individuals throughout the organization to commit to it. However, to be effective this sponsorship needs to be linked to a commitment to modelling coaching behaviours, as already noted. This can be an argument for bringing in external coaches who can support senior managers in developing and practising coaching skills. Where this does not happen, external coaches may find it easier than internal coaches to challenge and to encourage behaviour change.

Learning and development culture

A coaching initiative will be helped by a learning and development culture which is supportive of continuous and self-managed learning. In this culture, there is likely to be a commitment to reflective and double-loop learning and a willingness to challenge existing practices (these are all characteristics of learning organizations, introduced in Chapter 2). Where the organization's culture does not support these practices, however, coaching and mentoring may be experienced as counter-cultural and their benefits may not be recognized. In this case there might be an argument for not introducing coaching at all. The CIPD (2012:11) observes that 'coaching is not for every organization and indeed, in some cases can be counter-productive...'. However, sometimes coaching will be introduced in these circumstances precisely in order to produce cultural change in an organization. In this case it needs to be recognized as a cultural change programme and supported as such.

An example of a coaching intervention being used in this way is provided by the CIPD (2008:10) which reports that the Metropolitan Police Service has developed coaching capability 'to support a cultural change from a command and control environment to one that is compatible with a more relational approach to policing'.

There are other ways, too, in which the learning and development culture can create barriers to introducing coaching effectively. For example, where coaching has mainly been used to address poor performance rather than to improve already good performance, it is unlikely to be attractive to senior managers or to those identified as having high potential. Where this is recognized as an issue it can be addressed through explicit repositioning of coaching within the organization (CIPD, 2008). In fact, coaching is used rather more to support good performance (48 per cent) than to address poor performance (43 per cent), according to the CIPD (2011). A number of other measures can be adopted to help to embed coaching within the learning and development culture. Training a cadre of internal coaches can help, particularly if a substantial proportion of line managers are involved in this. External coaches may provide support for the development of coaching skills, both through training and supervision and by providing one-to-one support in the early stages of practice. Coaching behaviours can also be encouraged in line managers if the desired behaviours are included within competency frameworks and assessed and rewarded in performance reviews.

Resourcing

The majority of coaching in organizations is delivered by line managers and internal coaches (CIPD, 2011). Where an internal coaching capability exists, there is obvious financial benefit in making use of this, rather than buying in an external resource.

Practitioner viewpoint

There can be advantages to having internal coaches who already have an in-depth understanding of the environment in which the coachee is working. There are also other advantages, including significant cost savings from using internal rather than external resources, and these may be essential for some organizations. Not everyone makes a good coach – some will not have the appetite for it, or the aptitude. Those who do develop and use coaching skills, however, can often gain considerable job satisfaction from the coaching relationships. Where the coachee has regard for and confidence in the coach, internal coaching can be very successful.

Janet Turner, senior HR professional.

However, external coaches can also be a valuable resource when an increase in coaching capability is needed quickly. They can provide training for internal coaches as well as support, for example in the form of coaching supervision. Selecting external coaches, however, can be challenging. Coaching is not a regulated profession and there are a number of coaching qualifications available. Coaches may also come from very varied backgrounds and may draw on a range of models of coaching. However, there are a number of areas where those selecting coaches can have the same expectations of all coaches. These include being a member of a professional body, providing evidence of relevant coaching experience and references, providing evidence of continuing professional development and demonstrating a commitment to supervision.

The criteria used for selecting coaches will partly reflect the purpose of the coaching, and the skills and experience required will reflect the level of seniority of the coachee or coaches and the intended outcomes (improving poor performance or improving already good performance, for example). Where coaches are required to develop the skills of internal coaches, training or supervision skills may also be needed.

It would be usual for coaches to be interviewed by the sponsor of the coaching intervention in the first instance to establish suitability for the role or roles. Where the programme requires the appointment of a significant number of coaches it is common to select a number who are suitable for appointment from whom coaches can choose

Practitioner viewpoint

A critical consideration when using executive coaches is their ability to establish credibility with a senior audience. The challenge here varies. I have found when introducing coaches to 'up and coming' executives, where coaching is part of the development programme, that they are much more receptive and trusting of the coaches at the outset as they are introduced to them. Sometimes, though, I have used executive coaches for helping with performance issues with individual senior managers or for developing whole executive teams, combining group or individual coaching. Here the audience can be more cautious and people have more concerns about the extent to which they may be personally exposed in the process where position and politics can raise the stakes. The coach has to be someone who is both capable and confident in managing group dynamics as well as able to quickly establish rapport, engagement and trust with the participants. The positioning of the coach with the team is also important to establish a relationship of partnership and equality – it cannot work if the coach is seen as a 'servant' of a team and, and as I have seen, the best coaches I have worked with will not allow this to happen. The coach is likely to be challenged at some point, so experience and assuredness at working at executive level are key. I have never been in a scenario at senior management team level where this could be undertaken by anyone other than an external coach, and the most successful I have worked with have held senior line positions in organizations prior to specializing in executive coaching. In any case, in whichever scenario, it is always good practice to introduce the prospective coach and coachee to each other before any arrangements are confirmed and indeed, many coaches will insist on an introductory session to assess whether the chemistry can work between them.

Janet Turner, senior HR professional.

those they feel comfortable working with. This is often referred to as a 'chemistry' meeting. Alternatively, coaches may ask for a preliminary session so that they can ensure that mutual relationship needs can be met, recognizing the extent to which the relationship between coach and coachee can affect the coaching experience.

Team coaching

So far this chapter has focused on coaching for individuals. However, most organizations rely on teams of individuals in order to perform well and coaches are often asked to work with groups or teams to help them to improve their performance. Team coaching can lead to the development of a coaching culture within the team and can make an important contribution to organization-wide change or cultural change.

There is no single definition of team coaching, just as there is no single definition of either coaching or mentoring. Clutterbuck (2008:19) offers this definition:

> a learning intervention designed to increase the collective capability and performance of a group or team, through the coaching principles of assisted reflection, analysis and motivation for change.

Team coaching is likely to involve rather more interactions between the coach and team than the team development workshop outlined in Chapter 4. Rather like individual coaching, there may be an agreed number of sessions over time, with agreed objectives. There may also be a mixture of individual coaching (to help individuals to learn to work effectively in the team) and whole team coaching to help members to learn together and to share their developing understanding of how to work well together.

Practitioner viewpoint

There can be great value in the coach offering feedback on the team's performance and the contributions made by each individual member (this may happen in one-to-one coaching sessions). Coaching can help team members to learn how to listen to each other, to hold constructive discussions, to work through conflict and to manage multi-dimensional relationships. Many individuals are more comfortable and effective in one-to-one relationships and a combination of team and individual coaching sessions can help them to develop the skills they need to be effective in a team. This can also be true at board level and here too a combination of team and individual coaching can produce significant improvements in performance.

Elizabeth Walmsley, executive coach.

Team coaching can be used to help a new team, or a team whose membership has changed significantly, to work effectively. It can also be used, for example, to help a longstanding team to raise its game. Clutterbuck (2013) notes that most team coaching seems to be at leadership or project team level, although teams at all levels could benefit from it.

Some of the skills used in team coaching will be very different from those used in one-to-one coaching; working with groups and teams requires a good understanding of group dynamics, for example. These are skills that facilitators working with teams will use, and there is some potential overlap between the roles of team coach and team facilitator. Shaw and Linnecar (2007:92) observe that 'when team coaching is going well, the coach is acting more as a facilitator than a coach'.

Evaluating coaching and mentoring

While coaching and mentoring are offered by most organizations (CIPD, 2015), evaluation of their effectiveness is much more limited. In a survey of coaching evaluation, the CIPD (2010) drew on evidence from its learning and development survey of the same year to point out that only 36 per cent of organizations were evaluating coaching and mentoring. Even where evaluation was taking place it was not being carried out rigorously. The most popular methods used were participant reaction sheets ('happy sheets') and 'stories and testimony' (CIPD, 2010:4), while links to key performance indicators and assessments of return on investment (ROI) and return on expectation (ROE) were significantly less common.

In fact, at individual level it is reasonable to include self-reports by individuals (and teams) of their assessment of the value of the coaching they have received. While notoriously subjective, these reports cannot be disregarded. Line manager reports (or stakeholder reports in the case of teams) can also identify whether there have been improvements in performance. This evidence too is limited, not least because the benefits of coaching interventions may appear over time; it is also difficult to distinguish the effects of coaching from other factors which may influence performance. Nonetheless, triangulation of evidence from a range of sources can help to provide understanding of what has been achieved. 360-degree feedback may also be used to provide evidence of performance change after coaching (in the case of teams, this 360-degree feedback can be gathered from stakeholders).

Where a coaching intervention is planned as part of an intervention which spans the whole organization, or part of it, the objectives of the intervention should be identified as part of the business case, with indicators of success identified and timescales for achievement. This should make it possible to measure achievement against these objectives and to make an assessment of what the investment in coaching has achieved. Metrics which can be useful here include employee surveys and data on absence, retention, career development as well as productivity; financial data such as revenue and profits may also contribute to an understanding of the longer-term impact of coaching and mentoring. These can be complemented by feedback from stakeholders and their observations about what has gone well and what has gone less well from their perspective (CIPD, 2012).

Conclusion

Coaching and mentoring are well-established ways of supporting individuals (and teams) in managing their learning in the workplace. Their popularity shows no sign of waning. In fact, the skills both draw on are so highly prized that some organizations seek to establish a coaching 'culture' where practising and demonstrating these skills is expected of staff at all levels of the organization.

Where this culture exists, there is an emphasis on behaving in ways which support and encourage continuous learning to support organizational change and development.

There is no one agreed definition of coaching or mentoring and it is not always easy to distinguish clearly between them, although it is usually agreed that mentoring relies on the mentor drawing on his or her experience to provide support, while this not always the case in coaching. Neither coaching nor mentoring is easy. Helping others to learn always has its own challenges: coaches and mentors must make judgements about how to respond to the needs of the learner, how to balance the needs of the individual and the organization, and how to recognize the boundaries of their own competence. Above all, coaches and mentors must constantly review their own practice and their own well-being and fitness to practise.

Just as coaches and mentors support others in their learning, so they in turn need to be supported through supervision. They must also demonstrate a firm commitment to both developing their skills through continuing professional development and to ethical practice.

Learning and development professionals are often expected to work as coaches and mentors and so can be expected to have well-developed skills in both. They may also have to design and manage coaching interventions, whether as individual initiatives or as part of a larger change management programme. This means they need to be able to resource coaching requirements, making judgements about whether to employ internal or external coaches, and to select coaches. They may also need to be able to co-ordinate the contributions of a number of coaches, for example when they are working to a support a change programme, to ensure that they are working in a way that is congruent with its overall aims.

Reflective questions

How would you summarize the similarities and the differences between coaching and mentoring?

What are the main advantages and disadvantages of internal and external coaching respectively and in what circumstances might you choose to use each of them?

What are the arguments for and against line managers taking on the role of coach for their direct reports?

How can the skills of listening and asking questions help individuals to think through the issues they bring to coaching and mentoring sessions?

How can coaching and mentoring support organizational and cultural change?

References

AC and EMCC (2016) Global code of ethics for coaches and mentors [online] www.emccouncil.org/src/ultimo/Models/Download/4.pdf [accessed 16 April 2016]

Arney, E (2006) Distinguish between managers and coaches, *People Management*, **12** (25), p. 48

CIPD (2006) Coaching supervision: maximizing the potential of coaching, *CIPD* [online] https://www2.cipd.co.uk/NR/rdonlyres/5EBC80A0-1279-4301-BFAD-37400BAA4DB4/0/coachsuperv.pdf [accessed 07 August 2016]

CIPD (2008) *Developing Coaching Capability: How to design effective coaching systems in organizations*, coaching toolkit, CIPD, London

CIPD (2010) Real world coaching evaluation, *CIPD* [online] https://www.cipd.co.uk/knowledge/fundamentals/people/development/coaching-evaluating-guide [last accessed 7 July 2016]

CIPD (2011) *The Coaching Climate,* survey report, CIPD, London

CIPD (2012) Coaching: the evidence base, *CIPD* [online] https://www.cipd.co.uk/knowledge/fundamentals/people/development/coaching-report [accessed 7 July 2016]

CIPD (2015) *Learning and Development Survey: Annual report*, CIPD, London

Clutterbuck, D (2008) What's happening in coaching and mentoring? And what's the difference between them? *Development and Learning in Organizations: An International Journal*, **22** (4) pp. 8–10

Clutterbuck, D (2013) Time to focus on coaching the team, *Industrial and Commercial Training*, **45** (1), pp. 18–22

Clutterbuck, D (2014) *Everyone Needs a Mentor*, 5th edn CIPD, London

Clutterbuck, D and Megginson, D (2015) *Making Coaching work: Creating a coaching culture*, CIPD, London

Downey, M (2002) *Effective Coaching*, The Guernsey Press Company Ltd, Great Britain

Garvey, B (2004) The mentoring/counselling/coaching debate, *Development and learning in Organizations: An International Journal*, **18** (2), pp. 6–8

Hawkins, P (2008) The coaching profession: Some of the key challenges, *Coaching: An International Journal of Theory Research and Practice*, **1** (1), pp. 28–38

Hawkins, P and Smith, N (2013) Transformational Coaching, Chapter 16, Bath Consultancy [online] http://www.bathconsultancygroup.com/downloads/Transformational-Coaching-Chapter-16-v1.0-Feb-2013[313].pdf [accessed 7 July 2016]

O'Connor, J and Lages, A (2007) *How Coaching Works: The essential guide to the history and practice of effective coaching*, A&C Black, London

Open University (2016) B867 Workplace Learning with Coaching and Mentoring Unit 7, Open University, Milton Keynes

Pemberton, C (2006) *Coaching to Solutions,* Butterworth Heinemann, Oxford.

Purcell, J and Hutchinson, S (2007) Front-line managers as agents in the HRM-performance causal chain: Theory, analysis and evidence, *Human Resource Management Journal,* **17** (1) pp. 3–20

Shaw, P and Linnecar, R (2007) *Business Coaching: Achieving practical results through effective engagement*, Capstone, Chichester

Sherman, S and Freas, A (2004) The Wild West of executive coaching, *Harvard Business Review* **82** (11) pp. 82–90

Ulrich, D (2008) Coaching for results, *Business Strategy Series*, **9** (3), pp. 104–14

Whitmore, J (2002) *Coaching for Performance*, Nicholas Brearley

Evaluating learning and development in a knowledge economy

06

REBECCA PAGE-TICKELL

Introduction

Evaluation is the assessment of a process, event or product, in this case of learning and development, in order to identify its effectiveness, efficiency and value. As every learning and development practitioner knows there are a very large number of interventions, methods, consultancies and approaches that can be used to help develop a workforce. The CIPD 2016 L&D conference had around 100 exhibitors alone – each one with a specific take on L&D, perhaps a new tool, or an insight gained from practice. How can we choose between these – which works best? Which is most useful in a specific organization and which fits with a specific culture? These are the questions that evaluations set out to answer. Griffin (2011) reports the Learning and Skills Council's finding that organizations in the UK alone spend £37 billion a year on workplace learning. Questions about the value of this learning are therefore also important. Evaluation can assess how efficient and effective learning and development has been as well as supporting evidence-based choice for new programmes and interventions. There are a range of purposes for evaluation – but they can be coalesced into a few simple questions:

- How effective are our employees for a chosen business decision/strategy?
- How can we best communicate the quality of our employee value proposition and build our employer brand?
- How can we enable our learning and development providers to appreciate their own performance levels and enhance their provision?

Learning and development functions serve an important purpose within organizations. They provide a foundation for ongoing competitive advantage through building the people resource. Gubbins and Garavan (2009) note that 'organizations today operate in an external environment that is fast paced, uncertain and continuously changing', and Han and Boulay (2013:6) state:

> Understanding and quantifying impact is essential for the credibility
> of HRD interventions and an increasing necessity for organizations
> choosing among various investment options for their continuous
> improvement.

At both an individual and group level we tend to recognize the successes of development as the people and departments around us improve in specific ways. However, rarely do we ask whether this is enough – how much more could both individuals and groups of learners have developed? Is the development intervention as effective as it could be? Have initial expectations of the learning been met? Have the gaps identified by an initial analysis been sufficiently filled? These questions are all important and relevant and are likely to be the initiator for an evaluation. The input of stakeholders is an important factor here as different stakeholder groups may have differing aims and perspectives on the evaluation. Clarity of mutual understanding on the purpose of the evaluation between stakeholders becomes particularly important when discussing an evaluation process prior to the start.

This is important in a knowledge economy where competitive advantage lies in the knowledge that individuals and groups possess and use. The provision of learning and development needs to be fully aligned with the environment and culture of the organization to ensure that it is readily accessible and understood by the recipients. The mode of provision of learning and development also needs to be carefully considered to ensure that as well as providing the most relevant and appropriate interventions, they are delivered in modes, places and times that are effective.

On occasion, organizations may use their learning and development as a sort of comfort blanket, offering warmth and protection against a chill wind of change in the external environment. However, continuing the metaphor, if the blanket is made of material that is too thin or it isn't tucked in properly then it will not provide any protection against the cold. Similarly, learning and development that is not adapted to its purpose or delivered appropriately can counterfeit an effectiveness which closer inspection would indicate is an illusion. This is the most important reason for learning and development interventions to be evaluated – to answer the question, 'does it work?' And if so, how well does it work? The follow-up questions, of which elements are most effective – should we do more of that? Which parts are ineffectual – should we stop doing them altogether or can we change them?

Typologies of evaluation

Evaluation is a central part of the learning and development process in which organizations determine the merit of the learning and development interventions. Mavin, Lee and Robson (2010), in their literature review, identify useful definitions of evaluation, perhaps the most accessible of which is that provided by James and Roffe (2000:12) 'comparing the actual and real with the predicted or promised'. This indicates that evaluation is a typically reflective activity for organizations incorporating a sense of what we wanted, what we got and what could have been. This also hints at the range of stakeholder perspectives – each member of the organization may wish for something slightly different – as well as the degree to which all learning and development is embedded with the organization's mission, vision and values. Evaluation needs to be designed in the light of the organization's expectations and 'personality'.

Evaluation is typically the final stage of learning and development, but should be planned for from the very beginning. This is primarily because the learning to be achieved within organizations is typically embedded within the organization and usually relies on teamwork. Therefore, a measure of performance improvements depends on a wide number of causal links. The 'goalposts' for this are quite broad and can be quite non-specific. By first considering how incremental improvements in performance will be measured, a learning and development function can assess the effectiveness and value of the intervention.

Hartog (2010:225 notes that 'Hard measures (of evaluation) cannot capture the subtleties of learning processes such as improved relationships or a greater flow of information and knowledge in a firm.' She goes on to note the importance of contextualization in evaluation, particularly the importance of learning and development practitioners engaging with stakeholders to explain the various processes of learning and knowledge management and their link with learning and performance levels.

Evaluation of learning and development interventions needs to be considered within the competitive context of industry and macro-economics as well as at a more local level. The reason for this is that the longer-term impact of the development should be aligned with the impacts of the dynamics within the industry as well as wider economic trends. This is clearly very difficult to predict, but given the competitive advantage that learning and development interventions can confer, it is also particularly important. This has been developed further by the Australian Public Service Commission (APSC, 2005:3) who have identified that evaluation can take place at a number of levels, from strategic through to tactical and operational questions.

Strategic level evaluation includes questions about whether the learning and development interventions are enhancing competitive advantage or enabling the organization to meet service users' needs.

Tactical level evaluation includes questions about broader learning needs; for example, are junior manager development needs being sufficiently met to enable them to deliver high performance? Is the value of the learning and development package on offer to employees understood fully?

Operational level evaluation includes questions around the efficiency of the implementation of interventions; for example, is there good value for money, have the participants responded well to the learning, is there positive feedback from participants' line managers?

The more operational levels are considered to focus more on efficiency of the intervention itself – in essence, asking if it is doing what it was designed to do at an appropriate usage of resources. The more strategic levels concern effectiveness of the programme as a whole, considering whether it meets current and emerging organizational requirements. These levels can be applied through the contextualization of learning and development. This allows those levels to be applied through specific questions. They can also be enabled using a number of approaches. In essence, this allows the learning and development function to take a specific focus on the effectiveness and integration of the interventions from several different perspectives.

Internal validation

The first of these perspectives is internal validation. This involves ensuring that the intervention itself has met its objectives – essentially, has it done what it was designed to do? This is measured often using the ubiquitous happy sheet to try to capture the reaction of participants to the intervention. The accuracy of these happy sheets is difficult to assess as participants may be in a rush to leave and so quickly write the first thing that comes into their minds, rather than making a considered judgement about the effectiveness of the intervention. They may also be concerned about their views being related to their own managers or perhaps any negative views having an impact on later career opportunities. Additionally, participants may assess the degree of engagement they experienced during the intervention rather than its effectiveness in enabling them to learn. While these elements are related, they are not always causal.

The focus of internal validation is efficiency – is the intervention really doing what it was designed to do? How efficient is its use of resources; participant time, finance, facilitator time, etc.? How can this intervention be enhanced to be more efficient and productive? This often results in a change of method, for example to more online learning, or perhaps more use of wikis or face-to-face meetings, etc.

External validation

External validation considers, by contrast, the intervention within its wider context of a learning needs analysis. Therefore, the questions for evaluation focus on the effectiveness of the intervention as a whole for the organization. Have the specific learning needs been met to a sufficient extent? This can act as an evaluation of the learning needs analysis. If the learning intervention has been conducted effectively and the internal validation indicates that participants were satisfied and the learning met its objectives, then the learning need should be satisfactorily addressed. Where this is not the case, then either the learning needs analysis was not correct in its diagnosis, perhaps missed certain elements, or did not sufficiently address the root causes of the poor performance. For the L&D practitioner this is extremely useful as it provides a point of reflection concerning their ongoing practice and how they themselves can improve the effectiveness of the function.

The focus of external validation is effectiveness at an organizational level. Its primary focus is on the integration of the interventions within the organization and to an extent on the effectiveness of the learning and development choices for the organization's position within its wider environment.

Functions of evaluation

When an evaluation takes place of learning and development, it does so within the context of the organization. There are multiple stakeholders who will each have a stake in the evaluation. There are therefore a number of purposes or functions of evaluation. These have been discussed at length by Scriven (1991). He identifies a specific range of functions:

- *Pragmatic functions* – for example to fine tune the running of the intervention, to make sure that it meets its required objectives.

- *Ethical functions* – to ensure that all parties involved are benefiting from the intervention and that it is not causing any harm. For example, performing poorly at a development centre can be particularly detrimental to the career trajectory of a manager when it is not handled correctly. Other issues may include whether the events of the programme are being kept confidential.

- *Intellectual functions* – to assess the degree of learning and improvement in the knowledge and capability of participants. To ensure also that the learning remains cutting edge and participants are indeed being taught the optimal knowledge.

- *Social and business functions* – L&D interventions can provide opportunities for cross-organizational relationship building; this is an important area which can therefore be evaluated.

- *Personal functions* – there may be personal reasons for an evaluation which will vary between the people involved. For example, an evaluation is frequently used to demonstrate the value of a process by the process owner.

Applying these ideas to your practice

Spend some time thinking about evaluation of learning and development in an organization you know well. What have been the outcomes of the evaluation? Did it demonstrate both internal and external validation? How well do you think this organization made use of the results of the evaluation?

Feedback

Evaluation is a complex task which can be very time consuming. Therefore, organizations tend to be quite careful in both starting and using evaluations. One reason can be the pace of change – the learning needs that the intervention was designed to address simply may no longer exist, or have changed to an extent that is clear and an evaluation would be likely to add less value as a historical assessment. Evaluations can also become quite political, in particular where an organization-wide, high-status intervention is considered. In these cases, any negative results which demonstrate that the intervention was not effective may be swept under the carpet.

The process of evaluating learning and development

The process of evaluating L&D is explored from various overarching approaches through to the specifics of the 'who, what, where and how'.

The place of evaluation within learning and development processes and systems

The process and systems of learning and development are complex and context based. Learning is individual to both people and organizations and as such the organizations that seek to enhance learning through learning and development processes will carry out the activity in individual ways. There is sufficient continuity across industry for similarities, but equally there is significant variation. One of the similarities in process is that evaluation should always top and tail interventions, that is, they should be designed with consideration of how they will be evaluated. In this way, L&D professionals are consistently able to identify the results of their interventions, giving them the opportunity to continuously improve them.

Additionally, learning and development processes are part of the core activities of the HR function. As such, their evaluation should be carried out as part of a strategic review of the HR function as a whole. In some organizations, learning and development is considered to be quite separate from the human resource function. However, its product, developed employees, is central both to people strategy as well as specific elements of the HR function. For example, learning and development is a core part of a total reward strategy and should be evaluated from this perspective. This involves evaluation of entire programmes and the underlying organizational philosophy of development, rather than simply individual programmes – although, of course, this may also be part of the evaluation.

The reward perspective considers the contribution of learning and development to the employee perception of reward and the extent to which it supports the engagement of employees.

EVALUATION CASE STUDY Organization – outsourcing call centre

The situation

The organization was in a positon of growth, recruiting a high number of advisors, and this created a requirement for additional team leaders.

These positions were open to internal and external applicants and on average 70 per cent of the applicants who passed the shortlisting stage were internal. However, of these only an average of 10 per cent were successful.

To address this situation, we analysed the content of the assessment centre that was used as the main part of the selection process. This research highlighted that the internal applicants were at a disadvantage as it was clear that to meet the assessment criteria the applicants had to have previously held a team leader or supervisory role.

The organization did not want to dilute or change the process, so it was decided to use the assessment centre as a learning needs analysis tool to determine applicants for a fast-track development programme and then as a method of evaluating the programme.

It was agreed to evaluate the programme using the Kirkpatrick model, and we focused on levels 1, 2 and 3.

The process

The learning outcomes of the development programme were based around the team leader role profile and the activity criteria in the assessment centre.

A key element of the programme was secondments that enabled the delegates to apply the learning in real work situations. Following each of the secondments the delegates had to go through related elements of the assessment centre to test if there had been improvement in both knowledge and behaviours.

Any delegates who did not meet the requirements of the ongoing assessments were then removed from the programme.

The delegates who passed all the assessments were then shortlisted for future team leader roles.

The outcome

Although there were a number of delegates who failed to pass all of the regular assessments (25 per cent), of those that were shortlisted to attend the next available assessment centre, there was a significant increase in the number of successful internal applicants gaining team leader roles with two out of three roles going to these applicants.

Trevor Whaley
Director of Irwin Whaley Training Limited

Learning transfer into the workplace

The purpose of learning and development as practiced in business is essentially to enhance competitiveness. Donovan, Hannigan and Crowe (2001:221) note that 'Whether or not transfer of learning takes place depends on many factors including employee motivation, relevance of training and, notably, the work environment'. Mavin, Lee and Robson (2010) refer to Chiaburu and Lindsay (2008:199) when they note that 'training programmes are effective only to the extent that the skills and behaviours learned and practiced during instruction are actually transferred to the workplace'. Or, from another perspective, all learning is without value unless it is used to positive effect in the workplace. There are some forms of learning and development where this transfer of learning may be more opaque. For example, some leadership development activities focus on character-building activities and these should impact the workplace through, for example, confidence of decision making or willingness to listen to others. However, it is difficult to quantify the precise contribution of this change in a highly dynamic and complex organization.

Donovan, Hannigan and Crowe (2001) have designed a questionnaire to assess transfer of learning: the Learning Transfer System Inventory. This is a questionnaire-based tool which considers 16 different scales in four key areas:

1 ability to use knowledge and expertise;

2 motivation to use knowledge and expertise;

3 work environment supporting use of knowledge and expertise;

4 trainee characteristics (secondary elements).

One of the benefits of this approach is that it can be cascaded to any part of the organization to consider both individual differences as well as organizational characteristics in the transfer of learning. For example, specific questions consider the impact of the learning on various stakeholders as well as their role in enabling the transfer of learning. It also considers organizational factors such as organizational readiness to change, the presence of coaching and organizational rewards, or sanctions for the use of new learning. The stakeholders considered include peers, managers, and supervisors. It therefore takes into account the embedded nature of learning and is a tool that may support further alignment of learning and development interventions with organizational culture.

Challenges specific to learning and development

The challenge of valuing knowledge, learning and development is discussed with the challenges of evaluating L&D in the wider, economic, organizational and environmental context.

Anderson (2006) has identified two challenges in evaluation which are specific to learning and development: those of evaluation and those of value.

Challenges of evaluation concern the practicalities of evaluating learning and development as well as use of the appropriate methodologies and methods. Learning and development professionals recognize the need to evaluate for the wide range of purposes identified above. However, there are practical difficulties and constraints which Anderson (2006) details:

- Capturing the full value of the learning and development interventions for both organization and individual is very difficult. Much of this value may well be personal and individualized. The nature of adult learners is that they are heterogeneous and bring their own perceptions and experiences of education and learning to the intervention as well as their prior experience, capacities and ways of learning.

Their reception of the learning can be varied and the value that they accrue individually may not be measurable in the short term.

- Evaluation that is undertaken correctly is time consuming and costly. Where a learning and development function is under pressure to deliver learning interventions, then evaluation can take a back seat to more pressing immediate issues.

- Line managers may not always value or be interested in the results of an evaluation. Their interest may be enabled by presenting the data with a focus on their own group of employees.

Challenges of value concern the appreciation of the value of learning. The value here is related to both the effectiveness of the learning and development interventions, that is the extent to which they contribute to the bottom line and competitive position of the organization. It is also concerned with the efficiency of the learning experience and process. Anderson (2006) notes four separate conditions which may enable an organization to raise the value of its learning and knowledge:

- the degree of trust that senior managers show in the contribution of learning to organizational performance;

- the use of metrics in the measurement of learning;

- a focus on the contribution of learning interventions to organizational capability in the short term;

- a focus on the contribution of learning interventions to organizational capability in the long term.

Anderson goes on to note that variation in organizational culture, industry etc. indicates that these four characteristics may vary and the individual 'mix' needs to be understood by the learning and development function in order to ensure that it is in tune with the organization. This will enhance the reception and use of evaluation data that is produced. Bird (2008:20) notes: 'The value of training is demonstrated through the extent to which programmes and organizational goals are aligned'. She goes on to note that alignment, whilst well understood in principle, is less well applied, with little 'expertise in terms of processes and tools that help to embed alignment within an L&D function' (p. 11).

Methods of evaluating learning and development

Behavioural objectives approach

This is a form of goals-based evaluation which assesses whether the initial learning goals of the learning intervention have been met. This is the most commonly used form of evaluation as it compares performance on previously identified learning needs prior to and following the intervention. It is a key basis of Kirkpatrick's approach to evaluation which, whilst somewhat aged now, still dominates the industry in practice.

Responsive evaluation

This form of evaluation considers the perspective of all the stakeholders impacted by the intervention. It seeks an understanding of their perspective on the outcomes and their desirability. How has the intervention had an onward impact on the organization? For example, if there has been a focus on one specific group of employees, has it left other groups feeling demoralized? Amba (2005:279) notes that it is:

> a disciplined form of inquiry that results in qualitative evidence… this kind of evidence is important… because it enhances the understanding of human behaviour, it promotes holistic thinking, offers contextual information and brings in the perspective of the community or target group.

These benefits allow a more effective integration of learning and development interventions into the business and can support alignment with a range of people processes.

Goal-free evaluation

Goal-free evaluation focuses on the outcomes of the learning intervention as they are experienced. It is an emergent approach that assesses outcomes without consideration of inputs such as the objectives of the learning intervention, or a training needs analysis. The benefit of this is that the outcomes are identified in a manner that is free from the constraints of expectations. This allows for recognition of unexpected benefits. For example, in a management development programme conducted for first and second reports to C-suite in a telecommunications company, a feedback-based goal-free evaluation identified enhanced integration between engineering and service functions which was led by improved relationships among the management teams. This subtly positive outcome was not related to any of the pre-course goals but was a significant benefit to the organization. It is important with this approach to ensure that the evaluator is as objective as possible and uses a business-based focus to ensure that their findings are both relevant and reliable.

Participatory / collaborative evaluation

Participatory evaluation is that conducted by the learners themselves. This type of evaluation is particularly relevant as the learners are the owners of the learning. They are also experts in the process and tasks that they manage. Therefore, they are most likely to be able to identify incremental gains resulting from the learning. The evaluation is also likely to develop over time as the results of the learning become clear through application. The capturing of this knowledge can be managed by the learning and development function in a number of ways, with regular smaller evaluation collection and summary being perhaps the most efficient. Where a number of participatory evaluations can be collated, a detailed picture of what has been most effective about the learning and what needs to change can be gained.

Key measures in evaluation design

There are a range of measures for evaluation that can be used by the L&D practitioner. Amba (2005:280) identifies four 'generations' of evaluation measures: measurement, description, judgement and negotiation.

- **Measurement** includes the collection of various forms of data.
- **Description** concerns the practicalities and features of the intervention.

- **Judgement** suggests an assessment of the quality of the intervention, for example through comparing the intended and actual outcomes.
- **Negotiation** is engaging with the business, which Amba identifies as part of responsive evaluation.

Learning function efficiency measures

These measures identify the efficiency with which the L&D function carries out interventions. It can include measures such as whether courses are taught at full capacity – if a series of courses is taught at, for example, 85 per cent capacity, then it is likely that the organization will need to resource an extra course at potentially considerable expense. There are a range of measures that can be used to assess the efficiency of delivery. The most commonly used include:

- *Activity and utilization* – how much learning and development is taking place? How frequently are e-learning resources visited? How many hours of coaching is taking place per month? What is the amount of intervention employees undertake? Does this vary by function or level?
- *Cycle time* – how long does it take for a learning need to be addressed, from identification of the need through to its resolution?
- *Effort* – how much time and effort is required for the design and implementation of interventions – are resources used efficiently?
- *Cost* – what is the average cost per learner, what is the cost per type of intervention? How much is the L&D budget as a percentage of the total payroll?

Key performance Indicators

Key performance indicators are indicators which measure the successful delivery of learning. Usually focusing on a specific activity they identify whether a business-based measure has been achieved. This may be zero defects or a measure of customer satisfaction, for example. They are typically identified by the business and may frequently be related to generic performance measures such as the balanced scorecard.

Benchmark measures

Benchmark measures involve comparison with another similar situation. This is usually another internal function, for example comparing two accounts functions in the same organization but in different locations or with different client groups. Alternatively, it may include comparison between organizations. Collaborating organizations, such as customer and supplier, may on occasion be willing to allow benchmarking between two functions. This enables a rigorous evaluation of learning and development interventions between two different contexts. The lessons from each organization around what works and what needs to be changed can be shared for mutual benefit.

Key steps within the evaluation process

Each evaluation is unique and specific to the learning being evaluated as well as the organization in which it is being conducted. However, there are a number of characteristic stages that should be considered when preparing for an evaluation.

1 *Stakeholder engagement.* All stakeholders should be considered and engaged in the evaluation in order to understand their perspective. The stakeholders include those who are involved in the learning itself, both receiving and delivering, business leaders, those who will receive the effects of the learning such as colleagues in the value chain, customers, suppliers etc., and finally those who will make decisions based on the evaluation, eg functional heads.

2 *Purpose of evaluation.* Identify the specific purposes of the evaluation – for decision making, identification of value, assessment of efficiency, transfer of learning, etc. The purpose of the evaluation should provide a basis for the design.

3 *Identify resources available.* These resources may include time, finance, people, access to participants, managers, other stakeholders, etc. At this point you will have a clear idea of what you want to achieve for whom and with what. Now you can turn to design of the process itself

4 *Design of the evaluation.* Here the focus is on what you will actually do. What methods of evaluation will you choose? Careful consideration is required here to ensure useful results. Consideration and consultation now will pay dividends later. In what form are you planning to present the results? A formal report to board, or a briefing meeting, or…?

5 *Specific issues to consider*:

- **Who will you include in the evaluation?** Participants, managers, customers, suppliers, C-suite, etc.? How can you ensure that their views are as representative as possible? One option here is to stratify your sample, ie ensure that you have included a specific proportion of the stakeholders (eg 10 per cent) and have included representatives from each stakeholder group.

- **How will you gather data?** Questionnaires, interview, observation, focus groups, feedback, etc.? Remember to pilot any methods that you choose to use to check that they do work.

- **Is your data collection ethical?** Does it respect participants and offer both anonymity and confidentiality, ensuring that participants have a right to withdraw from the research and to be protected from harm?

- **How will you analyse the data?** This depends on whether you use qualitative, quantitative or mixed data.

- **What timescales will you apply?**

- **How will you use the findings?** For example, in redesign of interventions, change of mode of presentation, process for enhancing transfer of learning, etc.? Whilst these results cannot be known until after the evaluation data has been collected and analysed, preparing for the expected options in the design will help.

Sources of data

There is a range of types of data that can be used for an evaluation. The choice of which data to use is usually constrained by a range of factors within the organization. When planning an evaluation it is useful to ask a range of questions to identify the best sources of information for your specific situation:

- *What data is already available?* Eg have happy sheets from the ends of the courses been saved? Is there a process for assessing skills learned, such as through an apprenticeship or performance appraisal?

- *What processes is the organization familiar with?* There is likely to be a range of processes which the organization will readily accept as they are familiar, eg survey monkey, focus groups, one-to-one interviews, telephone interviews, etc.

- *Are there some times that should be avoided?* There may be times when the organization is already occupied with delivering information, for example during a data-gathering process for employee engagement or performance review when managers and employees are likely to feel that they have been required to turn their attention away from their daily tasks in order to complete people-related processes. They may well resent further requests for information from the learning and development function. Equally, at year end a finance function will not usually have capacity for anything other than the task at hand.

- *Who should be asked?* The data needs to come from reliable sources, so, for example, a manager new in post or employee new to the organization may not be able to provide useful information. The learners themselves should be consulted, as well as their customers (in the broadest sense) for example their line managers, internal suppliers/providers and possibly external contacts as well.

- *How many participants should we ask?* Ideally every learner and all those in the same value chain as them will be included in an evaluation. However, in practice this is unrealistic due to factors such as cost, time and distraction from ongoing tasks for both the learners and the learning and development team. The evaluation should include a sufficient number of participants in the sample for it to indicate all the views of participants.

- *What point in the organizational cycle?* When the organization is in the process of a re-organization or M&A, then particular care should be taken with gathering data. Learning and development activities, as a service to the organization, can become a political pawn and careful thought should be given during times of organizational upheaval as to who should be consulted and how.

Types of data

There are two broad types of data that can be collected: qualitative and quantitative.

Qualitative data

This is data that focuses on description and gathers words. It asks about the quality of an experience of learning. It has the benefit that it focuses on a person's experiences and can give a deeper insight into specific variations in individual experience. This is particularly relevant for the more complex types of learning and development interventions, for example leadership development, coaching for performance and mentoring. It is usually gathered using one-to-one interviews and occasionally focus groups. Surveys will also frequently include a section in which respondents are able to comment on their own experiences and preferences.

Qualitative data is usually analysed through thematic analysis. This is where the researcher identifies themes in the data that they have gathered.

For example, on interviewing a coachee about their experience of coaching, a researcher identified five core themes, of which struggling to be understood and sensing that the coach did not fully understand the business were particularly important to the evaluation process. A total of five interviews were carried out for coachees, with some agreement on the themes. When all the themes were compared across the process, the most important were:

1 a clear focus on long-term performance improvement;

2 a broad sense that the coach did not really fully understand the business;

3 coachees had generated focused goals and a clear plan to implement them.

Quantitative data

This is data that focuses on numbers and asks questions about quantity of an experience, for example how much, how often, when, etc. It has the benefit that the data is easily comparable and can answer senior management questions about financial value and skill levels attained. It is more useful for skills-based learning and development as well as the evaluation of bigger programmes and evaluation of large numbers of learners. It is usually gathered through surveys, observation, questionnaires, etc.

Quantitative data is analysed using statistics. Metrics such as the average are calculated with simple equations. Depending on the data this may include the mean (arithmetic average) median (the central point) and mode (the most popular response). These can be complemented by working out how similar or different responses are, using standard deviation to see if differences between groups are due to the learning or some other factor, and using T tests and correlation to identify trends in learning and outcome. These trends do not show cause and effect, rather they indicate broad relationships.

For example, data was collected from a series of health and safety courses to assess the usefulness of the content. Participants completed a simple questionnaire of 10 questions with a 1–5 scale where 1 = very useful and 5 = irrelevant. The fourth question – how useful was the content of the practical session? – showed that the mode (most popular score) was 2 (quite useful) although the mean (arithmetic average) and median (middle score) were both 3 = neutral. The implication of this is that on the whole participants thought the content could be improved but for some it was particularly relevant. Further analysis indicated that office workers had found this session less useful, but apprentice engineers considered the content quite useful. This led the providers to adapt the material for different participant groups. Further investigation among the apprentice engineers group correlated attendance on the module with number of workplace accidents and found that the number of accidents was significantly reduced, indicating that there was a genuine relationship between attending the course and safety in the workplace.

Qualitative and quantitative data are both equally useful for evaluating learning. In practice, both are often used in combination in evaluations as they complement one another well. This is known as triangulation. It allows the benefits of spread and breadth of data which quantitative data gives along with the in-depth understanding of qualitative data.

Applying these ideas to your practice

Spend some time identifying learning and development interventions in an organization you know well. Have they been evaluated by the organization? How would you go about evaluating them, given the opportunity? If possible, choose two contrasting interventions, eg mentoring or work-based learning and organized, structured courses. For each of them use this chapter to outline how you might go about evaluating them. How did you find this activity? What part was more complex and which was easier for you to think through?

Feedback

There are a number of complex decisions to be made when conducting an evaluation. This complexity itself can deter learning and development professionals from carrying out this activity. However, this risks the investment in learning and development being squandered on second-rate learning, and can put the organization at a competitive disadvantage. Review the evaluation plans you have outlined – how could you make them adaptable to the context of the organization to optimize the chance of completing the evaluation?

Sources of data collection

The design of data collection is a complex task which should be undertaken with care. The truism of 'rubbish in = rubbish out' is relevant here, with the added caution that a poorly designed questionnaire can be quite frustrating for participants to complete. When designing data collection, ensure that you:

- retain a tight focus on the purpose of the evaluation;
- trial questions to ensure that they are easy to understand and accessible;
- review questions and other sources of data in the light of the purpose of the evaluation;
- agree the collection of data with relevant managers as well as participants;
- allow enough time for data gathering as well as data analysis;
- build in prompts to remind respondents of the questionnaire in order to raise completion rates.

Questionnaires

Questionnaires are particularly useful for focusing on specific elements in an evaluation. They can be used to gather data from participants, their managers and others who work in the same value chain as the participant. They can be delivered online, perhaps via providers such as Survey Monkey or directly to e-mail, as well as through paper and pencil. The benefit of completion through paper and pencil is that you can guarantee who completed the questions, when and where, as well as answer any questions that respondents may have. For all their convenience, online questionnaires have none of these guarantees and so the data gathered may be questioned.

Feedback

Feedback is a qualitative method of data collection which can be carried out informally or formally. Informal feedback is intermittent but very valuable. It can allow specific issues to be raised which you may not have noticed, or may have been hidden from you. Whilst occasional, it is still useful and can be both part of ongoing monitoring and evaluation as well a kick start to an evaluation process.

Formal feedback includes the feedback from happy sheets as well as direct requests for feedback from participants and their managers as part of the process of ensuring the transfer of learning from the 'classroom' to the workplace.

Interviews

There are a range of interview types, typically one to one rather than panel for the purpose of evaluation:

- *In-depth* – this type of interview is focused on the experience of the learner and is relatively unstructured. It could be used in preparation for an evaluation, perhaps identifying potential questions or themes to be investigated. It may last for quite a long period of time and should reveal in-depth, useful information. It is inductive, that is, it usually seeks new information of which the organization is currently unaware.

- *Structured* – this type of interview follows a series of pre-determined questions to ascertain responses against specific criteria. In-depth information will be gathered to aid a fuller understanding of the strengths and limitations of the learning and development intervention. This will often be focused on the areas identified by the training needs analysis which was ideally conducted prior to design of the intervention. Where this is missing, which may well be the case, then this type of interview can be useful to identify the ongoing learning needs.

Focus groups

Focus groups accomplish the same purpose as interviews, but economize through the use of small groups to answer the questions. In this case, the impacts of the group can mean that the participants are less honest and can present their views as a group which can reduce some of the richness of the data. It is very important that the facilitator of focus groups is skilled in managing group dynamics.

Observation

Observation is a useful form of evaluation as the data collected is direct, performance-related data rather than secondary reported data. The opportunities for observation should generally be a natural part of the workplace and may well be automated, for example, assessing customer relations skills in a call centre. Observation can also include 'tests' of ability such as tests of understanding of a computer language which may be conducted at fixed intervals after a course.

Case study

Case studies are resource intensive and provide a detailed review of an individual example. They are useful for evaluation of unusual or individual forms of learning and development. An example may be C-suite coaching. The intervention is a one-off, and in-depth interviews held at short, medium and longer timescales may enable a clear evaluation of the learning attained through the intervention and its impact on the business.

Benchmarking

Benchmarking is a useful tool that can be used to gather data for evaluation of learning and development interventions. It can be used at a range of levels, for example, comparing the effectiveness of a shared intervention among different functions to identify what works particularly well and what needs to be worked on further. This can allow adaptation to specific functional issues which can enhance the effectiveness of the intervention. The question of what to assess and how to go about assessing it is very important here.

Taylor and Furnham (2005:171) note that one of the keys is in the calculation of the benefits of interventions. They note:

> Accountants do not take long to provide figures on the costs of training. HR professionals have a harder task in identifying the benefits in such clear terms. A board faced with the firm's figures, which directly affect the bottom line profitability or potential productivity of the organization, will find the training budget a tempting area for cuts.

Kirkpatrick's four levels of evaluation model

There are a number of competing models of evaluation. Each one can offer a 'window' on the effectiveness of the learning and development intervention. They vary in their applicability for different types of industry and the method should be chosen with care to match the specific situation as well as industry preferences.

The best-known model of evaluation is provided by Kirkpatrick (1967). This is the model that most learning and development practitioners will recognize and which is translated into a practical approach to evaluation with relative ease.

This model considers stages of evaluation in terms of the stages or levels of learning. It therefore has the benefit that it follows the participants learning journey, at quite a high level, and focuses on the extent to which it can be applied to make a difference in the workplace. The four levels are therefore divided primarily by the time within which they are relevant.

1. Reaction level

The earliest is a simple initial reaction to the learning and development intervention. Most appropriate when there has been a training course, typically a 'happy sheet' is used to gather participants' reactions to the training. This is usually a questionnaire which will ideally focus on the objectives of the training as well as participants' reactions to the hygiene factors, such as the quality of food, entertainment level of the trainers, etc. It essentially focuses on whether participants enjoyed the experience of learning. It also assesses to some extent whether they 'gelled' with the trainer. The ratings are therefore quite susceptible to a range of conflating factors. Examples I have known include poor ratings when a participant has stayed up very late enjoying the bar and is feeling bad the next day. The lead trainer typically receives the best ratings whilst those offering intermittent input are rated one step lower than the lead trainer. The impact of the hygiene factors such as the quality of the food and the comfort of the beds can have a surprising impact on the happy sheets. Clearly, a degree of comfort is necessary for learning, but it may also be questioned to what extent these elements genuinely impact the learning experience itself.

Taylor and Furnham (2005:172) note criteria for a questionnaire to follow to be of value:

- Word questions carefully. Pre-test all questions by administering them to a group other than the group that will be evaluated.

- Measure only one aspect of the training at a time.

- Make the responses to each item on the questionnaire mutually exclusive and exhaustive.

- Leave room for additional written comments.

2. Learning level

This stage considers the degree of learning itself and will usually be carried out shortly after the intervention itself. For example, in the case of a skills course the evaluation of learning will identify the improvements in the use of that skill, perhaps a few weeks later. This level of evaluation is most accessible and useful for the development of specific skills, either behavioural or technical. For this to be reliable it is important that a measure of the skills is taken before the intervention starts as well as afterwards. This opens up a whole can of worms including issues such as:

- What is the appropriate gap between the intervention and the measurement of learning? For example, in the case of a behavioural skill such as interviewing skills it may be that the learner needs an amount of practice before they can use specific types of question with ease. However, in the case of a technical skill such as the use of advanced excel applications then the earlier assessment of learning may be more appropriate. In fact, it may help to ensure that the learning is used and provide a bulwark against loss of learning.

- How standardized is the assessment? For the assessment of capability to be accurate then the same measure should be applied both before and after the learning. This is quite problematic as there are a number of factors that could impact the reliability of the assessment such as different people administering the assessment of skills, both across locations as well as prior to and after the training. There may also be a range of exercises used to assess the learning, especially when it is applied learning. Therefore, for the accurate evaluation of learning, the same assessment should be administered, ideally by the same person. Clearly, this is not often possible

- How flexible is the assessment? Whilst a training needs analysis will have been conducted prior to the training, it is the nature of adult learners that they are all different and so their initial skill levels and capacity to learn can be highly variable. The assessment of learning should take this into account.

- Is the learning assessable at this stage? Where the training is focused on more complex behaviours such as decision making or coaching skills then the assessment of learning itself is quite complex. It revolves around issues such as opportunity to practice the behaviours, heterogeneity of the coaching situations and a certain ambiguity about the success of the coaching itself.

- What does success look like? The measurement of a skill indicates that there is a pre-determined level at which it can be considered to have been successful. This is complex in the case of skills such as language learning and application and measurement of the skill can be complex, as can recognition of the level at which the skill has been accomplished.

- Is the assessment focusing on the skills or behaviours themselves? In some cases there may be reports from the training course about levels of skill which can colour the assessment itself. It is important that at this point the behaviour or skill itself is measured rather than reputation, rumour or any inferences about the skill itself. For example, if assessing the use of advanced excel then a discussion about the learner's enjoyment of excel is not relevant to an understanding of their skill level.

3. Behaviour level

Here the focus is on the application of learning in the workplace and whether performance levels in the workplace have been improved. That is, has the skill been used sufficiently to be incorporated into everyday life and to make a positive difference in the workplace? This is usually carried out through observation by managers and discussion with the learner around their implementation of the learning. The issues identified above are also of relevance here. For example, the range of skills that are assessed as part of the evaluation should match those identified as part of the training needs analysis. These skills should also have been assessed as part of the pre-course selection for each participant. In this case, the evaluator will gather a set of precise and accurate data which clearly shows the impact of the intervention for this group of participants. The issue that should be considered is whether every participant should be assessed, or whether there is an appropriate group or sample that can be taken who would represent the group as a whole. This provides a saving in use of resources, time, finance, etc., but potentially at the cost of accuracy.

The degree of accuracy that is required in an evaluation is a matter of policy that should be made by the management team. This is important to ensure that the evaluation focuses on the learning achieved rather than being compromised by poor practice which will affect the focus of the evaluation. However, this should be balanced by a review of the best use of resources. Evaluations are complex and can become very time consuming. They will often identify areas for improvement in the design and delivery of interventions. This can at times moderate the reputation of a learning and development function if not communicated carefully and can also detract from the provision of development itself.

This stage is of interest in that it also includes a focus on the application of the learning among the team itself. A core question that arises is the extent to which the learning can be directly attributed to the intervention itself. For example, the learning may be shared around the team to positive effect. This may also involve the trainer in providing some uplift to tweak the skills that have been learned.

4. Results level

This final stage considers the impact of the learning on overall performance in the job. This is a longer-term evaluation which should ideally feed into consideration of the ongoing design of learning and development as well as ongoing analysis of training needs. The primary focus here returns to the mission and vision of the organization. For example, where entry to new markets is a corporate goal, then this level considers the extent to which the learning and development interventions have facilitated the entry to the new markets. This is a particularly complex question as it involves the environment external to the organization, including competitive dynamics, shifting environmental factors as well as leadership choices and power dynamics within the organization. The complexity of this stage can mean that here soft data such as reputational reports can be as relevant and useful as hard data such as the quantity of sales or proportion of share in the new market.

Evaluation of Kirkpatrick's model

Whilst this model remains very popular among practitioners and is simple to use and easy to explain to managers, there are a number of criticisms levelled at it:

- There is an explicit link between enjoyment of a learning and development intervention and the capacity to learn. This link is not necessarily always the case. For example, in coaching interventions the discomfort caused by the recognition of a need to improve performance can be an important stage in gathering the intention to change.

- The simplicity of the model and its focus on behaviours is less well matched to a knowledge economy.

- The model does not fully recognize the complexity of learning and its application within the workplace. A social constructivist approach to learning focuses on the process of learning as constructing meaning in the context, ie workplace learning. Kirkpatrick's model circumvents this complexity through its focus on timescale, possibly due to its age.

- The unitary focus on learning has a tendency to bypass the more multi-faceted purposes of evaluation itself, such as making people-focused decisions.

Philips (1992) updated this model:

1 *Reaction and planned action.* As with Kirkpatrick's model, at this stage participant satisfaction is assessed. However, here there is also consideration of how participants in learning will actively apply the learning, so that their planned actions in implementing the learning are considered. This ensures that an element of context is taken into account and prepares for the transfer of learning.

2 *Learning measures.* The second stage focuses on changes in knowledge, skill and attitudes. This can be assessed via management action, so for example allowing people to implement their learning on new projects or tasks as well as via questionnaires to assess the degree of learning that has been achieved.

3 *Job application.* The third stage considers the measurable changes in on-the-job behaviour. This is usually passed through management observation and focuses on initial transfer of learning. This is the stage at which peers and customers should start to notice some improvements in the service delivery.

4 *Business results.* Finally, the impact of these changes on business results is considered. The measures will be related directly to the type of learning undertaken and will consider a range of variables relevant to the business. This may include, for example, quality of supplier relationships, number of sales, speed of resolution of customer complaints depending on the role under consideration. This is typically measured via a usual business measurement such as KPIs or, alternatively, via observation by managers and supervisors. This stage considers longer-term strategic results and can provide useful data for decision making at a business unit level.

5 *Return on investment.* This final stage evaluates the value of the benefits of the programmes compared with the costs. Direct costs to be included are the directly invoiceable costs such as design and delivery of the programme, use of facilities, participants' time, etc. The costs to be included can vary; for example, if there are multiple opportunities available then it may be important to incorporate some measure of opportunity cost which compares programme benefits to the costs. It can be difficult to isolate direct benefit against subsequent improvements.

CIRO

This model of evaluation developed by Warr *et al.* (1978) incorporates preparation and design of the learning and development intervention into the evaluation itself. It has four stages:

1 **Context**: obtaining information about the situation to decide if and how training can help.

2 **Input**: identifying the interventions most likely to achieve the desired results.

3 **Reaction**: what the trainees' opinions of the training are. Verbal or written feedback.

4 **Outcomes**: immediate (learning); intermediate (behaviour); ultimate (results).

The model focuses on using each of these elements as questions to identify the learning need initially and then to assess the effectiveness of the learning subsequently. Mavin, Lee and Robson (2010) note that one of the primary strengths of this model is its capacity to take the organizational reality into account, with the initial input measure concerned with resources available and the input questions concerned with the objectives of the organization. However, they go on to note criticisms of Tennant, Boonkrong and Roberts (2002) that there is insufficient focus on behaviours and it is more appropriate for complex, managerial-level learning than less specialized, more junior learning.

Key barriers to conducting the evaluation of a learning and development activity

There are a number of challenges that can act as barriers to undertaking an evaluation of learning and development within an organization. One of the primary factors is an unwillingness to identify where things could have been of a higher quality. Managerial courage is required to review learning and development activities in particular. Taylor and Furnham (2005:171) note that from the perspective of trainers and coaches the evaluation of training is quite personal: 'On the one hand they recognize its importance in the cycles of assessing learning needs and delivery. On the other hand, assessing their performance is never comfortable and has some of the awkwardness of the dreaded annual appraisal.'

The culture of an organization may exacerbate the difficulties, for example if it is a blame culture or a high-performing culture.

It is natural to want your reputation, as evidenced by the programmes you lead, to be established and so often a search for the 'good news stories' can replace a genuine evaluation. This is the case in particular where multiple stakeholders have conflicting requirements as well as political power in the situation.

The perception of the basis for resourcing learning and development interventions can also provide a barrier. If the organization frames the resource requirements as an investment, then financial disciplines of evaluating the use of resources may implicitly be engaged. Managers will therefore have an expectation of some measure of both effectiveness and efficiency. However, where the resource is perceived as a sunk cost, then an interrogation of what that cost has provided will implicitly seem a waste of time, almost like throwing good money after bad. This barrier to evaluation can be quite robust and learning and development practitioners may benefit from a clear focus on learning as an investment for both the individual and the organization.

Wills (1993) investigated the reasons for avoiding evaluation of learning and development in business schools. He carried out 10 semi-structured interviews with tutors, and whilst the original purpose of the research had been to investigate best practice in evaluation, he became more interested in the reasons why tutors avoided evaluation. Three major themes were identified.

1. The customer

Who is the evaluation for? Wills identified three key participants: the purchaser, the provider and the participant. Importantly, these stakeholders were identified as having potentially conflicting needs and were individually evaluating the training from their own perspective. A concern for reputation on the part of tutors was identified as leading to a reluctance to evaluate alongside a conflicting desire to demonstrate the value of the courses. Tutors also saw evaluation as focusing on the initial purpose of the training so that it caused them to consider fundamental issues around the training, which they could not always do as part of a busy role.

2. The evaluation of public versus in-house courses

Courses which are open to multiple organizations can have diverse participants with a range of development needs. One tutor referred to this as a 'type of circus'. By contrast, tailored programmes for specific organizations were identified as being preceded by a significant degree of diagnosis on which the design of the specific module was based. This indicates a greater need for evaluation.

3. Evaluation as an organic system

The place of evaluation as part of the entire development process rather than a 'check' at the end was discussed. The use of 'happy sheets' was not considered an effective evaluation. There was a resistance to what Wills identified as 'tweaking' of courses with a preference for a systematic approach to evaluation leading to continuous improvement.

Implications for practice

Consider your own organization:

1 Who are the primary stakeholders for learning and development? What are their specific needs? How could you access their individual evaluations?

2 How can you compare the effectiveness of public versus in-house interventions? From an organizational perspective, how could you assess the specific costs and benefits of each?

3 How could you build evaluation as a system that runs as an everyday part of your learning and development interventions? An organic system indicates that the evaluation develops as part of the L&D and is integral to its use – how could you build this in for your own organization?

The importance of evaluation in different types of economy

With the move from the service economy to the knowledge economy, it is important to explore how knowledge management strategy can maximize the value of L&D within an organization.

The knowledge economy identifies the recent economic trend towards service industries based on use of technology where the application of knowledge and expertise is the key to competitiveness. Leadbetter (1999) stated:

> The idea of a knowledge-driven economy is not just a description of high-tech industries. It describes a set of new sources of competitive advantage which can apply to all sectors, all companies and all regions, from agriculture and retailing to software and biotechnology.

This economy changes rapidly and is quite different from the tradition, manufacturing-focused economy. In this economy there is a larger proportion of different types of contract, for example zero hours contracts, part-time and fixed-term workers, consultants, etc. The focus for the L&D function here is on the management and development of knowledge and skills. These include implicit and explicit knowledge. Explicit knowledge includes the expected understanding; for example, an engineer would be expected to have a good understanding of forces and pressures in an engine. Tacit knowledge is the implicit knowledge which, while very important, is not taught formally, but is an important part of the role, for example, an engineer may know that one supplier is more reliable than another or may have a good relationship with certain customers which can lead to early discussion of any glitches in a project. This type of information is very valuable, but difficult to encode, teach or, importantly, evaluate. Ideally, tacit and explicit knowledge support one another and through a process of conversation and articulation can be shared throughout the team. This informal process may be difficult to evaluate.

Brinkley (2006) notes that a definition of the knowledge economy is elusive, and Garavan and Gubbins (2009:246) note Gratton's (2000) point that 'knowledge, skills and competencies are considered to be the drivers of innovation and change and thus key sources of competitive advantage'. They go on to indicate that HRD is therefore a 'lynch-pin' for sustained organizational success and competitive advantage. This additionally places a premium on the quality and efficacy of learning and development interventions, which is measured and understood through the evaluation process. Mohanta (2010) identified six characteristics that knowledge workers require:

1 factual and theoretical knowledge;

2 the capacity to find and access information;

3 the ability to apply this information;

4 strong communicate skills;

5 the motivation to use and develop these skills;

6 intellectual capability.

This range of characteristics provides a clear focus for evaluation both of performance and of the learning interventions that may be implemented to enhance that performance.

Evaluation of learning and development interventions is both valuable and important in all situations that involve learning interventions. These can include enabling informal learning as well as the more 'designed' types of interventions. Indeed, Garavan and Gubbins (2009) indicate that capturing and enabling social learning and networking competencies is an essential capability for both learning and development practitioners as well as other employees within large complex organizations such as multinational corporations. Purushothaman (2015:11) discusses this within the context of the Indian IT industry:

> The critical success factor for many Indian IT firms is their inquisitive approach of learning every day and moving from error correction to innovation and a paradigm shift. The key focus of the software firms is to leverage employees to disseminate their tacit knowledge and relentlessly engage them to accomplish individual and organization goals.

In a highly competitive environment in which learning and knowledge dissemination are the key competitive drivers, then ensuring that the learning offered is optimized becomes a core business focus.

However, evaluation of an entire culture of learning is highly problematic, and Purushothaman (2015:11) describes the culture of learning as one which:

> inculcates employees to softly navigate the edges of their comfort zone and actively disseminate tacit knowledge; thereby, constant learning churn is witnessed. It also persuades employees to get rid of the fear of losing their reputation in the organization once their valuable knowledge is shared.

Return on investment

Taylor and Furnham (2005:172) report Morrison's 2004 quote from *E-Learning Strategies* that 'ROI can be predictive or historical. The best predictive ROI will draw on historical ROI data'. Return on investment is the application of accounting techniques to assess the value derived from a specific investment. This can be very effective in a number of processes within an organization. For example, if considering the purchase of IT facilities, then a review of initial costs, compared with quality, downtime, service costs, future proofing, etc. is likely to be able to be summarized into a relatively simple set of figures which identify the top-line return on investment as well as the range of options and the return for each of these.

However, when this is translated into the provision of services for developing people then the question of value becomes more important. The use of financial metrics therefore can be quite controversial, and quantifying the results of the learning and development is not always easy. For example, what is the value of improved supervision? Is that value simply focused on the financial implications of, for example, less absence, or does it also incorporate other less measurable factors such as improved morale, increases in employee engagement and the onward impact of an enhanced psychological contract? It can appear that putting a financial limit on this is almost demeaning.

One approach to ameliorate this is to consistently apply the same metrics for financial measures over time and also across locations. This will allow the choice of metric to be made carefully and with a view of the relevance of that metric to the organization as a whole. For example, when evaluating the ROI of different delivery options for the CIPD intermediate module in legal issues, then the quality of legal decisions and the number and cost of ET applications could be considered as an appropriate measure. Always these measures need to be taken with a pinch of salt; for example, in a large organization one function, such as logistics, may be more litigious than another, such as accounting. This demonstrates the importance of consistency in the measure as it allows subtle variations to be identified whilst also allowing for broader differences which are observed consistently over time.

These challenges with ROI are exacerbated in the public and third sectors. Whilst these sectors maintain an increasing vigilance over value and the use of finance, part of the psychological contract may be considered to be an opportunity for personal development. The mission and culture of these organizations often involves a focus on values which can increase the sense of value being undermined and disrespected.

Return on expectation

Where complex interventions are concerned, particularly in the arena of leadership development, coaching, etc., then return on expectations may be a more useful measure than return on investment. This has the benefit of being a future-facing measure that, whilst robust, takes into account the growth and development of the organization.

Conclusion

This chapter has addressed the value of evaluation practices for an organization as well as the challenges and barriers to evaluation in practice. A range of methods for evaluating learning and development interventions has been presented along with a discussion of their appropriateness for differing organizations and economies. There are two underlying challenges for the learning and development practitioner to manage:

1 The first underlying challenge identified by Han and Boulay (2013) is to ensure that the results of evaluation are built into organizational decision making. They therefore need to be relevant, appropriate, easy to interpret and fully integrated with corporate strategy to ensure that they are fully utilized and learning and development interventions really do build sustainable competitive advantage.

2 Whilst the data that is used to populate an evaluation is backward looking, the results of the evaluation itself need to be forward

looking and predictive of both future economic situations and business challenges as well as the most advantageous resource-based responses to these challenges.

Evaluation is an essential tool in the tool kit of the learning and development professional. Used well it can provide a clear rationale for both enhancing learning and raising its acceptance in order to build organizational capability. As Bird (2008:20) notes.

'Learning and development (L&D) professionals who cannot articulate the real value of interventions to their clients (internal or external) will never earn themselves a place in the boardroom.' That is, they will be less able to influence at the most senior levels of an organization, thereby denying the organization the full benefit of learning and knowledge.

Reflective questions

Can you summarize what is meant by the term evaluation?

Which of the functions of evaluation do you think are most frequently evidenced in your workplace? Which do you think you hold primarily?

What type of data are you most comfortable in collecting?

How can learning and development professionals in your organization support the successful evaluation of interventions?

To what extent is evaluation part of the practice of L&D professionals in your organization?

References

Amba, T (2005) Responsive evaluation: its meaning and special contribution to health promotion, *Evaluation and Program Planning*, 28, pp. 279–89

Anderson, V (2006) The value of learning: a new model of value and evaluation, *CIPD* [online] http://www2.cipd.co.uk/NR/rdonlyres/94842E50-F775-4154-975F-8D4BE72846C7/0/valoflearnnwmodvalca.pdf

Australian Public Service Commission and the Australian National Audit Office (2003) Building capability: a framework for managing learning and development in the APS, Australian Public Service Commission and the Australian National Audit Office, Canberra [online] www.apsc.gov.au

Australian Public Service Commission and the Australian National Audit Office (2005) Evaluating learning and development: a framework for judging success Australian Public Service Commission and the Australian National Audit Office, Canberra [online] www.apsc.gov.au

Bird, H (2008) Articulating the value of training: linking training programs to organizational goals, *Development and Learning in Organizations: An International Journal*, **22** (2) pp. 20–22

Brinkley, I (2006) *Defining the Knowledge Economy: Knowledge economy programme report*, The Work Foundation, London

Chiaburu, D and Lindsay, D (2008) Can do or will do? The importance of self-efficacy and instrumentality for training transfer, *Human Resource Development International*, **11** (2), pp. 199–206

Donovan, P. Hannigan, K and Crowe, D (2001) The learning transfer system approach to estimating the benefits of training: empirical evidence, *Journal of European Industrial Training*, **25** (2/3/4), pp. 221–28

Gratton, L (2000). *Living Strategy: Putting people at the heart of corporate purpose*. Financial Times/Prentice Hall, London

Griffin, R (2011) Seeing the wood for the trees: workplace learning evaluation, *Journal of Industrial Training*, **35** (8), pp. 841–50

Gubbins, C and Garavan, T N (2009) Understanding the HRD role in MNCs: The imperative of social capital and networking, *Human Resource Development Review*, 8, p. 245

Han, H and Boulay, D (2013) Reflections and future prospects for evaluation in human resource development, *New Horizons in Adult Education and Human Resource Development*, **25** (2), pp. 6–18

Hartog, M (2010) Critical issues in learning and development: beyond 'the learning organisation', in *Critical Issues in Human Resource Management*, ed C Roper, U C Na-Ayudhya and R Prouska, Chartered Institute of Personnel and Development, London

James, C and Roffe, I (2000) The evaluation of goal and goal-free training innovation, *Journal of European Industrial Training*, **24** (1), pp.12–20

Leadbetter, C (1999) New measures for the new economy, *OECD* [online] https://www.oecd.org/sti/ind/1947910.pdf

Mavin, S, Lee, L and Robson, F (2010) The evaluation of learning and development in the workplace: a literature review, *HEFCE* [online] https://www.northumbria.ac.uk/static/5007/hrpdf/hefce/hefce_litreview.pdf

Morrison, D (2004) *E-Learning Strategies: How to get implementation and delivery right first time*, John Wiley & Sons

Mohanta, G (2010) Knowledge worker productivity improvement processes, technologies and techniques in defence R&D laboratories: an evaluative study, Bharath University, School of Management Studies

Purushothaman, A (2015) Organizational learning: a road map to evaluate learning outcomes in knowledge intensive firms, *Development and Learning in Organizations: An International Journal*, **29** (3), pp. 11–14

Raab, R T, Swanson, B E, Wentling, T L and Dark, C D, eds (1991) *A Trainer's Guide to Evaluation*, FAO, Rome

Scriven, M (1991) Evaluation Thesaurus, 4th edn, Sage, Newbury Park, CA

Taylor, J and Furnham, A (2005) *Learning at Work: Excellent practice from best theory*, Palgrave Macmillan, Basingstoke

Tennant, C, Boonkrong, M and Roberts, P (2002) The design of a training programme measurement model, *Journal of European Industrial Training*, **26** (5), pp. 230–40

Wills, S (1993) Evaluation concerns: a systemic response, *Journal of European Industrial Training* **17** (10)

Concluding thoughts 07

This final chapter will pull together the main themes of this book and consider some of the challenges facing learning and development professionals in the future. One important theme has been the constantly changing (and challenging) environment within which organizations operate and the impact of this on approaches to managing and developing people within organizations. Another has been the rapid change in digital technology which has made possible new approaches to learning and a movement away from face-to-face learning events. Changing ideas about learning itself have been an important theme too, with much greater emphasis on individuals taking responsibility for their own learning. This means that helping individuals to learn and to develop the skills of managing their own learning has become more important than simply training them – so there has been a shift to emphasizing learning rather than training.

These changes have transformed the role of learning and development professionals, with a new emphasis on supporting self-managed learning through facilitation, coaching and mentoring and on developing in themselves and others the skills of working effectively in online and virtual environments. Similarly, learning in the workplace has largely supplanted classroom teaching, so that what is learned can be applied quickly to produce improvements in practice. This means much more emphasis on facilitating the work of groups (including learning sets) and teams so that participants can work together to find and put into practice solutions to workplace problems. It also means much greater emphasis on reflective and practice-based learning, both often integrated into the accredited learning supplied by or in partnership with suppliers of further and higher education.

Perhaps most importantly of all, there has been a shift in the contribution learning and development professionals can be expected to make to the wider organization, with a much greater emphasis on their strategic role. As a consequence of this they are increasingly required to develop the skills of thinking strategically, of contributing to the development of business strategies and of ensuring that their own objectives, policies and activities are fully aligned with wider business objectives.

The term VUCA was used in the introduction to this book to describe an external environment which is volatile, uncertain, complex and ambiguous. The pace of change in this environment means that organizations are under constant pressure to find new ways of working so that they can compete in a global marketplace. Many are heavily knowledge intensive and rely on highly skilled workers. This is the case for most manufacturing industries remaining in the UK (CIPD, 2013), since those which are labour intensive have moved to parts of the globe where labour is cheaper. It is also true of IT industries and of service industries in the financial, legal and consultancy sectors, for example. All these organizations need well-developed skills in reading and responding to changes in the external environment and the agility to change themselves and their ways of working. They also need to be able to constantly create and recreate new knowledge and understanding in response to changing circumstances and possibilities.

All this puts learning and development professionals centre stage in organization development and change. To be successful they need to have the knowledge and skills to contribute to strategic thinking about the organization's future and to support the learning and development of its employees in ways that make that future possible. This book has been, in large part, about how they can achieve this.

Digital technology and the future of learning and development

The pace of change in the use of technology both in the workplace and in society more generally has been dramatic. By 2014 almost all (95.8 per cent) of businesses in the UK had internet access (ONS, 2014). Workplace practices have altered with remote working, including home working, increasingly possible and accepted. Citizens' lives outside work have been affected too, with even civic transactions (such as paying income tax and vehicle tax) now often carried out online. By 2016 more than 80 per cent of adults were using the internet every day or nearly every day compared with 78 per cent in 2015. The comparable figure in 2006 was only 35 per cent (ONS, 2016). Curiously though, this digital revolution seems to have had only a limited impact on learning and development in the workplace. CIPD's annual learning and development survey reported in 2015 that while three-quarters of organizations were using learning technologies, there were wide variations in practice. The report's authors commented that:

> one in three of those who use learning technologies currently deliver more than three-quarters of their L&D activities completely through face-to-face experiences and more than two-thirds report that less than a quarter of activities are delivered through learning technologies or blended learning (CIPD, 2015b:15).

The picture seems somewhat better in public sector organizations where 88 per cent use learning technologies (CIPD, 2015b) and in larger organizations generally, which is perhaps not surprising given that the high levels of investment often needed to design and deliver online learning materials may be more easily accessed in these organizations.

Confidence and skill levels among learning and development professionals also seem to be a cause for concern. Only a quarter report feeling '"extremely" or "very" confident in their ability to harness technology to increase the effectiveness of their L&D interventions' (CIPD, 2015b:4). Overton and Dixon (2016:7) found that slightly less than a quarter of L&D leaders thought their teams had 'the right skills to exploit technology for business advantage', with half saying their staff lacked 'knowledge about the potential use and implementation of technology' and little more than a quarter believing them to be confident in 'incorporating new media in learning design'.

There are some obvious benefits in using digital technology to support learning and development. These include offering flexibility to learners, enabling them to study at times and in places which suit them, whether at home, while travelling or while working away from the home or office. More traditional models of learning which require presence at a physical location, such as evening classes and day-release schemes, seem much harder to justify when more easily accessible options are available – although this is not to say that they never have a place.

There is also potential in online learning to allow learners to customize their learning, for example by providing diagnostic tests which enable them to identify where they need to access extra tuition or conversely where there are materials which they don't need to study.

There are also challenges in online learning, already discussed in this book. Access to the internet is essential and is still problematic in some locations. Perhaps more important though are the skills needed by both learners and those who support them to be effective in a virtual environment. Of these, the most important, for both facilitators and learners, may be the ability to communicate well and to build relationships within the constraints of virtual classrooms and online discussion forums. Without these, online collaborative and social learning are not possible. Those who design online learning also need to have the skills (and resources) to incorporate interactive and collaborative activities. They may also build in access to video and audio materials which can enrich the learning experience and make it more enjoyable.

The skills of learning in a virtual world are not markedly dissimilar to those of working remotely using digital technology, so there can be an obvious value for learners in developing digital skills which they can transfer to their working life. For multinational organizations, for example, there is a strong case to be argued that workers need well- developed digital skills if they are to be effective in a workplace which spans the globe.

Applying these ideas to your practice

Spend some time now thinking about your own experience of online learning in the workplace or in private study. Make a note of any skills you developed through this study which might be relevant to working in an online environment. If you can, try to think of skills you haven't yet developed but which could help you to further improve your effectiveness in working in a virtual world.

Feedback

You might have identified that you have developed skills in relation to communication and relationship building, and using collaborative tools such as wikis and blogs (these were all discussed in Chapter 2), or that you have learned how to manage particular types of software which are new to you. You might also have found that you have learned how to access information online, using databases, for example, or scanning the internet for information, and how to evaluate the value of the information found there (these are the sorts of activities that can easily be incorporated into online learning). You may also have found that you developed an understanding of what works well and what works less well in online learning design. For example, how comfortable were you with reading on screen and were there times when you preferred to download and print materials? In this case, how easily available were print-friendly materials? How much interaction did you want with the materials in the form of online quizzes for example? How helpful did you find (or would you have found) access to podcasts and videos to vary the experience of online study? And how valuable was it (or would it have been) to be able to discuss your learning with fellow students in a discussion forum?

Meeting the needs of the business

If learning and development professionals are to adopt a strategic role this means, as a minimum expectation, that learning and development objectives must be aligned with those of the wider business. It also means that learning and development professionals must have the skills to contribute to strategic thinking and be able to demonstrate that the activities they design can have a direct and immediate application in the workplace.

Only a small minority of organizations (6 per cent) report that there is no alignment between their learning and development strategy and that of the wider business, while a quarter say they are 'extremely aligned' and another two-fifths that they are 'broadly aligned' (CIPD, 2015b:7). These figures do suggest, though, that there remains considerable scope for improvement in aligning learning and development and business strategies.

Loon (2014) emphasizes the importance of L&D professionals influencing as well as aligning with organizational strategy. He identifies that to achieve this they need to understand the business, the organization and its contexts, to be able to work with colleagues and to deal with the organization's systems, processes and politics. It is these qualities which enable them to develop policies and practices which meet the organization's needs and which demonstrate their ability to provide advice and guidance on business goals and strategies. On the subject of technology, for example, he comments:

> it is not about having the latest and greatest technology but it is about fit, which can only be achieved if L & D practitioners are savvy about the business, the organization and the context (Loon, 2014:13).

The credibility of learning and development activities can be enhanced if learning can be shown to deliver improvements in workplace performance through practice-based and reflective learning, as discussed in Chapter 2. Evaluation of the outcomes of learning activities (as discussed in Chapter 6) can also provide useful evidence here. However, while evaluation of some sort is widely practised, only a small proportion of organizations say that they evaluate 'the wider impact on business and/or society' (CIPD, 2015b:25).

Learning and development in context

While much has been said in this book about changing approaches to learning it is perhaps worth pointing out here that debates about learning, about how to help others to learn and about the nature of knowledge itself are far from new. Plato wrote about all these in about 380 BC in his most famous work *The Republic*. In this text he described Socrates' debates about education and other topics of civic importance with fellow Athenians and visitors to the city state. The conclusions Socrates reached in these debates were very different from the ideas discussed in this book, since for Plato knowledge was immutable and real understanding given only to the few. Nonetheless his work had great influence for centuries on thinking about teaching and learning.

Mentoring too has a long lineage, the term being first used in Homer's Odyssey. As Odysseus left on his journey he charged his friend and adviser Mentor to take care of his son, Telemachus, and to teach him 'everything he knew, so that he would be prepared for life' (Pemberton, 2006:43). The story has been told and retold over the centuries, most notably in Fenelon's *Telemachus*, first published in 1699, which explains how, under the guidance of Mentor, the young man learns the skills he will need to become ruler of Ithaca. From these stories, incidentally, it is clear why the term mentor still has the meaning of passing on experience.

The debate about how best to help others to learn has continued for centuries and at its heart are debates about ontology and epistemology. Ontology was introduced in Chapter 1 (in the discussion about dialogic and diagnostic organization development) and concerns our understanding of reality. Does it exist independently of our experience of it (as Socrates argued) or is it socially constructed, so that we each see and understand the world differently? Epistemology concerns our understanding of knowledge, and this has been a theme throughout this book. Is knowledge, and therefore learning, really concerned with discovering facts that already exist independently of us whether we know about them or not, or is knowledge created by and individual to each? Judgements about learning and the best ways to help others to learn follow from the conclusions we reach about ontology and epistemology. Throughout this book there has been a strong emphasis on learning as a personal and social process, whether for individuals or groups, and on learning through activity (for example in action learning) and through connecting and collaborating with others. This is simply because these are approaches which best support innovation and change. They are firmly in the tradition of constructivist approaches to learning which hold that reality and knowledge are socially constructed. However, this is not to dismiss the tradition where reality is believed to exist independently of our understanding of it and knowledge is achieved through observations of this external reality – for example through scientific measurement and mathematical calculation. This is the positivist approach and much teaching, learning and research is in this tradition. In the case of research, it is often associated with quantitative methodologies and learning and development professionals will often need to demonstrate skills in these when carrying out needs analyses (particularly at organizational level) and providing evidence of the contribution learning and development has made to business performance. In both cases the evidence used may rely on rigorous analysis of quantitative data such as statistics.

All this provides further evidence of the importance for learning and development professionals being able to view learning and knowledge from different perspectives and to choose which works best for their particular purposes.

Critical thinking

In addition to all the skills already outlined, learning and development professionals need well-developed skills in critical thinking so that they can make judgements about the value of new ideas about learning and development. This means questioning the assumptions upon which they are based and looking hard for the evidence that they are or are not of value. This is not the same as being negative or critical in the usual sense but is more about paying careful attention to information and data. Many of the topics covered in this book can usefully be the focus of critical thinking (this was suggested for example when ideas about generations in the workplace were introduced in Chapter 2). As new ideas about learning and development emerge, they too need to be carefully reviewed and assessed for value in individual contexts. At the time of writing, for example, insights from neuroscience are being drawn on by some to inform thinking about how to help people to learn. These include the ideas that areas of the brain increase their capacity when they are used actively, that there is a positive correlation between physical exercise and brain performance, and that gaming can enhance learning. All these propositions are outlined in a research report published by CIPD (2014), with supporting evidence, and all have obvious potential for influencing practice in learning. The field of neuroscience has also provided, in the past, examples of uncritical use of insights from science to create what the OECD has termed 'neuro-myths'. One of these was the idea that the left brain and right brain were responsible for different types of thinking, associated with logical and verbal information, and creativity and visual information respectively (OECD, 2002). Goswami (2004) points out that in fact 'there are massive cross-hemisphere connections in the normal brain and both hemispheres work together in every cognitive task so far explored with neuroimaging, including language and face recognition tasks.'

None of this is intended to suggest that learning and development professionals need to be (or can reasonably be expected to be) experts in neuroscience, but past confusions in this field do demonstrate well the importance of critical thinking.

Applying these ideas to your practice

Spend some time searching the internet for materials on neuroscience. What potential do you see for the argument that insights from neuroscience should influence the practice of learning and development and what evidence would you seek to satisfy you that this would be a useful practice?

Preparing for the future

So far in this chapter, and in this book, a wide range of skills have been identified for learning and development professionals. Both strategic thinkers and facilitators of learning, they are expected to have a well-developed understanding of the business and the ability to manage relationships and processes within the organization so that they can influence outcomes and demonstrate that they can deliver improvements in performance. In addition to all this they need to be effective in a digital world and to help others to be so as well. This may seem a counsel of perfection, and of course in reality many will specialize in particular areas rather than the whole range. However, expectations of the function as a whole are wide ranging and demanding and there has been a marked shift in the roles undertaken by learning and development professionals. CIPD (2015a) noted a shift towards performance consultancy rather delivering learning, with all that implies for the ability to understand and respond to business needs. Overton and Dixon (2016:8) went further and described the role of the learning and development professional in the future as 'facilitator and creator of network connections, social mentor and curator of knowledge and learning resources'. This implies a very high level of skill and agility – and above all the ability to constantly learn and relearn new skills.

There is some cause for concern that skills levels are not yet where they need to be to enable this to happen (CIPD 2016). The relative slowness in the uptake of digital learning, already discussed, is one example of this and limited use of evaluation to demonstrate the business benefits of learning and development is another. Part of the response to this may be more investment in learning and development and there is some evidence that this is happening. Overton and Dixon (2016) reported for example that across their research sample 38 per cent of organizations had increased their training budget and another 36 per cent expected to do so in the following two years. It may also help to bring into the learning and development function those who have operational experience and need to learn about helping others to learn – this might strengthen the mix of skills in the team. Above all, though, learning and development professionals need to be determined and proactive in managing their own constant learning and self-development through a programme of continuing professional development.

Applying these ideas to your practice

In this last reflective activity of this book, spend some time making notes about the skills you want to develop next and how you will go about doing so. You might want to use the skills development form provided in Chapter 4 to help you with this.

Constant learning and development of new skills is expected of all organizations, all employees and all citizens and it is learning and development professionals who can help them to achieve this.

References

CIPD (2013) *Megatrends: The trends shaping work and working lives*, CIPD, London
CIPD (2014) *Fresh Thinking in Learning and Development: Neuroscience and learning research insight*, CIPD, London

CIPD (2015a) *L&D: Evolving Roles and Enhancing Skills*, research report, CIPD, London

CIPD (2015b) *Learning and Development 2015*, survey report, CIPD, London

Goswami, U (2004) Neuroscience and education, *British Journal of Psychology*, **74**, pp. 1–14

Loon, M (2014) *L&D: New challenges, new approaches*, CIPD, London

OECD (2002) Understanding the brain: towards a new learning science [online] www.oecd.org/edu/ceri/31706603.pdf [accessed 12 August 2016]

Office of National Statistics (ONS) (2014) E-commerce and ICT Activity: 2014 [online] https://www.ons.gov.uk/search?q=E-Commerce+and+ICT+Activity+2014 [accessed 1 September 2016]

Office of National statistics (ONS) (2016) Internet access: households and business: 2016 [online] http://www.ons.gov.uk/peoplepopulationand-community/householdcharacteristics/homeinternetandsocialmediausage/bulletins/internetaccesshouseholdsandindividuals/2016 [accessed 31 August 2016]

Overton, L and Dixon, G (2016) In Focus: preparing for the future of learning, *Towards Maturity* [online] www.towardsmaturity.org/in-focus/2016/futurelearn [accessed 27 August 2016]

Pemberton, C (2006) *Coaching to Solutions*, Butterworth Heinemann, Oxford

INDEX